PRECARIOUS EATING

PRECARIOUS EATING

NARRATING ENVIRONMENTAL HARM IN THE GLOBAL SOUTH

BEN JAMIESON STANLEY

UNIVERSITY OF MINNESOTA PRESS

MINNEAPOLIS • LONDON

The University of Minnesota Press gratefully acknowledges the generous assistance provided for the publication of this book by the University of Delaware.

Portions of chapter 1 are adapted from "Paddy, Mangoes, and Molasses Scum: Food Regimes and the Modernist Novel in 'The Tale of Hansuli Turn,'" in *Modernism and Food Studies: Politics, Aesthetics, and the Avant-Garde*, ed. Jessica Martell, Adam Fajardo, and Philip Keel Geheber (Gainesville: University Press of Florida, 2019), 261–76; reprinted with permission of the University Press of Florida. Portions of chapter 3 are adapted from "South African Ecocriticism: Landscapes, Animals, and Environmental Justice," with Walter Dana Phillips, in *The Oxford Handbook of Ecocriticism Online*, ed. Greg Garrard (Oxford: Oxford University Press, 2017), doi.org/10.1093/oxfordhb/9780199935338.013.154; reprinted with permission of the Licensor through PLSclear.

Excerpts from Divya Victor's "C is for Comorin and not Chutney," in *Kith* (Toronto: BookThug; Albany, N.Y.: Fence, 2017), are reprinted with permission of the author. Materials from the Western Cape Archives and Record Service (WCARS) are reproduced with permission.

Published by the University of Minnesota Press
111 Third Avenue South, Suite 290
Minneapolis, MN 55401–2520
http://www.upress.umn.edu

ISBN 978-1-5179-1579-7 (hc)
ISBN 978-1-5179-1580-3 (pb)

Library of Congress record available at https://lccn.loc.gov/2024024814

Printed in the United States of America on acid-free paper

The University of Minnesota is an equal-opportunity educator and employer.

Contents

Introduction

Narrating Precarity through Food and Hunger

In September 2020, as confirmed Covid-19 cases in India surpassed five million, the Union Government pushed three Farm Acts through parliament.[1] Dismantling minimum prices for agricultural products, this new legislation would allow farmers "to sell their goods to anyone for any price."[2] Farmers' unions launched a protest in Punjab, arguing that the acts would "push the small and marginal farmers out" by letting corporations deflate prices.[3] Moving to Delhi's outskirts in November, Punjabi farmers were joined by counterparts from numerous states to voice two demands: repeal the 2020 Farm Acts and legislate minimum support prices. Pop musicians proclaimed support, along with "sports personalities, retired army personnel, poets and writers, middle-class intelligentsia," and members of India's diaspora.[4] States governed by opposition parties passed resolutions rejecting the Farm Acts.[5] After nearly a year of protests and talks, Prime Minister Narendra Modi announced the repeal of the Farm Acts (just ahead of state elections, in which his party would need farmers' votes).[6]

To achieve this repeal, an estimated six hundred protestors died of causes including exposure and violence, illustrating a culture of "supreme sacrifice for a common cause."[7] Protests against the 2020 Farm Acts crystallize as part of a larger resistance to India's economic restructuring since 1991, which promised "to transform the economy from agrarian to industrialized," but never created sufficient jobs in the industrial sector.[8] Agriculture represents a shrinking slice of gross domestic product (GDP), but 85 percent of rural Indians still depend on smallholder farming; many

1

besides are landless agricultural workers.[9] Small farming has become more precarious as droughts and big dam projects collide with patented seeds, loans, and disadvantageous trade terms. A certain vision of prosperity linked to urban wealth and financialization has moved on from farming, leaving behind workers for whom this new economy offers a stark choice: continue to farm despite adverse circumstances or pursue unstable employment in crowded cities (where urban-led economic growth has benefitted only some, leaving many urban dwellers in informal settlements with poor services). This scenario raises the cruel irony of food producers going hungry, as the neoliberal state renders both food production and food access vulnerable to global economic fluctuations and environmental disruptions.

While the Farm Acts were consonant with thirty years of economic liberalization, protestors questioned the "extreme freedom . . . [of] corporate capital" and the dismantling of the public sector.[10] Their alternative worldview resonates with global grassroots mobilizations such as the food sovereignty movement, which rejects the "freedom" of corporations and links environmental resilience to the right to healthy, culturally-appropriate food. The controversy over India's 2020 acts exemplifies how attitudes about food production anchor larger debates, in which neoliberal agendas clash with social and environmental justice perspectives—and in which small farmers are galvanizing figures for leftists of various stripes. Such global debates invoke fundamental ideological questions: for example, can poverty, hunger, and climate crisis be resolved by market mechanisms? Or should these problems be addressed by challenging global capitalism? The farmer protests thus speak to the entanglement of environmental precarity, social hierarchy, and relations with food.

Punjabi farmers' concerns about the economics of agriculture might seem distant from either environmental conditions or food consumption. Showing how these three elements intertwine, however, is a facility of fictions such as Mahasweta Devi's 1978 "Shishu" ("Strange Children"). This short story unfolds in Lohri, a drought- and famine-stricken district in 1970s Bihar, India, where an unnamed hunger-relief officer has been assigned. He finds Lohri a frustrating place where relief supplies disappear in the night, stolen by "abnormal" children.[11] Nonetheless, the relief officer endeavors to "rehabilitate . . . in farming" the local Adivasi population, the Agariyas (238). A self-described "honest, well-meaning official" outraged when two sacks of grain go missing, he sees no hypocrisy in distributing basic supplies while himself enjoying "the best quality rice for dinner. Fresh peas in the fried rice, meat, pickles, and dark-brown syrupy *gulabjamuns*," since his "uncle [is] a state minister" (238, 234). Contrasting miserly food relief to opulent eating, "Shishu" questions the possibility of "honest" action within this system of tiered access to food.

At the story's climax, the relief officer chases the thieves into the forest, only to discover that these diminutive people are not children, but "adults!" (240). "We're the Agariyas of Kuva," they say as they encircle the relief officer (240). Hiding since their village was "burned down by the police" after a massacre twelve years ago, the Agariyas of Kuva have barely survived: "Our bodies have shrunk. . . . That's why we steal food. We must eat to grow bigger again" (231, 240). The relief officer concludes that they want "retaliation . . . against his five feet and nine inches of height, against the normal growth of his body" (241). He protests: "I'm only an ordinary Indian. The size of my body is much less than those of the Americans, the Canadians, or the Russians. . . . Never have I eaten much more than the number of calories that is an absolute minimum according to the World Health Organization" (241). Leveraging the nutritional rhetoric of global institutional authority, the relief officer acknowledges inequalities among nations but denies rampant inequality *within* postcolonial India. Yet he privately wonders whether "the body of an average Indian, what he has always considered . . . puny and short," is in fact "the most heinous crime against human civilization, and [whether] he is to blame personally for the hideously stunted forms of these once-proud adults" (241). Eating enough calories and having a normative body come to represent all that is withheld from the have-nots of the postcolonial nation. Confronted by bodies that disrupt his expectations, the relief officer questions his entire worldview: "Everything else is false: the Copernican system, science, the twentieth century, the Independence of India, the five-year plans" (240). The progress narratives of modernity cannot accommodate these hungry bodies, which exceed notions of India as a decolonized, modern democracy.

Like many Indigenous people, small farmers, and otherwise marginalized persons, the Agariyas of Kuva are victims both of state failures and of a broader consensus of capitalist modernity dominated by the global North (even before India's liberalization). What strikes me about

"Shishu" is how Mahasweta registers such national and geopolitical forces via depictions of hungry bodies.[12] "Shishu" expresses that, by doing something as quotidian as eating enough calories, the more privileged among us benefit from harm to others whom we may never encounter. This is the uncanny weight of our global food system, which connects one body to another economically and physically, even incorporating bodies into other bodies, in a network of power relations stretching across and beyond the human species.

But what does this have to do with the environment? "Shishu" anticipates a particular kind of environmental writing: what I will describe as "consumption fiction." In the story, outsiders see Lohri as "cursed land" with "poison in its soil" (232, 235). But Lohri's "natural" conditions are neither inherent nor separable from human influences: instead, nonhuman forces interact with political and economic pressures. The massacre at Kuva, it transpires, was provoked by resource extraction: an expedition for iron ore "blasted" the mountain where the Agariyas' gods lived (232). In response, the Agariyas of Kuva "butchered" the government party (232). Police burned Kuva village, "poured salt over its soil," and beat up the other Agariyas (232). In this account of state-sanctioned violence against Adivasis, environmental harm (mineral extraction) enters the story by sparking conflict between marginal and hegemonic worldviews. Similarly, while Lohri is suffering "drought and famine," the causes of hunger exceed dry land (230). One government officer gripes: "If you gave [the Agariyas] land, they would sell it to the moneylender. Then they would . . . complain, 'Where's water? Where's seed? . . .' But even if you gave them those things, they would sell everything to the moneylender and then argue back, 'What are we supposed to eat until the crop is ready? We'd borrowed to eat. We have to repay the loan with the land'" (230). While the officer finds this irrational, his description reveals that the Agariyas are exploited by moneylenders—one of many sources of precarity for agriculturalists. Economic hierarchy intertwines with drought to produce hunger that cannot be resolved by government sacks of rice and milo.

This is a different account of environmental crisis than we might see in a narrative about privileged people confronting climate change. Rather than environmental problems driving Mahasweta's story, they become relevant as they interact with social and economic forces to structure hunger and precarity. National and transnational inequalities register on the tangible scale of the hungry body, centering injustice among humans even as the story invokes beyond-human relations. Such an environmental discourse resonates with the politics of smallholder agriculture in India (as I elaborate in chapter 1) and with postcolonial and environmental justice viewpoints, rather than with "climate fiction" or "Anthropocene" paradigms. "Shishu" exemplifies the importance of eating and hunger to narratives from the global South that represent environmental precarity from within a paradigm of unequal resource access and maldistributed environmental risk.

This book expands ideas of the "environmental" by foregrounding eating, a key interface among human and nonhuman actors. *Precarious Eating: Narrating Environmental Harm in the Global South* contends that ideas about eating, hunger, and food production are central to antihegemonic cultural narratives of how capitalist globalization shapes environmental precarity. While I focus on South Africa and India since their 1990s liberalization, I begin with the earlier story "Shishu" to locate how depictions of food and hunger can render narratable the often-abstract forces of global environmental inequality: by focusing attention on body-scale experiences of deprivation. Throughout the book, I examine texts from India and South Africa that evade in-vogue categories such as "Anthropocene fiction," yet are in several cases canonical to the postcolonial environmental humanities. I identify an environmental canon from the global South bound together by logics less about the rupture and largeness (the Anthropocene-ness) of contemporary crisis, and more about the continuity of this crisis with consumer-capitalist globalization, imperialist dispossession, and experiences at the scale of the body. Rather than conflating environmental problems with emergency, this is a canon attentive to quotidian and small-scale manifestations of precarity. These logics characterize what I call "consumption fictions": neoliberal-era novels that track the enmeshment of environmental precarity with globalized capitalism through representations of eating, hunger, taste, and agro-food systems.[13] *Precarious Eating* is about how contemporary South African and Indian writers and thinkers explore "consumption" as a way to process environmental and social impacts of liberalization.

The word *consumption* can refer to the purchasing of goods, the use of environmental resources, or the act of eating. These three meanings are not really separate: humans cannot eat without using resources, and most people in a global capitalist system cannot eat without buying something. Depictions of eating can thus organize thought lines around environmental injustice and economic inequality, and it is this feature of eating that I intend "consumption" to evoke. Consumption also describes the ideological relation in which the global North sees the South as available to use: materially in the sense of resource extraction and labor exploitation, but also via cultural appropriation in arenas such as tourism and cuisine.

In consumption fictions, representations of cultivating, fishing, cooking, dining, grocery shopping, and going hungry are strategies for documenting how globalized capitalism molds uneven environmental precarity. Consumption fictions take interest in the materiality of food systems themselves; however, they also employ eating as a metonym to invoke broader forms of "consuming," foregrounding asymmetrical access to resources such as water, land, and housing (issues closely linked to food access). Using discourse about eating to make room for worldviews beyond the neoliberal consensus, these novels ask readers to confront how the satiation of the privileged comes at the expense of the hungry, both literally and figuratively. Those hungry are above all the poor in the global South, making consumption an important lexicon for fictions concerned with environments and lives in the global South, including, in this project, novels by Tarashankar Bandyopadhyay, Amitav Ghosh, Zakes Mda, Zoë Wicomb, Henrietta Rose-Innes, and Prayaag Akbar.

Consumption fictions resonate with activist mobilizations that situate the global agro-food system as an environmental injustice. Agrofood systems can express extractive logics or shape alternatives, whether through small-scale projects in food justice or larger visions of dismantling capitalism, as embraced in the food sovereignty movement. "Food sovereignty" provides a conceptual framework for many of my readings, which draw inspiration from activist notions of food as central to agency, community autonomy, environmental justice, and possibilities beyond the neoliberal consensus. In addition to borrowing activist concepts, *Precarious Eating* amplifies eco/food movements by recounting histories such as protests against genetically modified (GM) seeds in India, or the birth of the South African Food Sovereignty Campaign (SAFSC). At the same time, I am aware of the tendency for scholarship in food studies to idealize movements for food sovereignty; I seek to avoid this by centering literary and cultural texts that are alert to the complexities and tensions of food movements. Each chapter in this book considers a central pair of South African or Indian cultural texts in conversation with materials such as activist declarations, cookbooks, archival letters, ethnographic narratives, scholarly debates, field observations, and reportage. This diverse archive allows me to explore how novels, nonfiction, and film form part of the broader cultural field that I call "consumption culture": a constellation of narratives and expectations about eating, coproduced by cultural representations; trends in food production, cuisine, and diet; and dynamic environmental and economic pressures. Consumption culture takes many forms, as different expectations about eating express different political, aesthetic, and environmental attitudes; I observe both a globally dominant neoliberal consumption culture and various consumption cultures in resistance to neoliberalism as they manifest across my archive. Even as I attend to specific trajectories of the novel, my concerns extend beyond the literary-critical: I am interested in broader questions about the narratives that surround food and their implications for pursuing environmental justice.

Linking the Postcolonial Environmental Humanities with Food Studies

This book brings together three interdisciplinary fields—environmental humanities, postcolonial studies, and food studies—as well as literary criticism on the global novel. Consumption fictions speak to these fields' overlapping concerns with power, representational and conceptual scale, and how to think relations within and beyond the human in an era of anthropogenic (caused by *some* humans) climate change. In this section, I begin to situate how this study draws out an intersection between postcolonial environmental humanities and food studies.

But why this focus on food? Food and taste have structured imperial projects and shaped globalization since at least the fifteenth century, when the spice trade motivated European incursions in South Asia, South Africa, and beyond. Sugar cane from South Asia was brought to the Americas by imperialists, as were enslaved and indentured people from Africa, India, China, Portugal, and Java who would work sugar plantations to satisfy European appetites.[14] Monocultural farming arose with plantation agriculture, slashing agrobiodiversity and increasing the likelihood that crop failure could cause famine. Indeed, food and famine were weapons of European control, as when Britain mismanaged famines in India and Ireland.[15] With twentieth-century decolonizations, "food power" became a mode of neocolonialism: the United States won overseas markets by pushing "food aid," disrupting local foodways while sowing foreign debt.[16] The industrialization of farming helped American hegemony supersede that of Europe. In the 1970s, the "Green Revolution" readapted America's sway over the global South, which became less reliant on American food but more dependent on fertilizers, pesticides, and seed varieties owned by Northern-based multinationals. Ostensibly intended to "eliminate starvation," the Green Revolution "in many cases contributed to malnutrition, famine, social instability, and large-scale ecological problems."[17] According to many scholar/activists, biotechnology patents and new land grabs are the latest modes of neocolonial and neoliberal exploitation, characteristic of a corporatized food system that is a major driver of climate change.

Food, then, is key to power. Food production and distribution are crucial intersections of the environmental, corporeal, and social, as Elizabeth DeLoughrey and George Handley describe in explaining "postcolonial ecologies": the "material resources of the colonies literally changed human bodies and national cultures" as foods from the "New World" were transplanted "all over the globe, while Asian and African crops such as sugarcane and coffee became integral to the plantocracies of the Americas." DeLoughrey and Handley conclude that "tracing out these histories of nature is vital to understanding our current era," in which climate change is motivating new land grabs.[18] They articulate the large-scale reasons why food should matter to the postcolonial environmental humanities: a focus on food illuminates the globalizing, consumptive logic that connects earlier moments of colonial environmental transformation to the present.

As an arena of neoliberal harm, agro-food systems have appeared peripherally in scholarship foundational to suturing postcolonial studies and ecocriticism, such as Rob Nixon's *Slow Violence and the Environmentalism of the Poor*.[19] Agro-food systems also animate recent work that draws on postcolonial studies and environmental humanities to articulate the "Plantationocene" as an alternative to the Anthropocene thesis, work that acknowledges that "environmental problems cannot be decoupled from histories of colonialism, capitalism, and racism," and that "industrial monocrop agriculture leads to extractive regimes of labor and exploitation."[20] In a more zoomed-in sense associated with culture, identity, gender, and sexuality, food is central to postcolonial work by scholars such as Anita Mannur and Shameem Black; as Graham Huggan and Helen Tiffin assert, "food . . . has long been a staple of postcolonial criticism" in the sense of attending to food's value as a common "signifier for ethnicity."[21] Such analyses of food's symbolic and cultural meanings bear reintegrating with questions of the social and environmental damages wrought by a globalized food system.

Bringing such threads together, I find fundamental the macro questions outlined by DeLoughrey and Handley and by Plantationocene scholars, but I am also invested in the micro: the material and affective details of everyday lives; the local and body-scale impacts of planet-scale dynamics. I am interested in how novelists, activists, scholars, and even cultivators and restaurateurs activate the local and somatic to conceptualize a planetary environment structured by uneven globalization. This book furthers the postcolonial environmental humanities by engaging eating, hunger, taste, and agro-food systems as part and parcel of environmental culture.

At the same time, this book extends food studies' engagement with justice and environment. Centering on authors from the global South and building on work by Mannur, Allison Carruth, Parama Roy, Kyla Wazana Tompkins, Susie O'Brien, Desiree Lewis, Psyche Williams-Forson, Sarah D. Wald, Jonathan Bishop Highfield, and others, I add to growing emphases in food studies on hunger, agricultural labor, colonialism, food sovereignty, power, and also literature.[22] Rather than food studies entailing a preoccupation with the gastronomy of the privileged, I identify unexpected associations of gastronomy with marginalized figures whose unfulfilled appetites point to the imbalances in consumption that cause uneven environmental crisis. "Taste," then, matters in this study alongside farming, fishing, famine, corporate food power, disordered eating, and the environmental impacts of agro-food systems. Much as scholars such as DeLoughrey, Nixon, O'Brien, Jennifer Wenzel, Byron

Caminero-Santangelo, Huggan and Tiffin, and Anthony Vital have interrogated impasses between postcolonial studies and ecocriticism to establish an integrated field of postcolonial environmental humanities, I pursue the mutually enriching potential of the postcolonial environmental
humanities and food studies—fields with shared concerns that have so
far remained largely separate. Integrating these conversations clarifies
the material and metaphorical importance of food to global environmental justice.

From Food Regimes to Consumption Culture

Cultivation, fishery management, drought, biodiversity, climate change,
and genetically modified organisms (GMOs) are important to consumption fictions, as are other environmental topics related to food production.
But consumption fictions also depict seemingly less "environmental"
features of what Tompkins calls "eating culture," meaning "practices and
representations of ingestion and edibility."[23] Butcher shops, restaurants,
recipes, dietary preferences and proscriptions, disordered eating, and
cuisine loom large in the texts studied here. These topics matter to an
environmentalist consideration of food systems: to understand the social
and environmental impacts of food production, we must also look at
consumption, which is structured by access, trends, and taste. I describe
behaviors, expectations, and narratives around eating as "consumption
culture" in order to emphasize how they engage broader resource-use
patterns.

This work builds on a multidisciplinary set of intellectual and activist traditions that have placed food and hunger at the center of power
relations and environmental justice. In the 1980s, sociologists Harriet
Friedmann and Philip McMichael coined the term "food regime" to
describe the geopolitical system in which "forms of capital accumulation
in agriculture constitute global power arrangements, as expressed
through patterns in the circulation of food."[24] Food regime theorists designate 1870–1914 as the "Settler-Colonial" food regime: Britain funneled
cheap food to European working classes by importing grains and livestock from settler colonies, where they pushed monocultural farming at
the expense of local food systems, peoples, and environments. After the
First and Second World Wars a "Surplus" regime emerged: agricultural

industrialization yielded surpluses in the United States, which were sent overseas as the aforementioned "food aid," often destabilizing local agriculture and locking postcolonies into foreign debt. A "neoliberal food regime" has arisen since the Green Revolution, intensifying with the 1990s formation of the World Trade Organization (WTO), which dismantles barriers to agricultural liberalization.[25]

In addition to consolidating global Northern power and facilitating economic disruptions, industrial agriculture spurs climate change and other environmental problems (such as groundwater contamination). The global food system produces anywhere from 21 percent to 37 percent of total net anthropogenic emissions of greenhouse gasses, second only to the fossil-fuel industry.[26] Conversely, climate change threatens foodways: if current trends of production and consumption continue with medium population growth, the Intergovernmental Panel on Climate Change (IPCC) projects a median increase of 7.6 percent in cereals prices by 2050, increasing the risk of hunger; "vulnerable people will be more severely affected." These impacts could, however, be mitigated by sustainable food production, agroforestry, and the reduction of food waste.[27] How we produce and distribute food, then, is an urgent environmental justice question.

While likely to intensify with climate change, hunger is not an aberration. Instead, hunger and environmental damage are structuring features of a global food system rooted in extractive imperialism. This idea has been explored by thinkers such as the Brazilian physician and nutritionist Josué de Castro and the Indian economist Amartya Sen, who have long argued that famines do not result from "natural" events, overpopulation, or declines in available food, but from structural inequalities (see chapter 1).[28] In the neoliberal era, scholar/activists such as Vandana Shiva have decried corporate claims to "cure hunger" by pushing agricultural technologies such as chemical fertilizers and then transgenic seeds.[29] Many argue that the liberalization of agriculture, patenting of seeds, and globalization of retail have made our food system more vulnerable to climate shocks.[30] Even when the system is working in its normal fashion, the IPCC estimates about 821 million people are suffering hunger or malnutrition while 25–30 percent of food is wasted. With two billion adults overweight, epidemics of obesity, diabetes, and heart failure are connected to processed foods and disparities in food access (in type as well as quantity).[31] Many who labor in the food system—farmworkers, smallholders, fishers, meat-packers, restaurant employees—are subjected to grueling work, health risks, and trauma while receiving little compensation or job security.

And yet, food can be an avenue to hope. From Oakland, California, to Durban, KwaZulu-Natal, urban gardeners are re-greening vacant lots with motivations that range from "wholesale rejection of notions of ownership and private property, to more basic and limited claims of social justice and necessity."[32] In India, the Right to Food Campaign (RTFC) has mobilized to ban food exports, prohibit the corporatization of food and agriculture, and address childhood malnutrition.[33] In South Africa and Native North America and around the world, farmer-activists are gathering under the umbrella of food sovereignty to decry land grabs, GMO patenting, the privatization of water, and the liberalization of agriculture, and to grow concrete pathways for agroecology, community foodways, seed saving, and more.

Precarious Eating situates such activist mobilizations in an uneasy dialogue with what Americanist food scholar Julie Guthman calls a "new politics of consumption" since the 1980s, "manifested as eating green, eating locally, and fair trade."[34] This politics coincides with the rise of "foodie culture," an array of pleasure-oriented trends in restaurants, food-shopping, home cooking, tourism, and blogging in which context "fair trade," "local," and "organic" can become little more than buzzwords dressing up middle-class consumerism as ethical.[35] Wenzel describes this phenomenon as "postconsumerism": the aspiration to "help the poor or save the planet by buying things."[36] As Wenzel points out, we can hardly fix poverty or environmental degradation by participating in rarefied consumerism, since a global capitalist system creates those problems in the first place. Many co-ops and farmers' markets do advance social and environmental justice, yet such pursuits can be undercut by a "lack of critical reflexivity about foodie privilege, especially in relation to the larger global food system."[37] The "new politics of consumption" may intensify a tiered food system in which wealthy consumers access tastier, healthier, greener food choices, whereas poor consumers are exposed to processed junk and risks of food toxicity.

While analyses of "foodie" phenomena often center on the United States, places such as South Africa's Western Cape also boast upscale restaurants glorifying "farm-to-fork," foraging, "indigenous foods," veganism, and other dining trends; culinary tourism has surged here since the 1990s (see chapters 3 and 4). Citizens of the global South are variably incorporated into this sector as consumers, as laborers, and as sources of "authentic" gastronomic knowledge. Meanwhile, Northern eco/food movements draw on often-elided cultural sources, such as Native North American and Vedic agroecological techniques used in organic farming.[38] The alternating refusal and commodification of "ethnic" food animate the reception of non-Anglo literatures and even bodies, as Parama Roy, Shameem Black, Anita Mannur, and Graham Huggan have documented. Culinary tourism, large-scale organics, and "ethnic" cuisine often go hand in hand with exploited labor, as foodies exercise privilege by assimilating cuisines from "different" communities while remaining "reluctant to invest in larger structural changes."[39]

Building on the aptitude the genre of novel has for interweaving large-scale structures with individual experience, I approach culinary cultures through the lens of the literary. This approach offers a way to integrate ideas about food as an economic and geopolitical system (a "global food regime") with concepts of eating as a cultural, personal, embodied, and even metaphoric vector, often a way of marking ethnicity, exploring sexuality, or "managing difference" in narrative.[40] In consumption fictions, scenes of cooking or eating can express racial, gendered, place-based, or sexual identity; or can combine with depictions of global food systems to highlight differentiated experiences of environmental precarity in different bodies. The lens of "consumption" can thus transcend "local versus global" debates that have encumbered both the environmental humanities and the study of the novel, as I will discuss.

Of course, the appropriation of the global South's cultural resources by the North (and by settler communities in the South) can manifest not only in cuisine, but also in novelization and novel-reading. Most of the fictions discussed in this book are elite commodities: they are Anglophone texts by cosmopolitan authors who are based at least partially in the global North and craft narratives that fit publishers' sales formulas. This selection bias is a structural feature of the canon I am naming:

consumption fictions are characterized by marketability and appeal to literary critics in the global North. The authors of these texts have in some ways benefitted from neoliberalism, even as they castigate its environmental and social damages. Perhaps for this reason, consumption fictions are often self-reflexive about how to reconcile their critiques with their commodity status.

Engaging with consumption fictions requires me to also self-reflect about the appropriation possible in such a project. I want to acknowledge my positionality as a white transmasculine settler based at a U.S. university, and consider how that perspective has shaped this book. Not unlike my approach as an educator, the orientation of *Precarious Eating* is to amplify voices and contexts from the global South in order to push for globally minded and justice-focused conversations about the environment. I believe this is a useful goal, yet there is an important sense in which I am not the right person to tell stories of environmental injustice in the global South. Recognizing this, I attempt a mode of inquiry that addresses such stories not in spite of my positionality, but in dialogue with it. My location and training have led me to approach environmental justice and postcolonial inquiry from the angle of how we talk, write, and teach about planetary environmental problems and about the global South within the United States. Interdisciplinary environmental conversations in the U.S. academy need to engage more often and more subtly with thinkers and contexts from the global South, which is why this book often relates South African and Indian circumstances and stories to contexts (political, cultural, and scholarly) that might feel more immediate to U.S. Americans. I hope that, by taking anticolonial activists, scholars, and novelists from the global South as respected guides, this book can encourage careful rethinking of environmental politics in a challenging present. Part of this effort is the book's contribution to transcending a polarity in the environmental humanities between local and planetary scales.

Scalar Challenges in the Environmental Humanities

"Sense of place," or commitment to a local landscape, occupied a privileged space in first-wave U.S. ecocriticism. Celebrated by writers as different as Wendell Berry, Louise Erdrich, and Peter Berg, "sense of place" is not a monolithic concept: an insistence on the cultural importance of place can empower Indigenous critiques of how colonialism has reshaped Native lands, even as an appropriative sense of place can deny how settler places have been created through such world-altering violence.[41] Overemphasizing local places and sensory data can also occlude other paths to environmental consciousness, as Ursula Heise argued in her 2008 *Sense of Place and Sense of Planet*. From a postcolonial perspective, insular attentions to the local may ignore transnational practices that change environments, such as energy and mineral extraction by multinationals, the exporting of hazardous waste, or the imposition of agribusiness technologies, methods, and chemicals. (As Cajetan Iheka notes, "it is practically impossible to identify any locality without some global embeddedness," making notions of local isolability simply inaccurate.[42]) On the other hand, a postcolonial accounting of landscapes impacted by such processes can use "the concept of place to question temporal narratives of progress imposed by colonial powers," according to DeLoughrey and Handley.[43] O'Brien similarly suggests that, while (first-wave) ecocriticism focused on a more static sense of (rural) place, postcolonial criticism turns to concepts such as cosmopolitanism to emphasize "the provisionality and the constructedness of our relations to place."[44] This formulation suggests the multiple possibilities of sense of place, which *can* include examining how postcolonial places are shaped by the often-violent forces of globalization and global environmental damage.

As ecocriticism has wrestled with these contradictory senses of place and increasingly engaged the physical sciences, a counterpoint has emerged: the Anthropocene concept, popularized by biologist Eugene Stoermer and atmospheric chemist Paul Crutzen. If "sense of place" emphasizes the local, "Anthropocene" stresses the enormity of environmental crisis: humans are not just social, economic, or biological agents, but geological agents reshaping the earth. But understanding humans on a geological scale tends to cast humanity as a holistic agent. Scholars in postcolonial, decolonial, Black, and Indigenous studies instead think in terms of empire and racial capitalism. In these registers, humanity is not homogenous: different bodies and populations have different relations to power, environmental problems, and precarity. For postcolonial historian Dipesh Chakrabarty, the climate crisis prompts a difficult question: how can we engender "species thinking"—facing a planetary catastrophe that will eventually affect humanity as a species—while still analyzing inequality among humans?[45] Certainly climate crisis cannot be explained apart from capitalist globalization, because "financialized carbon capitalism and imperial practices" *cause* climate change.[46] Observing that seven corporations controlled global oil supply across the twentieth century, Vishwas Satgar and Jane Cherry are among many scholar/activists who argue that the global North and carbon-intensive corporations (which would include food-industry giants) owe a "historic climate debt" to the global South.[47] The term "Anthropocene" has galvanized interdisciplinary conversations, but has also come under fire for its tendency to occlude such differentials. Numerous scholars have proposed ways to rethink, reperiodize, or rename the Anthropocene, emphasizing how racialized divisions among humans enabled the extractive violence and enslaved labor that capacitated planet-altering industrialization.[48]

Rather than simply zooming out from "sense of place" to an Anthropocene scale, then, how can we represent varied human interactions with the nonhuman in ways that overcome a local–global binary? Geographers such as Katherine McKittrick have explored what forms of place-making are possible in light of world-shattering processes such as enslavement, diaspora, colonization, and neocolonialism.[49] Ecocritics have proposed conceptual strategies such as "cosmopolitan bioregionalism" (Byron Caminero-Santangelo), "telecoupling relationships" (Sverker Sörlin), and "fractal topographies" (Thomas Lekan).[50] These probings suggest something challenging but necessary about thinking across the small and the very large.

I write within the space that such conversations have created: space not only to reframe the Anthropocene or sense of place, but to express our global environmental and societal crisis through other frameworks entirely. Food is simultaneously intimate and geopolitical, allowing the frameworks of consumption fiction and consumption culture to pivot between embodied experience and global crisis. Combining this multidimensionality of food with the novel's facility for multiscalar thinking, consumption fictions put front and center how globalization both produces and textures environmental precarity; this relation is epitomized by the shifting global foodscape and expressed in patterns of eating. Thinking with the rubric of "consumption fiction" thus creates new ways for the environmental humanities to transcend the local–planetary dichotomy. This approach also offers a new direction for literary-critical conversations about how to represent the large and heterogenous systems of globalization and climate change.

The Novel, Globalization, and Climate Change

If novels once imagined the nation (following Benedict Anderson), then contemporary novels often imagine the globe, expressing a cultural shift toward thinking on a global scale. This is not to suggest that the nation has become irrelevant: indeed, we are witnessing new surges of exclusionary nationalism. Nonetheless, globalization has become the primary frame of reference in many texts, as scholars have argued using various terms: "global novel" but also "world-shaped novel" (Rebecca Walkowitz), "plot of globalization" (Alexander Beecroft), and "world novel" since "around 1989" (Debjani Ganguly).[51] Like those in the environmental humanities, conversations about the novel and globalization often splinter around how to negotiate between global systems and local heterogeneity. Heise explains both debates based on how thinkers perceive the relation between "globality" and "difference": world literature theorists subordinate "cultural difference as internal" to "global systems, networks, and cultural economies [seen] as structures that already exist"; others, such as postcolonialists, see "cultural difference" as "foundational," and "global culture and citizenship" as "imaginative goals to be reached by negotiating fundamental differences."[52] In ecocriticism, this relation "plays itself out not only at the borders of human communities but also at the interface of human and nonhuman systems": some ecocritics treat local differences as mere "variations in a context of globally shared environmental concerns," whereas, in postcolonial ecocriticism, difference "play[s] a crucial role."[53] Heise's schematization is helpful. Yet in my view, "globally shared environmental concerns" and attention to local difference are more readily integrated than this schema would imply, if we take our cues from texts with a postcolonial view of more-than-human globalization.

In this study, "globalization" refers to a beyond-human network: the transnational circulation of capital and ideas, but also organic and inorganic matter, in a web of intertwined economic, cultural, and also environmental systems. As reflected in this definition, I put the imbrication of economic and cultural globalization with planetary changes at the center. I share with many "global novel" scholars an interest in how fictions shoulder the difficulty of understanding our interconnected reality—but interconnected, I would suggest, across species as well as national borders. Consumption fictions are about the asymmetries of this more-than-human globalization in which transnational economic and cultural exchanges are bound up in processes such as resource extraction, ecological exchange, toxification, seed patenting, climate change, and biodiversity loss.

On the heels of "global novel" scholarship, recent literary-critical interest has swerved toward the novel and climate change. Is fiction good at representing climate change? Which fiction? What role might novels fulfill in confronting climate change? Part of this book's background work is my own thought process about how the study of the novel and globalization might inform (rather than be supplanted by) these inquiries. In other words, how might literary critics address climate change in its full imbrication with globalization? Too often, the "climate fiction" conversation centers on authors from the global North, eliding how the contours of empire have shaped climate change (see chapter 2). Within the rubric of consumption fiction, a distinct critical framework from climate fiction, I focus on novels of the global South and apprehend environmental problems in their interrelations with globalization.

Consumption fiction is an important subgenre of what we might call the "global environmental novel," referring broadly to novels that attempt to map relations between globalization and environmental crisis; I argue that tracing consumption has emerged as a particularly apt strategy for narrating these enmeshments. By foregrounding intimacies between individual eater, global economy, and nonhuman environment, consumption fictions bypass the epistemic pitfall in which thinking on a planetary scale would elide power imbalances within the "human." Building on the ability of the novel form to connect individuated characters to larger systems, consumption fictions depict patterns of eating as a way to trace extractive logics across space and time, even as they attend to local and embodied contexts. As I address in chapter 2, this multiscalar facility enables consumption fictions to tackle the global/planetary scale regarded by some as an impediment to representing climate change, while addressing the unevenness of globalization and environmental precarity. Representational difficulty, meanwhile, can offer lessons about imaginative difficulty: consumption fictions dramatize the conceptualization of how local and global, human and nonhuman interlock as a crucial and elusive aptitude in this globalized and environmentally devastated world. Thinking about food systems is a mode of developing and demonstrating that aptitude.

Connecting Contemporary South Africa and India

This book addresses consumption culture across South Africa and India, particularly Cape Town and the Cape region, West Bengal, and Maharashtra's capital, Mumbai, all places that offer specific points of comparison and South–South connectivity. India and South Africa are key contexts in which to explore the ideological consumption of otherness, because the global North so often reduces South Asia to "Indian food" and because South Africa has heightened media visibility, standing in for "homogeneous 'Africa'" in the Northern imagination.[54] Even as South Africa may remain synonymous with racial injustice for many global Northerners, the country has become a tourist destination celebrated for its biodiversity, megafauna, wine, and gastronomy; Cape Town has recently also become a cautionary tale for water management (see chapter 5) and resource inequality remains rampant. These contemporary patterns build on segregationist and apartheid histories in which racialized governance overdetermined land usage, conservation practices, and access to food, water, and electricity. The Indian subcontinent likewise animates conflicting ideas in the North: extreme poverty, iconic Bengal tigers, sectarian tensions, rapid economic growth, delicious food. Mumbai, India's largest city and financial center, combines glitzy corporate construction, the celebrated *dabbawalla* system of delivering home-cooked lunches to office workers, and sprawling informal settlements with precarious water access.[55] West Bengal is mythologized for its agrarian histories and is still home to many small farmers and fishers, and yet it is India's second most densely populated state, with more than fourteen million people in Kolkata. It is a place where glamorized conservation projects would obscure a history of famines and atrocities. Here and elsewhere in India, rural livelihoods have been endangered by unregulated mining and forestry, debt cycles (with marginal agriculturalists exposed to global price fluctuations and encroaching multinationals), and the withdrawal of state support for small-scale agriculture—along with the dismantling of many welfare programs.[56]

Both South Africa and India are postcolonies with substantial foreign investment and widespread poverty; both transitioned to neoliberalism "late" under pressure from external financial institutions. Dawning with 1970s–1980s structural adjustment programs in Africa and Latin America, neoliberalism is the political-economic ideology that "market competition is the most efficient mechanism for generating prosperity and protecting individual liberty," expressed in policy agendas that deregulate markets and dismantle social safety nets in favor of "free trade," tax cuts for corporations, private property rights, and privatized services.[57] In South Africa, neoliberalism arrived with the 1990s transition from apartheid to multiracial democracy: the African National Congress (ANC) defaulted on the socialist demands of anti-apartheid activism as it became the ruling party. At the behest of mining and finance capitalists including the World Bank, the ANC government protected private property rather than nationalize land, banks, or mines; promoted export industries and free trade; and privatized many municipal services. On land reform, the ANC adopted a "willing-seller, willing-buyer" stance in which the state merely subsidizes the purchase of land by black clients.[58] Only 7.5 percent of land had been redistributed as of 2017. Programs with modest redistribution goals, such as Black Economic Empowerment (BEE), have retained a market-centered and entrepreneurial logic.[59] The end of racial governance did foster a black middle class; however, the majority of black South Africans remain in poverty and the wealth gap has grown, making South Africa "one of the most unequal societies in the world."[60] India similarly faces severe stratification as a result of capitulating to external financial institutions: the country's July 1991 liberalization was a condition for an International Monetary Fund (IMF) bailout from economic catastrophe. While India is often narrated as a neoliberal success story, this "success" is defined narrowly in terms of GDP, ignoring that inequality has intensified.[61] Among India's urban elite, consumerism and investment opportunities have grown, whereas unemployment, precarious self-employment, and debt have increased among the poor.[62]

Framing Indian fiction in relation to these developments, Mukti Lakhi Mangharam describes India's post-reform period as "marked by disappointment," which millennial writers manifest by connecting the dots between colonialism and neoliberal-era exploitation.[63] Similarly, South Africanists note a fixation in postapartheid literature with deferral, disappointment, and waiting as the country endures an incomplete transition.[64]

My focus falls on the contemporary (or postliberalization) era: I primarily examine texts from the 2000s and 2010s, decades in which South African and Indian writers engage eating as a way to parse fallout from 1990s liberalization in dialogue with concerns about environmental imperialism and climate crisis.

Activists too have been wrestling with how neoliberalism both reinvents global class inequality and perpetuates never-resolved colonial, racial, gendered, and caste-based oppressions, as well as the environmental violence of extractive capitalism. A number of coalitions are demanding access to culturally appropriate food and traditional food-gathering pathways that have been obstructed by corporate land grabs, seed patenting, or fishing quotas. Not only have India and (to a lesser extent) South Africa been hypervisible sites in activism against GMOs, but subaltern groups in the two countries have also connected through organizations such as the World Forum of Fisher Peoples (WFFP). Founded in India in 1997, this group met in Cape Town in 2014 to advance the rights of traditional fishing communities, critiquing quota systems that advantage large-scale commercial fishing (see chapter 3).[65] WFFP claims to represent more than ten million small-scale fishers who can be "part of the solution to solve the climate catastrophe" by "providing affordable and nutritious foods" through "low carbon emission practices."[66] Such eco/food-activist networks constitute a neoliberal-era reimagining of earlier South–South anticolonial solidarities.

Indeed, South Africa and India have a long history of interconnection through migration and agricultural labor, expressed in South Africa's Indian-influenced cuisines. Imperialists brought indentured South Asians to work sugarcane plantations in what is now KwaZulu-Natal, where they created Durban's signature "bunny chow": curry served in a loaf of bread to take into the fields. As this example suggests, cuisine can express often-silenced histories of violence surrounding agro-food monocultures, such as practices of indenture. While Durban is regarded as the center of Indian South African life, Cape Town restaurants such as Bo-Kaap Kombuis and Faeeza's Home Kitchen also serve curries, roti, samoosas, falooda, and other "Cape Malay" renditions of Indian-influenced food. ("Cape Malay" refers to a Muslim community at the Cape with diverse origins, including Malaysian but also Arab and South Asian.)

Like the still-extant Bo-Kaap ("Upper Cape") neighborhood, Cape Town's District Six once testified to South–South culinary connections.

This working-class area was populated by descendants of formerly enslaved and indentured people who intermarried with Khoena and San people, and subsequent immigrants from places such as India, St. Helena, Ireland, and the Philippines. Cuisine was crucial to District Six's convivial hybridity, as recalled in Rozena Maart's short story collection *Rosa's District 6*:

> On Good Friday, the smell of onions sautéing in oil and turmeric took over the streets; palm-sized pieces of fish would be fried then placed in the turmeric sauce.... Christian families attended the three-hour mass... and returned home to eat their pickled fish. Muslim families went to mosque in the morning; they too would go home to enjoy their pickled fish.... Food in District Six was not divided along religious lines. Many families kept halal homes because they had extended family that were Muslim, and eating was such an important part of District Six life.[67]

With ethnically diverse Muslims, Christians, and Jews living side by side, District Six became a target for segregationist and apartheid regimes: the British used the bubonic plague as an excuse to remove black dockworkers in 1901, and between 1966 and 1982, the neighborhood was demolished, scattering residents across the Cape Flats.[68] Cuisine undergirds contemporary recuperation efforts at the District Six Museum, where workshops with displaced residents produced the 2016 *District Six Huis Kombuis: Food & Memory Cookbook*. This volume features recipes alongside portraits of District Sixers who reminisce about buying *snoek* (a South African fish) on "tick" to be repaid Friday, making a *lang sous* (stew lengthened by adding water) to feed more mouths, folding samoosas and eating North Indian food at the Crescent Restaurant, "the only place in Cape Town where people of colour could have a quality sit-down meal," and setting a "tafel," an open table that welcomed all diners during Christmas choirs.[69] For resident Aboubarker Brown, "that was the spirit of District Six. We shared food whether it was Eid or Christmas."[70] This working-class cosmopolitanism has been memorialized as the ultimate contrast to apartheid. Reviving food traditions is a way to honor that vision for South Africa, a vision intertwined with South–South connections to places including India.

Such culinary connections express community-building but also exploitation, pain, marginal livelihoods, and getting by. Recognizing how violent histories subtend cosmopolitan food cultures, *Precarious Eating* asks how cuisine can be an arena for thinking through environmental and societal ramifications of those histories. In the literary archive chosen, narratives about cuisine and dietary "choice" can reinsert acknowledgements of violence into sanitized accounts of colonial and postcolonial history, revealing how hegemonic expectations about diet impinge on efforts to rethink the unfair allocation of resources (chapters 4–5). Politicizations of hunger and gastronomic desire, meanwhile, enable subaltern environmental discourses to contest white, Western-style, and/or neoliberal variants of environmentalism (chapters 1–3).

The novels addressed here were all published prior to the Covid-19 pandemic, which continues to unfold as I write this introduction; the pandemic has only underscored the urgency of these stories by highlighting stark inequalities in food access and environmental precarity. Covid-19 has disproportionately killed in communities with degraded air quality and limited healthcare, has imperiled access to food, and has put many agro-food-industry workers into heightened-exposure scenarios. In South Africa, pandemic shutdowns prompted a food-access crisis, leading to widespread food protests and "looting" by the hungry—acts that were often criminalized in media and government responses.[71] India's lockdown caused migrant workers to flee the cities, walking hundreds of kilometers to home villages in scenes reminiscent of the 1947 Partition. The pandemic also unleashed new waves of food-linked Islamophobia, with "wild rumors" accusing Indian Muslims of "deliberately infecting food and water to spread the virus" and others rationalizing Covid-19 as "a righteous punishment for those who eat meat," meaning Muslims and Dalits.[72] These pandemic-era developments underscore the need to address environmental and food justice in dialogue with the politicization of diet, recognizing that pandemics will again impinge on food access as climate change accelerates, and that the management of such disasters will be informed by biases about who deserves access to resources. An investigation of consumption can parse these imbrications of globalization and environment, thinking across the scales of individual eater, community, nation, and planet, as this book explores across five chapters.

Outline

While this book focuses on Anglophone texts post-1990, I begin with histories of famine and a Bengali modernist novel to illustrate a longer and broader tradition in which representations of hunger and gastronomy illuminate combined environmental, social, and economic precarity. I then delve into realist and satirical novels (canonical to postcolonial literature) concerned with neoliberal India and South Africa. I end with emergent writers who speculate about future diets, water management, and climates.

Part I, "Eating and Environmental Precarity in India," includes two chapters that establish how eco/food rhetorics illuminate precarity and inequality in the Indian context, with implications for transnational analysis of neoliberalism's impacts in the global South. The first chapter is "From Famine to Farmer Suicides: Precarity and Gastronomic Desire in Representations of Indian Agriculturalists." Here I address narratives of marginal farmers in India, engaging a varied archive of fiction, film, and scholarly and activist discourse. I link the Bengal famine of 1943 and the 1990s, two moments of paradigm shift in agro-food systems, spurred by respective transitions from feudalism to capitalism and then to neoliberalism. I first discuss representations of the 1940s subaltern agriculturalist become famine victim, focusing on the intellectual legacy of the 1943 famine in Amartya Sen's economistic masterwork *Poverty and Famines* and in Tarashankar Bandyopadhyay's 1946–1951 novel *Hansuli Banker Upakathā* (translated by Ben Conisbee Baer as *The Tale of Hansuli Turn*). I then analyze the neoliberal-era figure of the "farmer suicide" in its resonances with Tarashankar's agriculturalists and in light of debates about GMOs. Scrutinizing social-scientific accounts of rural death in contemporary India alongside Anusha Rizvi's 2010 satirical film *Peepli Live*, I consider how seed patenting, masculinity, disappointment with neoliberalism's failed promises, and drought all intersect in the figuration of the farmer suicide. I argue that the hungry agriculturalist is a paradigmatic figure for combined economic, social, and environmental precarity in India, especially for inequalities entrenched by postcolonial economic growth. But I also find that motifs of labor exploitation, deprivation, and starvation have been twinned by a surprising trope of gastronomic desire on the part of the marginal agriculturalist. Gastronomic desire that cannot be satisfied (or that leads to death) indexes the precarity that global capitalism produces for marginalized actors confronting environmental instability. Advancing a broader argument of this book, then, chapter 1 pinpoints a pattern in which food, hunger, and agriculture become central to ideological contestations over how globalization intersects environmental change.

Staying with the focus on postliberalization India that concludes chapter 1, I clarify the genre stakes of studying "consumption fiction" in chapter 2, "Nutmeg and Disordered Eating: Reframing Climate Change." This chapter brings together Amitav Ghosh's fiction and nonfiction to consider how a focus on food and the global South might recast debates about "climate fiction," rethinking the novel's representational possibilities in an era of climate change. To this end, I consider the differing ways to describe planetary crisis offered by Ghosh's 2016 polemic *The Great Derangement*, his 2004 canonical environmental novel *The Hungry Tide*, and his 2021 nonfiction work *The Nutmeg's Curse*. While *The Great Derangement* proposes that "serious fiction" struggles to represent climate change because of its focus on the individual, both *The Hungry Tide* and *The Nutmeg's Curse* illustrate the benefits of describing planetary crisis in ways that center on appetites and food commodities (rather than climate change). To make this argument, I contextualize Ghosh's work in relation to both scholarly debates on "cli-fi" and received ideas about food in perceptions of Indian literature and culture. Where cuisine is often invoked as an index of ethnic or national identity, *The Nutmeg's Curse* participates in a different tradition of commodity-tracing texts such as Sidney Mintz's *Sweetness and Power* or Mark Kurlansky's *Salt*, in which a single comestible illuminates world history. I consider how such logics also inhere in *The Hungry Tide*, tracing the novel's references to food commodities such as tea, bananas, and Ovaltine in dialogue with material and cultural histories that attach those commodities to empire, exploited labor, and environmental transformation. I also rethink the affordances of novelistic individuation by reading the main character of *The Hungry Tide* as a disordered eater. This characterization models a mode of exploring the individual psyche not to avoid planet-scaled issues, but instead to represent them in a way that marks uneven power relations. By invoking climate change obliquely rather than centrally, I conclude, consumption fictions such as *The Hungry Tide* and nonfictions such as *The Nutmeg's Curse* can reemphasize the concatenation of climate change with factors such as empire, globalized commodity capitalism, political violence, and refugeeism.

Moving to a different national context, I continue to explore how food-focused representations expose neoliberalism's production of environmental precarity in Part II, "Environmental Politics of Consumerism and Cuisine in South Africa." Part II homes in on how speaking to hunger, parodying foodie culture, and engaging received ideas about cuisine can instantiate powerful (if sometimes problematic) modes of resistance to the racial, class, and gender dynamics of the neoliberal world order. Chapter 3, "Hunger versus Taste: Fishing and Foraging in a Tourism Economy," sketches how environmental politics and eating collide after apartheid. I focus on fishery regulations and "indigenous food" practices as they operate in dialogue with South Africa's liberalization and stratifying tourism economy. The chapter begins with the "abalone war" in the Western Cape in the 1990s, a conflict over fishing rights and valuable commodities that illuminates structural issues with neoliberal approaches to environmentalism and social transition. Just as neoliberal conservation policies can "greenwash" marginalization of the poor, gastronomic trends constellated around indigenous foods and foraging often claim to protect biodiversity and/or advance social justice—claims that are sometimes justified, but elsewhere exemplify neoliberal consumption culture's tendencies toward cultural appropriation and unscalable "alternatives" to industrial food. I approach these dynamics via representations of fishing and foraging in a range of media, including the gourmet cookbook *Strandveldfood*, activist declarations by the South African Food Sovereignty Campaign, and environmental novels by Zakes Mda. Mda satirizes neoliberal consumption culture by bringing to the fore tensions between hunger (caused by inequalities in food access) and "taste," or the aesthetics of food. His 2000 novel *The Heart of Redness* questions the social-justice efficacy of ecotourism through a submerged narrative of feminist food sovereignty, rooted in local traditions of oyster and mussel harvesting and guided by Xhosa and Khoena women. His 2005 *The Whale Caller* features playful portraits of ritualized supermarket shopping and restaurant dining, which I read as satirical sketches of how neoliberal consumption culture effaces hunger and the racialized wealth gap. In sum, Mda's novels exemplify how consumption fiction from the global South can politicize hunger and taste to reject neoliberal and consumerist approaches to eco/food politics, demanding a reprioritization of food sovereignty.

Chapter 4, "Queer/Vegan Reading: Consumption and Complicity from Supermarket to Butcher Shop," considers how racialized gender and sexuality are expressed through ideas about veganism/meat-eating, culinary history, and supermarkets in postapartheid South Africa, as well as the implications for environmental and food justice. I approach this problematic through two novels by Zoë Wicomb that track how meat-eating and supermarket shopping can reinscribe globalized capitalism and white supremacist misogyny, yet also encode cooking, eating, and butchering as sites of resistance. First, I analyze her 2006 *Playing in the Light* in relation to supermarketization, scholarship on South African temporalities, and queer theory. *Playing in the Light* uses supermarket shopping as a metonym to emphasize how capitalism regiments middle-class cisheterosexual whiteness through temporalities of consumption. Yet at the same time, the novel uses fruit from the supermarket to connote queer desire and disruptions to rigid racial/class categories. *Playing in the Light* thus locates consumption as site of both normativity and transgression. Next, I place field observations of South African vegan restaurants in dialogue with the burgeoning field of "vegan studies" and Wicomb's 2014 *October.* I argue for postcolonial analyses of meat-eating and veganism that would address how the politics of "environmentally friendly" diets intertwine with race and geopolitics, as well as speciesism and gender. Eating meat can express patriarchal, white supremacist, and speciesist violence in specific contexts; however, vegan advocacy becomes hegemonic when it loses sight of context, as I discuss in relation to two controversies in South Africa. In *October,* Cape cuisine and meat-eating express multiple violences of globalization across time, and yet Cape-style sausage-making becomes a process of antihegemonic empowerment. With this complex revaluation of a tainted food, Wicomb sidesteps paradigms of activism that stress ethical eating, instead foregrounding a need to engender resistance from *within* the oppressive food cultures of globalized capitalism.

To bring the book to a close, Part III, "Gastrohydropolitics and Climate Imaginaries," reconnects South Africa and India in a comparative concluding chapter that connects representations of the neoliberal present to speculative futures. In chapter 5, "Purity and Porosity: Speculating

Urban Water Justice and Future Diets," I ask how consumption culture intersects water management in an era of intensifying climate change and resurgent right-wing nationalisms. To this end, I trace how expectations about diet irrupt into narratives of water crisis in Cape Town and Mumbai. Many governmental, media, and "expert" narratives about water in these cities either assert technocratic mastery over water or claim that climate change makes water emergencies so unpredictable that government cannot be held responsible. Seeking narratives that instead reckon with how power relations govern access to water and drainage, chapter 5 compares the 2011 *Nineveh* by South African writer Henrietta Rose-Innes and the 2017 *Leila* by Indian author and editor Prayaag Akbar. I advance a conception of "gastrohydropolitics": a sense that struggles around hydro-infrastructures and water access can mirror, or can be structured by, the encoding of societal conflicts into notions of eating etiquette, proper food, and disgust. To illuminate this gastrohydropolitical viewpoint, I read *Nineveh* and *Leila* alongside ethnographic and urbanist scholarship on water infrastructures such as Nikhil Anand's 2017 *Hydraulic City*, as well as interdisciplinary scholarship that has situated "gastropolitics" as a key node of identity and power relations within and beyond South Asia. I pay particular attention to the role of gastropolitics in right-wing Hindu nationalism, to competing masculinities, and to politicizations of veganism, vegetarianism, and meat-eating. I suggest a gastrohydropolitical viewpoint as a nonemergency narrative that can apprehend possible climate futures in terms of both present-day injustices in hydro-infrastructures and hierarchical attitudes expressed through expectations about eating. Chapter 5 concludes the book with future-facing meditations on the speculative role of consumption fictions in imagining evolving food cultures and hydro-infrastructures as climate change intensifies.

As the comparative approach of this book reveals, the importance of food and hunger to environmental narratives is not specific to one national culture, but is rather a broader response to global conditions of neoliberalism and environmental destruction. Hunger and malnutrition are inseparable from this planetary order. At the same time, *Precarious Eating* remains specific about how these global patterns manifest in particular locales (where national policy failures also matter), leaving open the possibility that scholars of the Caribbean, East and West Africa,

Southeast Asia, Latin America, the Pacific, and beyond might explore eating in other environmental cultures in the global South. Both India and South Africa are home to a split environmental consciousness. Celebrated conservation efforts have operated at the expense of the poor. Extractive industries and large dam projects continue to devastate landscapes where poor people live. Rather than allow such problems in contemporary postcolonies to be ignored, consumption fictions provide nuanced accounts of how the geopolitics of environmental extraction and neoliberalism manifest locally, throwing into relief interconnected injustices that fester anew as our planet heats up. In so doing, consumption fictions offer a broad invitation to rethink neoliberal approaches to hunger, inequality, and environmental precarity.

PART I

Eating and Environmental Precarity in India

1

From Famine to Farmer Suicides

Precarity and Gastronomic Desire in Representations of Indian Agriculturalists

When South Korean farmer Lee Kyung Hae stabbed himself at the 2003 World Trade Organization (WTO) ministerial in Cancún, his death bespoke a gruesome open secret: neoliberalism's deadly impacts on rural food producers. Holding a sign that read "WTO kills farmers," Lee embodied an activist narrative that holds WTO policies accountable for intensifying hunger, poverty, environmental degradation, and misery. According to this narrative, so-called "free trade" has hurt marginal agriculturalists and numerous other workers, especially in global South countries that have little say in WTO decisions.[1]

While unusually famous, Lee's suicide is not unique. In India alone, hundreds of thousands of indebted farmers have killed themselves since the 1990s. Farmer suicides symptomatize both changes in agriculture itself and the tendency of urban-centered economic growth to make rural India "the underside of development."[2] Rural India was once narrated as culturally central, with villages "marshalled as relevant microcosms for understanding the greater Indian culture and society."[3] Granted, such narratives romanticized agriculturalists: elite nationalists used the peasant's oppression to symbolize the evils of colonialism without consistently addressing agriculturalists' material concerns (inflected by caste, class, and gender inequality).[4] But now, low-caste and poor farmers are excluded both materially *and* symbolically from the Indian nation, according to a number of public commentators. Rakhshanda Jalil writes that, whereas the farmer once "held pride of place" in Indian literatures and cultures, today rural India is ignored because "it flies in the face of the narrative of development and progress."[5] With rapid urbanization, cities are touted as centers of growth and national identity—even as 67 percent of Indians still live in rural areas and 70 percent of rural households depend primarily on agriculture, with 82 percent of farmers "small and marginal."[6] Invisibilized in urban-centric narratives, agriculturalists are paradoxically also hypervisible. A twin narrative of "agrarian crisis" and "rural distress" has also "infused public life and the media" in India since the 1990s, most spectacularly in the discourse on farmer suicides.[7] Contending with often sensational media representations of suicides and with urban disinterest in the rural, Indian activists, writers, and filmmakers are drawing attention to ongoing rural poverty. Contemporary representations of rural India echo longer traditions of cultural response to famine and agrarian distress and can shed light on global problems at the intersection of food politics, neoliberal globalization, and environmental damage.

This chapter addresses representations of marginal agriculturalists in India, connecting the Bengal famine of 1943 with controversies over farmer suicides and genetically modified organisms (GMOs) arising in the 1990s. Assembling a varied archive of fiction, film, activist discourse, and scholarly accounts, I argue that the hungry agriculturalist in India has been and remains a paradigmatic figure of combined economic, social, and environmental precarity. Hungry agriculturalists epitomize unjust distributions of labor's rewards, given the irony of food producers starving. But I also find that motifs of hunger are twinned by surprising depictions of the farmer's gastronomic desire, where yearning for rarefied food expresses an aspiration to elevate one's status. The desire to consume emerges as a crucial structure of feeling in neoliberal-era capitalism, highlighting disparities between "haves" (who can indulge this appetite) and "have nots" (who cannot, or who do so at their peril). To consume lavishly is both the promise held out by capitalist ideology and a forever-receding horizon illustrating this ideology's falsehoods. Indeed, when marginalized subjects do indulge in gastronomic delights, this can result in punishment by angry bosses or exploitative lenders, or death. Gastronomic desire that cannot be satisfied (or that leads to death) becomes a key representational vector for diagnosing the precarity that global capitalism heightens for marginalized actors confronting environmental instability. This chapter thus establishes a key argument of *Precarious Eating*: ideas about agricultural production, hunger, and gastronomy are central to contemporary cultural narratives of how capitalist globalization intersects with environmental crisis and who suffers as a result.

While this book focuses on the neoliberal era, this chapter begins with the 1943 Bengal famine to illustrate a longer tradition in which gastronomic language and representations of hunger illuminate combined environmental, social, and economic precarity. Food has been a vector of power for centuries, rising to spectacular importance in flashpoints such as famines. Cultural and scholarly narratives of the 1943 famine offer an important prehistory to the representational and material importance of food, eating, hunger, and taste today. For scholarship on famine, 1943 is an iconic case that continues to shape understandings of relations among food, power, capitalism, and environment. Moreover, in emerging at the threshold between two different agro-food systems—one feudal and one capitalist—the famine of '43 anticipates newer shifts occasioned by the Green Revolution, economic liberalization, the advent of transgenic seeds, and the controversy around India's 2020 Farm Acts. Cultural narratives of 1943 thus offer conceptual resources for navigating shifting agro-food systems (arrangements for producing and disseminating food, from cultivation to consumption) in the present. I take particular interest in how Tarashankar Bandyopadhyay's 1946–1951 *Hansuli Banker Upakathā,* as a literary narrative of the famine, presages contemporary consumption fictions. Tarashankar's mid-century novel anticipates my postmillennial literary archive in several ways: by illuminating combined environmental, economic, and social precarity through food-related representations; by conjoining depictions of hunger and food-producing labor with gastronomic language; and by using representations of food to travel across scales from the somatic to the global. Such patterns reverberate across the contemporary fictions discussed in this book, in which depictions of eating encapsulate how localized environmental calamity intersects with globalization.

India ostensibly has not experienced a major famine since 1943–1944. Conversations about hunger, poverty, and food production have migrated in new directions, including impassioned debates about GMOs and farmer suicides. Yet starvation remains an intractable feature of rural life. In the second half of this chapter, I situate controversies surrounding genetic modification and depictions of farmer suicides as paradigmatic sites of contestation in neoliberal-era environmental politics, tracing how narratives of hunger have transformed but persisted. Noting that GM controversies often turn on differences in how the problem is framed, I argue that such communication breakdowns symptomatize a need to redefine globalization as a more-than-human process of environmental and social change, or conversely to understand environmental change as operating through globalization's stratification of access to resources. After discussing GM controversies, I build on sociological and anthropological accounts of farmer suicides to establish how environmental, social, and economic factors conjoin to produce agrarian precarity. Finally, I examine Anusha Rizvi's 2010 dark comedy film *Peepli Live*, in which satire of the "farmer suicide" discourse communicates genuine concerns about rural poverty and starvation. The farmer suicide has come to represent all that is left by the wayside as India regurgitates the rhetoric of international financial institutions, presenting neoliberalism as a panacea and carbon-intensive agriculture as the way to feed the world. Yet the farmer suicide figure emerges not only through discourses of debt, starvation, and degraded environments, but also in relation to gastronomic desire. This emphasis on appetite underscores how neoliberal ideology promises modes of accumulation and consumption that India does not actually deliver to most citizens. In this way, the farmer suicide emerges as a key figure of the global present, combining food-producing labor and an appetite to consume with precarious access to food, water, and capital. This chapter thus uses the signal issues of famine, GMOs, and farmer suicides to exemplify a pattern in which food becomes central to ideological contestations over globalization and environmental change.

The Famine of '43: Origins, Inequalities, and Intellectual Legacies

The Bengal famine of 1943 was not a "natural disaster" or sudden rupture, but rather a flashpoint when gradual political and economic changes collided with a cyclone and with World War II. Rural living conditions in Bengal declined across the late nineteenth and early twentieth centuries whilst the region's agro-food system transitioned from feudalism toward capitalism. Under the zamindari system, tenant farmers paid rent to landowners (zamindars) expected to help in times of difficulty. However, zamindars increasingly ignored these obligations as British imperialists discouraged feudal "indulgences."[8] Tenant farmers nonetheless had a better deal than landless sharecroppers and wage-laborers, classes emergent in the 1870s and 1880s that could not form patronage relationships with zamindars. Rice, a staple and primary export, became scarce as early as 1862. A growing share of Bengal's rice was marketized to feed Calcutta and its expanding suburbs while population increased and production faltered, making rice harder for villagers to afford. Tenant farmers and sharecroppers could eat from their own crop, but wage-laborers depended on the market. The Great Depression arrived in 1930, fueling calls to abolish the zamindari system that colonialism had entrenched.[9] Yet this system would remain until after World War II.

The famine of '43 was a culmination of these changes in the organization of labor and distribution of food, also bound up in imperial policy: Britain prioritized the war effort in ways that caused starvation. Production of war materials boosted industrialization in Bengal, but profits were confined to urban areas, to sectors relevant to the war effort (jute, iron, steel, mining, textiles, tobacco), and to certain Indians. For example, owners of jute mills benefitted from increased demand, but these profits did not trickle down to mill workers or peasant cultivators. Likewise, a 1943 upsurge in rice prices (provoked in part by policies that delayed the movement of food grains to rush war materials) did not augment wages for rice growers, whose buying power was outstripped.[10] The Priority Classes Scheme, launched in 1942, aimed not to systematically combat hunger but to discourage industrial unions from joining the Quit India nationalist campaign. The measure therefore set aside subsidized grains, but only for urban workers in war-related industries, encouraging rampant prices in rural areas.[11] Rice *exports* from Bengal continued even as Bengalis were starving, feeding the British Indian Army and strategic priorities such as Ceylon and Mauritius.[12]

The government of Bengal also enacted "denial policies" in case of a Japanese invasion, requisitioning bicycles, stocks of grain, and 66,500 boats.[13] Rice denial authorized unsupervised agents to buy up grain, encouraging hoarding and speculation.[14] Boat denial devastated fishers and paddy cultivators; when civilians in Midnapur resisted, officials responded by destroying boats. Amidst this turbulence, as well as political repression and rape and looting by soldiers, a cyclone in October 1942 plunged Midnapur and neighboring areas into acute famine.[15] Rural dwellers could not escape cyclone-induced floods without their boats; district authorities rescued officials but left thousands of civilians to drown or starve. Relief work, including anti-famine measures and the removal of bodies, was delayed out of "desire to punish" for political agitation.[16] American and British soldiers and state-backed police continued to perpetrate atrocities, raping thirty-three women in two Midnapur villages in January 1943. Uproar resulted, citing the hypocrisy of British propaganda that lambasted Japanese brutality while heroizing Allied soldiers and police.[17]

Famine vulnerability, then, interwove with political and sexual violence and was structured by gender, class, caste, and the urban–rural divide. Waged agricultural laborers were the primary victims, followed by fishers, transport workers, paddy huskers, and craftspeople.[18] Urban populations were largely protected via the war economy; Calcutta "saw the famine mainly in the form of masses of rural destitutes, who trekked . . . into the city."[19] These migrants were likelier to survive in Calcutta because of relief kitchens, yet the relief was so inadequate that "unattended dead bodies could be found everywhere."[20] Many female famine victims resorted to sex work or were sold by family members.[21] Rather than addressing hunger, the British administration issued a vagrancy ordinance, expelling unsightly beggars to prevent "embarrassment" before Allied troops.[22] Stocks of requisitioned rice rotted rather than being distributed.[23]

As the Raj sought not to relieve famine victims so much as to hide them, contemporaneous explanations of the famine were highly politicized. The official account blamed a food shortage, produced by low carrying of stocks from 1942, a cut-off of Burmese rice imports when Japan conquered Burma, and the cyclone that damaged the *aman* (winter rice) crop.[24] Commonsense opinion instead called the famine "man-made," blaming "abandonment" at several levels: patriarchs cast off dependent family members, landlords ignored their feudal obligations, and the government of Bengal abandoned the rural poor.[25] To say the famine was shaped by "purposeful human conduct" was to reject British famine-commission reports, which repeatedly attributed famines to India's "unstable monsoon climate."[26]

Supporting the popular account of a "man-made" famine, scholars now refute that modern famines are primarily caused by natural events, or even by food shortages. The famine of '43 remains fundamental to the study of hunger because it dramatically illustrated starvation's roots in social inequality. Amartya Sen's 1981 *Poverty and Famines: An Essay on Entitlement and Deprivation*—arguably the most influential piece of scholarship on famine—opens with the famous insight that starvation results from "some people not *having* enough food to eat" rather than "there *being* not enough food to eat."[27] Using the famine of '43 as a case study, Sen's "entitlement approach" to famines "concentrates on the ability of people to command food through the legal means available": famines result when some segments of society are not accorded sufficient "exchange entitlements" to legally procure food.[28] Thus, while stresses to food supply can pressurize unequal entitlements, famines result not from food shortages, but from the social inequalities that tier access to food. Sen admittedly "makes no attempt to include . . . illegal transfers" such as looting, but notes that modern famines usually occur "in societies with 'law and order,' without anything 'illegal.'"[29] Indeed, legal forces tend to uphold inequitable entitlements, "guarding ownership rights against the demands of the hungry."[30] In 1943, Bengalis "who died in front of well-stocked food shops protected by the state were denied food because of *lack* of legal entitlement, and not because their entitlements were violated."[31] Extending this thought further would imply that famine is not an aberration, but a structural feature of modernity. Legal structures function to apportion starvation to certain people who are supposedly not "entitled" to food.

Influenced by Sen's chilling explanation, scholars have transitioned from thinking about starvation as caused by failures in food availability to recognizing famines as politically perpetrated. Scholars of the 1943 famine vary on the relative influence of illegal activities versus government policies, and of British versus Bengali actors, but the consensus remains that famine resulted from imbalances in power.[32] Famine scholars uphold that modern and "postmodern" famines in general are not caused by "natural factors," but by politics. Stephen Devereux credits Sen with galvanizing a "paradigm shift" from thinking of famines "as failures of food availability" to considering them "failures of access to food," and advocates a further shift to analyze "failures of accountability and response."[33] This "'new famine' thinking" explains the continuance of famines despite sufficient global food supplies and, for Devereux, disrupts common arguments in favor of biotechnology, such as when proponents of GM agriculture claim that transgenics will avert hunger by increasing agricultural yields, an argument that assumes that hunger results from insufficient food availability (whereas famine scholars have been arguing otherwise since the 1980s).[34]

Responses to the famine of '43, then, continue to inform ideas about hunger, food access, and now biotechnology, constituting an important intellectual heritage for food studies and the postcolonial environmental humanities to engage. Indeed, Sen's point that modern societies mark certain bodies as unentitled to eat illuminates the radical power of a simple claim made by food sovereignty activists: that access to healthy, sufficient, and culturally relevant food is a fundamental right. Influenced both by Sen and by the food sovereignty movement, this book understands tiered food access as an architecture of power, inequality, and environmental injustice fundamental to a petro-capitalist world order.

That India has avoided famine (by some definitions) since independence is frequently chocked up to the Green Revolution. But while the introduction of high-yield rice and wheat varieties in the 1970s may have increased agricultural yields, this has by no means prevented hunger. Contemporary India has "large central food surpluses yet localized pockets of dearth," a scenario that recalls 1943, suggesting a problem of distribution rather than supply.[35] India's success in averting famines should be considered alongside its failure to prevent quieter forms of hunger: chronic malnutrition and undernutrition persist, as do deaths by starvation.[36] As Sourit Bhattacharya puts it, "there is hardly any change in caste and class relations since independence. . . . The famine [of '43] is officially over, but for the impoverished it has now turned into an everyday condition of being."[37] Moreover, a different epidemic of rural death has become visible: farmer suicides. The second half of this chapter will contemplate how narratives of agrarian hunger have transformed but persisted. First, however, I will consider how hunger, gastronomic desire, and global capitalist incursion intersect in Tarashankar's novelization of the famine of '43.

Labor, Hunger, Delectation, Language: *Hansuli Banker Upakathā*

Beyond casting a long shadow in scholarship, the famine of '43 prompted a literary outpouring in Bengali and English from authors such as Bhabani Bhattacharya, Manik Bandyopadhyay, Kazi Nazrul Islam, Ela Sen, Bijan Bhattacharya, and Tarashankar Bandyopadhyay. Many famine writers were Bengali elites who belonged to the Progressive Writers' Association linked with the Communist Party. According to Rajender Kaur, such writers saw the famine as epitomizing the evils of British colonialism, spurring "utopian" nationalist narratives that eclipsed how inequalities within Bengali society would remain after independence—even as famine writers also noted how vulnerability was structured by class, caste, urban–rural location, gender, and religion.[38] Sourit Bhattacharya instead emphasizes how famine writers interrogated both colonialism and the rise of speculative capitalism, which allowed some Bengalis to benefit financially from the famine.[39] In Bhattacharya's account, famine prompts innovations in literary style to "capture the immediate horror" while also analyzing long-standing causes, and the resulting expanded realism incorporates naturalistic imagery, journalistic documentation, melodrama, analytical accounts (in which characters scrutinize causes of famine), episodic structures, and autocritical "reflection on the modes of representation."[40]

The latter self-reflexive technique is striking in Tarashankar's *Hansuli Banker,* which depicts the slow evolution of agrarian precarity even as it self-consciously questions the capacity of its elite author to represent this experience. *Hansuli Banker* was published in Bengali in installments between 1946 and 1951, straddling India's decolonization and partition, and translated into English by Ben Conisbee Baer in 2011 as *The Tale of Hansuli Turn.* I am indebted to Baer's translation and critical commentary. As I have argued elsewhere, Tarashankar dramatizes the incorporation of peasants into a global capitalist economy as a clash of the oral "tale of Hansuli Turn" against written genres, including official histories and the novel itself.[41] With this representational strategy, Tarashankar both acknowledges limits to his novelistic portrayal and positions famine and the shifting agro-food system as part of a broader clash of worldviews informed by the power dynamics of whose story gets recorded and how. Deaths of peasant women noted as uxoricides (killings of wives) and femicides in the subaltern "tale" get recorded in police ledgers as accidents or suicides; peasants accustomed to doing "business . . . by word of mouth" are misled by the gentry's written "documents" and "deeds" into signing away their land.[42] Divergent perspectives also register in the polyvocality of the original *Hansuli Banker Upakathā,* such as the use of dialect by rural lower castes while the narrator uses standard Bengali, a difference Baer preserves by drawing on various English vernaculars.[43]

While the present chapter focuses less on heteroglossia or metafiction and more on Tarashankar's integration of gastronomic and agrarian registers, *Hansuli Turn* exemplifies novelistic form's capacity to stretch in order to follow food and environmental crisis across differing cultural contexts and representational scales. Tarashankar's formal choices situate the famine as a symptom of how worlds collide and social, economic, and environmental forces combine to produce precarity.

Hansuli Turn sits at the intersection of famine writing with Indian agrarian fiction, a broad literature including works in Hindi, Bengali, Urdu, Oriya, English, and more that address the exploitation of agricultural laborers, debt, loss of land, hunger, and peasant insurgencies. Agrarian fiction stretches at least from the 1920s into the present, encompassing authors such as Munshi Premchand, Mulk Raj Anand, Gopinath Mohanty, and more recently Vikram Seth and Neel Mukherjee. Like famine literature (in Kaur's account), colonial-era agrarian novels sometimes mythologized peasants in the service of elite anticolonial nationalisms that wanted peasants' support but were inconsistent in pursuing their "economic demands or their fight against the zamindars."[44] Since India's independence, however, many agrarian novels have critiqued postcolonial social inequality. Indeed, recent writers often relate their present to prior shifts in the agro-food system, identifying how promising watersheds such as independence, universal suffrage, or the abolishment of the zamindari failed to improve conditions for marginal agriculturalists.[45]

Prescient of postcolonial agrarian literature, *Hansuli Turn* charts the reconfiguration of low-caste agriculturalists' oppression amidst World War II, the famine, and the demise of the zamindari system. It is also a compelling precursor to contemporary consumption fiction, saturated with representations of eating (as well as agricultural labor) that link local and global crises. Writing in an Americanist context, Allison Carruth has observed that the humanities tend "to treat as separate objects of analysis, on the one hand, culinary practices and gastronomical rhetoric and, on the other, agricultural production and agrarian discourse," reflecting a gendered separation between the reception of female versus male writers.[46] I suspect that this separation also reflects scant attention to writers from the global South in American food studies, and a perception that gastronomic language is relevant only to privileged relationships with food. But gastronomy, agricultural production, and famine all come together in the portraits of marginal cultivators in *Hansuli Turn,* an agrarian and famine novel bulging with mangoes, molasses, potatoes, and rice paddy. I'll discuss gastronomy in two main ways. First, I use the terms "gastronomic language" and "gastronomic rhetoric" to indicate language about deliciousness, culinary refinement, and the pleasure of food, whether applied to food itself or used metaphorically. Second, when referring to "gastronomic motifs" or "representations of gastronomic desire," I am naming scenes of artisanal culinary crafting, descriptions of appetites for sumptuous food, and moments in which social status is attached to eating certain foods. In *Hansuli Turn,* motifs of gastronomic indulgence intermingle with a narrative in which perennial deprivation crescendos into famine.

These interlocking representational vectors—gastronomy or "taste," agricultural labor, and hunger—illuminate a question important to *Precarious Eating*: how literary forms grapple with very large systems, especially globalization and the global environment. Globalization's vast scale and heterogeneity introduce a representational problem, analogous to the representational challenges of climate change: how to describe such a big monster without homogenizing the many localities involved. I argue that the representation of food is one mode of overcoming these challenges. Food resonates on the most localized scale, the somatic: eating and digesting are visceral means by which individuals interface both with nonhuman matter and with cultural systems. At the same time, food scales up: hunger and delectation cannot be divorced from the global agro-food regime, which apportions different qualities and amounts of food and labor to different populations, and which is a primary arena of human impact on the planet.

Set in western Bengal in the early 1940s, Tarashankar's novel depicts the Kahars, a community of agricultural laborers who live in "Hansuli Turn": a river bend that resembles a sickle-shaped hansuli necklace. Colonial agriculturalists created the Kahar caste to serve as palanquin carriers and armed guards; Hindu landowners remolded the Kahars as landless sharecroppers; wartime industries transformed them into wage laborers.[47] Tarashankar chronicles the latter transition through a conflict between Bonwari, the traditionalist Kahar headman, and Karali, a rebellious youth who embraces factory labor to challenge the landlords. Bonwari's fidelity to the zamindars proves futile as the existing order erodes. However, the novel ends not with the Kahars' liberation, but with their reconfigured oppression as a waged proletariat. Personal conflict between Bonwari and Karali allegorizes tension between adherence to the residual feudal system and urban proletarianization.

Unlike many famine novels, *Hansuli Turn* defers the famine until late in the narrative. First, the novel details the Kahars' social position under the zamindars and the economic shifts that accompany World War II:

> It's no profit to [the Kahars] if prices of paddy, rice, molasses go up. They eat by working in the masters' fields and receive a one-third share of the harvest . . . don't have paddy or rice to sell. Neither sell nor buy. A few greens in the backyard; snails and shellfish in lake, pond, ditch, and river— catch and bring. The price of coal rises; the Kahars never burn a piece of coal in their lives, they gather twigs and sticks. (106–7)

This early passage presents the Kahars as living almost outside capitalism. They "neither sell nor buy" and live mostly by sharecropping and subsistence gathering. A collective Kahar consciousness, focalized in this passage, perceives benefits to this scenario: why worry about the price of coal if you couldn't afford it in the first place? Yet this is a passage about exploitation. Landowners are profiting from the Kahars' labor as the prices of paddy, rice, and molasses spike. Tarashankar is both satirizing the supposed beneficence of a feudal system and documenting the onset of a war economy that intensifies stratification. An initial perception that "war makes no difference at all to the Kahars" becomes untenable: soon "not a single cow or goat [is] left in Kaharpara. War broken out. . . . Price of a ten-rupee cow thirty rupees. . . . Not the price of milk, not the price of plow-pulling power, the price of meat. War has made the Kahars forget their cow tending and milk selling; it's wiped that business out" (107, 367). War alters the type of "business" available. The Kahars initially profit by selling their cattle for meat, but to "forget" prior uses of cows (to plow and produce dairy) is to take short-term profit at the expense of longer-term food security. The causes of a stratified famine are already present, both in the feudal system that predates the war and in the Kahars' disadvantageous incorporation into capitalism.

Towards the end of *Hansuli Turn,* a cyclone and resulting flooding destroy homes, fields, and food. (*Hansuli Turn* is set in Birbhum district, close enough to Midnapur to be affected by the cyclone of October 1942.) Famine begins when rice prices soar and the landlords take advantage: "Price of paddy has gone from four to eight rupees. . . . No one in the land of India has ever heard of such a thing, it is unthinkable. . . . Bosses are jumping for joy; they'll sell paddy and make money. . . . They only give [the cultivators] reminders of dues" (336). Such passages expose how landlords and speculators exacerbated the Kahars' precarity by finagling the agricultural system. Consonant with both scholarship today and popular opinion in 1943, Tarashankar presents famine as produced by social inequality. By deferring the famine until late in the novel, *Hansuli Turn*'s narrative arc models the idea of famine as piqued by the war but brewing for many years. Tarashankar centers not on the famine itself, nor on its immediate triggers, but on chronic inequities and gradual changes to social and agro-economic organization. In this way, the novel sits between famine literature and agrarian literature, connecting catastrophic hunger to long-standing labor exploitation.

Hansuli Turn also links large-scale questions of resource distribution and economic organization to the creation of social status through eating practices. The Kahar community processes societal changes by debating the relationship between caste and eating, prompting readers to understand social status as a matter of who eats what when. *Hansuli Turn* thus highlights what Kyla Wazana Tompkins has described as "the production of social inequality at the level of the quotidian functioning of the body."[48] Important to the Kahars' degraded social status is the practice of eating leftovers from the gentry's feasts. Such informal payments are expected within the zamindari system: "Bosses do a lot in times of crisis. . . . They'll even come visit, make small loans, give such things as aged fine-grain rice, preserves, dried fruit" (83). The Kahar leader Bonwari accepts this system, grateful that the gentry give the Kahars leftovers that they "eat with pleasure next day" (278). Alimentation hinges on the Kahars staying in good favor, as the feudal system construes food as a gift rather than a right. By presenting this paternalistic food injustice as a social norm that the Kahars have accepted, Tarashankar situates famine as continuous with structural inequalities under the zamindars.

Leftover food becomes key to community debates about status, when the young Karali rejects paternalism by refusing to eat leftovers. He declares that "caste goes away by eatin', pickin' up, others' leftovers" (195).

Karali understands eating leftovers as not only a precarious means of obtaining food, but a performance of inferiority; to contest material subjugation requires resistance to such symbolic oppression. When Karali becomes a factory union organizer, he instructs his followers to boycott leftovers: "Eat leftovers, lose caste. The Kahar that eats others' waste falls into outcaste" (279). Karali positions caste as produced by quotidian practices such as eating, and therefore insists that the Kahars can resist their subjugation by eating differently. Bonwari is "dumbstruck" to learn that Karali rejects leftovers: "He cannot imagine such defiance" (279). Bonwari is shocked not because he disagrees that eating leftovers signifies impurity, but because Bonwari accepts this impurity as correct for his station. Eating leftovers (*jootha*) was a form of "ritual degradation" frequently "mandated to give concrete form" to the supposed "inferiority" of Dalits in nineteenth- and twentieth-century India.[49] Moreover, the forced violation of food taboos was a sore point between high-caste Hindus and their colonizers: the 1857 mutiny in the Bengal Army started because sepoys feared losing caste by biting rifle cartridges soaked in cow and pork fat by the East India Company. Food is "a significant vehicle of pollution in a high-caste Hindu gastropolitical order, . . . rendering the Brahmin male subject most vulnerable to penetration."[50] Karali reasserts the dignity of the Kahars not by rejecting a caste-based system, but by insisting that Kahars, just like higher castes, should resist degrading eating practices. Leftovers highlight the entanglement of systemic deprivation from food with daily performances of status.

Not only does Tarashankar represent differentiated eating practices as material and symbolic means of producing power relations, but he also texturizes structural inequality as a part of the individual's somatic experiences of hunger and gastronomic desire. In this way, *Hansuli Turn* exposes unjust social and economic structures via their expressions at the scale of the body. A flashback to Karali's childhood, when he is accused of stealing mangoes, represents differentiated food access as a somatic experience involving both savor and pain. The boss, Middle Ghosh, sends Karali to the train station fetch "a basket of extra special mangoes." A little girl begs Karali for a mango, and he gives her two. But, "as Karali was leaving, . . . the guard grabbed him, . . . cut off a bit of mango, ate, sang its unending glory, made Karali taste a slice of mango, and only then released him. There's his crime. Ghosh . . . caught him because of the smell of mango on his hands and mouth." To render this injustice palpable, the passage coaxes the reader's salivation with delectable sensory language, describing how the "sweet smell" of the mangoes "was lusciously filling the goods room. If you so much as entered the room that scent would go in your nose and fill your chest, dragging saliva from the back of your tongue until your mouth was wet and drooling" (47). Tarashankar's gastronomic language invites the reader to salivate and share the somatic experience of Karali's temptation, making tangible a global agro-food system that might otherwise seem abstract. Bonwari, however, condemns Karali: "Shame shame shame. There's God, there are Brahmins, there are respectable householders—they're your bosses; they may eat, but don't they give you the favor of their leftovers?" (47–48). Endorsing food entitlements differentiated by caste, Bonwari helps Middle Ghosh thrash and expel Karali, and this incident seeds a lifelong antagonism. The mango memory motivates the adult Karali's refusal of farming in favor of factory labor, as well as anticipates Karali's view of eating leftovers as quotidian subordination. Karali's experience of forbidden mango enacts on an individual, somatic scale the injustice of differentiated food access in a colonial regime where caste underwrites who can enjoy delectable foods and who starves.

These structural inequalities are expressed in embodied experiences not only of gastronomic desire, but also of agricultural labor. Appetite and farming intersect in a scene where a cultivator named Pana harvests potatoes (and hides a few for his wife to dig up later):

Pana dug potatoes. The potatoes of Pana's boss are really big. Pana's wife will . . . dig potatoes too. [Pana has] stashed four fat potatoes in a hole in the ground marked with a sign. He'll tell his wife to hide them. . . . It's boss who always gets the fattest potatoes. Large potatoes to be eaten with rice; [Pana will] get this little extra in his own share. The real pleasure is in getting this bit more. (85–86)

Pana's low-caste position bars him from eating the products of his labor, which are described in the fleshly language of gastronomic desire as "big," "large," "fat," and "fattest," highlighting the boss's surplus in contrast to Pana's "little extra." Focalized through Pana, the passage juxtaposes these descriptions of potato size with references to manual labor, emphasizing that the boss gets the best potatoes while Pana does the work. Pana wants to reclaim not just sustenance, but the "pleasure" of food. But the boss finds the potatoes that Pana had hidden and retracts Pana's puny share as punishment. The Kahars are food producers, yet they go hungry—a grim irony underscored by Tarashankar's gastronomic lexicon. Tarashankar represents unfulfilled gastronomic desire in order to expose the injustices of the agro-food system as experienced on the scale of the body.

The novel's connective logic between somatic experiences and larger systems crystallizes in a sequence on molasses production that evokes the enmeshment of individual, regional, and global scales. Bonwari "is better than anyone at making molasses; in Jangol, Bansbadi, the villages on the other side of the Kopai, Goyalpara, Ranipara, Ghoshgram, Nandipur, Karmamath, in all these seven villages Bonwari has no equal" (105). Bonwari situates himself regionally (in relation to other villages) via gastronomic ideas about food quality. But molasses-making also expresses Bonwari's place in a wider world, as Tarashankar interweaves the minutia of molasses production with both local caste conflict and Bonwari's musings on the war:

A fire burning fiercely in a great stove. . . . Bonwari sitting on a mound. . . . [Other Kahars] feeding sugarcane husks into the furnace mouth to fuel the fire. Boiling sugarcane juice bubbles and rises. . . . The Mister Mondols sitting over to the side . . . keeping a hard eye on the molasses. War's broken out across the world. . . . Won't the value of goods go up! Paddy, rice, molasses, beans, the value of all these things will rise. Thus the Mondols are 'viggilint,' not a single thimbleful of molasses must be swiped. . . . Privately Bonwari feels a little 'urt' about this. . . . Even he's mistrusted. So let them. Bonwari quietly concentrates on making molasses. He thinks about war. (105–6)

This scene directs attention to material details of molasses-making: sugarcane husks, boiling juice, feeding the furnace. But references to war interrupt, underscoring intimacies between small-scale food production and geopolitics: "concentrat[ing] on making molasses" and "think[ing] about war" overlap. World War II is creating spikes in commodity prices, but Bengal's food producers will not see the profit: the Mondols already own the molasses that these laborers are making. While Bonwari accepts this structure, he resents the implication that the Kahars might steal, raising the question of who is really stealing from whom in this arrangement. Evoking how global war exacerbates this local power dynamic, this scene invites us to contemplate the geographies of exploitation behind many delectable commodities.

Hansuli Turn not only notes power relations that structure food production and access, but also flags how food-related rhetoric can encode power into everyday speech. A prime example is the repetition of the word *scum*, which underscores parallels between material and discursive subjugation. *Scum* literally refers to the substance skimmed off while making molasses, but most frequently appears as a slur that the wealthy direct at the Kahars. The food byproduct becomes a metaphor that categorizes the Kahars as social detritus, even though their labor sustains the food system. When a sudden rainstorm threatens the molasses, Pana tells "juicy stories" that become "more luscious with his sense of pleasure at the ruin of Hedo Mondol's molasses. . . . Let the bastard's molasses turn ta crap. A right bastard scum" (122). The language of gastronomic pleasure ("juicy," "luscious") codes Pana's vengeful delight as a paltry compensation for his culinary labor: he produces molasses but cannot enjoy it, so he must instead relish the feeling of vengeance. By calling Hedo Mondol "scum," Pana reclaims the word and turns it against the higher castes. When Karali saves the molasses from the rain, Hedo Mondol responds, "Scum's gotta be called hero now—yep, scum's a real hero" (123). Praise comes with a reminder of Karali's inferiority, of his status as "scum." Karali denounces this language to Hedo Mondol's face: "Whatcha sayin' scum-my-scum for?" (123). This insubordination shocks the other Kahars:

> Karali's made them speechless. The lad's got guts for sure! . . . What Karali said was right too. Those phrases *are* always . . . on the tongues of the gentry sires. They won't say it if they're angry; it'll be fondly. They'll say—Oh very nice, scum. They will ask "How's it going?" affectionately by saying— Hey there bastard, how you doing? What Karali's saying is right. Yet—. Yet . . . you have to respect the difference between great and small. (124; emphasis original)

The narration again conjures a collective Kahar perspective, which disapproves of Karali's brashness yet acknowledges his point. Tarashankar represents qualms about rebellion as a hesitation to speak: the Kahars are "speechless," which is complicated in ways by the punctuation. Baer preserves Tarashankar's use of the long dash (—) to introduce direct speech: "They'll say—Oh very nice, scum"; "by saying—Hey there bastard." This usage is a convention of the Bengali novel.[51] The dash following the first "Yet," however, is followed by a period ("Yet—. Yet"). Rather than initiating direct speech, this particular dash marks a foreclosure of speech as the collective focalizer balks at completing the thought. Rendering this moment of speechlessness as a typographical mark raises "can the subaltern speak?" and "can we hear?" questions about Tarashankar's novelization of marginal lives, and about Baer's translation. Atypically for Baer's translated text, English-style quotation marks also appear in this passage. They do not designate quoted speech from the scene itself; instead, the phrase "How's it going?" employs conventions familiar to English-speaking readers in order to typify the colloquialisms for which the gentry substitute rude expressions when talking to the Kahars. While this English expression takes quotation marks, the usual dashes offset the "scum" and "bastard" phrases, as if to reemphasize their Bengali particularity. The scum incident thus sparks a multilayered reflection on food, language, and power: on the role of food-related rhetoric in the lexicon of paternalism; on the Kahars' hesitance to resist paternalistic language; on the limitations of subaltern speech's transmutation into novelistic discourse; and on further reformulations that result from translating such an incident from Bengali to English.

Scum, the material object, repeatedly attaches to Bonwari, figuring how the system treats him like scum; simultaneously, *scum* explains the meanings of other words. The molasses sequence closes with Bonwari "thinking about this Karali business as he stood beside the stove skimming off the crud, that's to say the scum. . . . All those bastard-scum phrases *are* awful, for sure" (124–25; emphasis original). Appearing twice here, *scum* has a material referent (molasses scum) and a linguistic referent ("bastard-scum phrases"), connecting the materiality of food and labor to a lexicon of oppression. Indeed, the distinction between linguistic and material uses of *scum* blurs with the first reference, "the crud, that's to say the scum": *scum* does not *directly* designate the residue of molasses-making, but serves as a linguistic gloss to define the word "crud." Likewise, *scum* defines "gunk": "Bonwari straining out the 'gunk,' that's to say the scum, with a sieve" (105). The recurring phrase "that's to say" is Baer's translation for the Bengali word *arthāt,* which Tarashankar uses whenever he is defining a creole word by using a synonym in standard Bengali. Baer suggests that Tarashankar uses *arthāt* to link a "glossary" of creole words and phrases throughout the novel.[52] This procedure underscores that the Kahars' use of dialect is, like their eating practices, a mark of alterity. Juxtaposing several meanings of *scum*—linguistic gloss, slur, and food byproduct—enmeshes the manual labor of skimming molasses with the word's role in encoding power dynamics in language. *Scum* exposes a linguistic system that naturalizes the Kahars' exploitation in colonial and then postcolonial agro-food regimes.

Hansuli Turn situates discursive power (such as the cultural representation of food, eating, and hunger; or the power to translate and the linguistic hegemony of English) as operating in dialogue with material power. Power in the agro-food system takes material forms: who can access which foods; who labors to produce food and at what costs; who eats and whom is eaten. Power in the food system also takes discursive forms, like what expectations are created or naturalized and what cultural understandings and assumptions are furthered or elided in how we write and talk about food. These modalities of power are interpenetrating: whom is narrated as un/entitled to eat has deadly effects, as spectacularly expressed in the famine of '43. To attempt a multimodal account of power is a reason both to study food (whose multiple resonances can themselves signal both material and discursive operations of power) and to approach food through a literary and cultural lens. Throughout this book, I cultivate an attention to how food is both a material artifact of labor and resources and also a complex representational system, with the view that such an approach can hone our attention to multiple formations of power and precarity.

Also relevant here is another network of power, both material and discursive: the privileged circulation of the novel genre and of Anglophone and Europhone texts. Gaps yawn between Tarashankar's elite novel and folk traditions, and between *Hansuli Banker Upakathā* and *The Tale of Hansuli Turn.* I myself can read only Baer's English translation, meaning my reading of *Hansuli Turn* is mediated by Baer's sense of the novel. (Because Baer's translation is recent, *Hansuli Turn* has received little critical attention in English.) I have written elsewhere on how to contemplate Baer's translation as a repositioning of the novel, worthy of study in its own regard for illuminating the construction of troubled and still-unfolding critical categories such as "global modernism."[53] While *Precarious Eating* is primarily a study of Anglophone texts, I include *Hansuli Turn* in part to trouble the Anglophone as category, considering a non-English-language prehistory to contemporary Anglophone writing about food, environment, and power.

Not only does *Hansuli Turn* bring forward intersections between discursive and material power through its engagements with food, but the novel also models how the lens of consumption can enable thinking across representational scales. *Hansuli Turn* depicts famine as a slow-onset event, attending to the gradually shifting economics of food production and food access. Gastronomic motifs join with this depiction of a changing agro-food system to convey local and regional expressions of global forces, documenting how large-scale processes cause social inequalities that are experienced at the scale of the body through exploited labor and differentiated eating. These representational patterns invite two important reorientations for food studies and the postcolonial environmental humanities. First, *Hansuli Turn* destabilizes the idea that gastronomic language necessarily fixes attention on privileged perspectives, instead combining representations of gastronomy, appetite, and labor relations to contest the consignment of subaltern agriculturalists to hunger. Second, *Hansuli Turn* models how attention to eating and starving can enable representational and conceptual movement across multiple scales, recentering lived experiences of unequal access to resources in accounts of how globalization shapes environmental precarity. Tarashankar zooms in on the inequalities *within* Bengal that are spurred by the colonial apparatus and exacerbated by the rural–urban dynamics of global war, a globalizing agro-food system, and environmental disruption. His gastronomic motifs concretize macroeconomics as they manifest on the intimate scales of appetite, labor, and alimentation. This perspective can help us grapple with more recent developments in the global agro-food system and in environmental politics, as I'll now explore.

GM Controversies and Beyond-Human Globalization

Accounts of the famine of '43 offer important prehistories to neoliberal-era narratives. While very different, both the 1940s and the 1990s–2000s were eras in which new policy structures transformed the economics of agriculture, intensifying long-standing exploitation. Both, I'll show, are also moments in which gastronomic desire and rhetoric counter-intuitively express deprivation. Thinking through such echoes, I'll now consider representations of agriculturalists and food politics in post-reform India (1991–present) with a focus on controversies over GMOs and farmer suicides. These have become hot-button issues in clashes over globalization and the environment, illuminating how the politics of eating matters to a beyond-human concept of globalization.

It is hard to imagine a more controversial subject than GMOs in environmental politics since the 1990s. The disagreements center on transgenics, a subset of biotechnological applications in which genes are moved from one species to another.[54] Scientists may be motivated to pursue transgenic research because they believe these technologies can save lives by increasing food availability, nutritional content, or climate resiliency; or by reducing chemical inputs.[55] This line of thought frames hunger, malnutrition, and climate change as technical problems amenable to technical solutions; social scientists and scholar/activists, however, tend to situate these as social, economic, and political issues requiring nontechnical redress. Devereux, for example, frames the "biotech debate" as exemplifying the need to reconceptualize famine as "a failure of policies and politics that requires a political economy analysis and political solutions."[56] Ian Scoones suggests that hunger and agrarian crisis remain pressing in India, but "how GM crops are supposed to address such issues, no one is sure"—in large part because GM seeds are not affordable for small farmers without high-risk loans.[57] Resonating with these analyses, Annika J. Kettenburg and colleagues argue, in a case study illustrative of broader debates, that the communication breakdown surrounding transgenic Golden Rice can be attributed to differences in "problem framing" between natural scientists and social scientists.[58] Anti-GM arguments are sometimes dismissed because concerns about impacts of GM foods on human health are seen as paranoid or ill-informed, but these are not the only concerns of anti-GM politics. Whether and how the technical potentialities of GMOs translate into real-world benefits (and for whom) is complicated by transnational corporations holding patents on GM technologies, and more generally by the uptake of biotechnologies in an asymmetrical regime of global capitalism that has rarely helped marginalized people or environments in the global South.

As Tarashankar documents, global capitalism was already changing the lives of subaltern agriculturalists in the era of World War II. These disruptions took new forms in the "Green Revolution" beginning in the 1970s, which brought hybrid seed varieties, monocultural farming, and the intensive use of chemical fertilizers and pesticides to places such as India. While proponents of the Green Revolution narrate these as ways to combat global hunger, leftist thinkers are likelier to question the effectiveness of such strategies and emphasize their costs: "laborers spraying pesticides and paying for it with their health, urban consumers paying for it with cheap, poisoned food, land paying for it with soil toxicity, farmers paying for it with their lives. . . . [or] their very ability to farm in the future."[59] In this context, calls from prime ministers for a "second" Green Revolution in the form of a biotechnological economic package will sound like further harm. The echo of the Green Revolution has helped to make GMOs controversial, prompting grassroots mobilizations for "an alternative trajectory, viz. an agro ecological transition."[60]

Much controversy about transgenics has centered on the American biotech company Monsanto, owner of the Bt technology contained in virtually all cotton seeds (from various companies) available to Indian farmers. ("Bt" stands for the *Bacillus thuringiensis* gene used to make plants resistant to pests, especially bollworms. Bt cotton is cultivated both in South Africa and in India, where it constituted 90 percent of the cotton grown as of 2017.[61]) The epidemic of suicides by Indian farmers since the 1990s has been linked to debt, which scholar/activists argue is incurred by buying Bt seeds and other expensive inputs. Monsanto has targeted small farmers in North America too, suing for patent infringement in cases such as that of Percy Schmeiser, a Canadian farmer whose fields of non-GM canola were cross-contaminated by a neighbor's GM crop. The court found in Monsanto's favor that Schmeiser "had no right to the Roundup Ready canola growing amidst his own nonmodified varieties and visibly indistinguishable from them, even if its presence there was the work of accident."[62] Concerns about GM implementation and human health impacts of Roundup and Agent Orange have made Monsanto the enemy for many activists. Monsanto's acquisition in June 2018 by the German pharmaceutical company Bayer has not discouraged critics.[63]

Among the most controversial ideas in transgenics are Genetic Use Restriction Technologies (GURTs). V-GURTs (dubbed "Terminator" genes by activists) are technologies in which inserted genes make the plants' future seeds sterile.[64] Such technology was designed to protect the intellectual property of multinationals by physically preventing farmers from saving seed year to year. (Seed saving, which is fundamental to traditional agriculture, is currently "practised by 100 million farmers in Latin America, 300 million in Africa and 1 billion in Asia," and accounts for 15–20 percent of the world's food supply.[65]) Because V-GURTs would protect intellectual property in perpetuity, they would "bypass . . . the intellectual property regulatory framework" that mandates expiration dates for patents and licenses (usually after twenty years).[66] Creating perpetual monopolies, this would rewrite the global balance of patent regulations (which has already tipped to increase the power of patent-holding corporations since the nineteenth century, and more rapidly since the 1995 international TRIPS agreement [Trade-Related Aspects of Intellectual Property Rights]) and would circumvent the sovereignty of nations that disallow certain foreign patents in order to protect their own economies.[67] V-GURTs also raise fears that the unintended spread of transgenes to other plants (e.g., through pollen) could sterilize "nontarget" plants, threatening biodiversity and non-GM crops.[68] Because of all the ways in which V-GURTs would privilege multinationals over small farmers, countries in the global South, and biodiversity, this technology triggered both concerns in the scientific community and a global outcry from anti-GM activists.

Monsanto's Bt cotton was the first transgenic introduced in India, with field trials in 1995; the prospect of a "Terminator" gene sparked national media attention in 1998. The Research Foundation for Science Technology and Ecology (RFSTE), led by scholar/activist Vandana Shiva, presented a court petition for stronger regulation of Bt technology, prompting extensive hearings. A public-relations battle ensued between Monsanto and nongovernmental organizations (NGOs) who launched a "Monsanto Quit India" campaign. This slogan echoes the anticolonial nationalist movement "Quit India" of 1942, exemplifying how activists situate mobilization against GMOs and global capitalism as a contemporary anticolonial struggle. Bt cotton nonetheless became commercially available in 2002 in India, to a storm of new protests, and in South Africa in 1997.[69] A "Terminator" gene, however, was not used: activism motivated a "*de facto* global moratorium" on GURTs by the Fifth Conference of Parties

(COP5) meeting in Nairobi in 2000; India followed suit by banning "Terminator" technology in 2001.[70] To the author's knowledge, no plants with V-GURTs are commercially available as of 2023. Farmers, however, can still be compelled to buy expensive seeds year after year when patent regulations cover future plant progeny as well as seeds themselves, and the TRIPS agreement has pushed countries in the global South to align their patent laws with regulatory frameworks developed in the North.[71]

GM debates symptomatize broader ideological clashes over globalization and environmental change: conflicting ideas about how we should adapt food systems for climate resiliency or combat poverty; philosophical questions about what can or should be owned; or quandaries about the future of capitalism. In Shiva's view, the patenting of seeds and other life forms constitutes a "second coming of Columbus."[72] Patented biotechnologies, she argues, are a new device to justify appropriation, akin to the charters that supported European colonization:

> The principle of effective occupation by [C]hristian princes has been replaced by effective occupation by the transnational corporations supported by modern-day rulers. The vacancy of targeted lands has been replaced by the vacancy of targeted life forms and species manipulated by the new biotechnologies. The duty to incorporate savages into Christianity has been replaced by the duty to incorporate local and national economies into the global marketplace.[73]

For Shiva, global capitalism is the new idol, and GM patenting is the new colonialism. The doctrine of *terra nullius* (used to justify European colonialism) is the ideology that non-European lands were vacant and unproductive, needing enclosure to make them useful (to Europeans). Shiva suggests that *terra nullius* has been adapted to enclose particular "life forms and species" regarded as needing biotechnological intervention to maximize their productivity. Her implication is both that transgenic science crosses sacrosanct boundaries by harnessing nonhuman nature to an ideology of productivity optimization (for the benefit of some humans) and that a biotechnological attitude ignores the amazing activity that earth and seeds already engage in, just as *terra nullius* ignores the ecosystem services and the food value for Indigenous peoples provided by preconquest lands. Shiva thus frames peasant resistance to GMOs as a movement to return genes—like land, water, and other contested resources—from the privatized realm to the "commons."[74] This politics clearly exceeds technical questions about whether transgenics can improve yields or pest-resistance (even as those technical issues are themselves contested). GMOs are an "iconic" issue for transnational activists, "representative of a wider set of struggles" against the commercialization of agriculture, disenfranchisement of the poor, and destruction of biodiversity.[75] Anti-GM activists in India, South Africa, North America, and elsewhere leverage "issues of sovereignty, inequality, rights, [and] justice" to garner media attention for "an alternative 'grand narrative,' one counterposed to the mainstream neoliberal worldview."[76] This counternarrative rejects the privatizing logics of neoliberalism and counterposes an idea of the earth as a commons that deserves respect and careful tending.

GM debates even raise conflicts over what we're talking about when we discuss globalization, as illustrated in the 2005 documentary film *Bullshit* by Per-Åke Holmquist and Suzanne Khardalian. Opening with gratuitous shots of bulls literally shitting, *Bullshit* takes its name from the "Bullshit Award for Sustaining Poverty" to which Shiva was named by Barun Mitra, a lobbyist based in Delhi and London. (Shiva apparently responded by praising cow dung as an excellent organic fertilizer.) Mitra challenges Shiva's work on grounds that she denies the centrality of "globalization" to her career:

> She has become a product of globalization, known across the world, fighting against globalization. Just imagine: twenty years ago it would have been impossible for her to become what she is. There wouldn't have been TV, there wouldn't have been satellite, there wouldn't have been communication. . . . So she has harnessed the power of the market, the forces of globalization, to become an icon, and now . . . prevents everybody else from accessing similar benefits.[77]

Mitra is certainly right that Shiva has become a transnational icon, speaking out against GMOs internationally and even cropping up in the heirloom-seed catalog from Missouri that I receive in the mail.[78] Mitra finds Shiva's stance "against globalization" hypocritical because her own status is "a product of globalization." But Mitra is describing globalization as information-dissemination through digital technologies ("TV," "satellite," "communication"). This is not the "globalization" that Shiva opposes. She refers to her antagonist as "the global corporate economy" and "economic and corporate globalization."[79] Shiva is problematizing the unchecked spread of corporate capitalism, not taking issue with all forms of transnational connection. Indeed, in an interview with Bill Moyers, Shiva criticizes GM science for looking at "genes in isolation" and claims, "the real science is the science of interconnection; . . . everything is related. Farming, for example, you must see the soil, the plants, the pollinators, the food that's produced, all of it in the whole." Playing devil's advocate, Moyers challenges that "some people" see "globalization, the movement of ideas, of people, of money, across arbitrary boundaries . . . [as] an economic equivalent of what happens in the world of nature in that everything is connected. And you can't stop it, Vandana Shiva." Perhaps missing an opportunity to differentiate the "movement of ideas" or "people" from the movement of "money," Shiva rejects this comparison of economics to nature: "This is not interconnectedness at the ecological level. It's an extremely artificial, corporate rule. . . . All that's flowing around is commodities."[80] Shiva's distinction is important: it is spurious and dangerous to leverage ecological rhetoric in order to abdicate responsibility for how we regulate (or deregulate) economies. And yet, these conversations suggest that at stake in GM debates, and in broader debates about neoliberalism, are *both* economic and beyond-human forms of global "interconnection," which may be more entangled than Shiva would like to admit.

I want to suggest that debates around GMOs illuminate struggles to narrate both globalization and a changing global environment. These phenomena are so large and heterogeneous that any narrative risks flattening or universalizing, inhibiting careful conceptualizations (not to mention thoughtful responses). Among the contentions of *Precarious Eating* is that we can work toward the more nuanced narratives that are prerequisite for justice-minded policies or social transitions by recognizing that environmental change and globalization co-constitute one another, as food-focused writing can illuminate. Waves of globalization alter human and nonhuman matter and change relations among humans and nonhumans. These multivarious types of change are enmeshed, as illustrated by the environmental and social impacts of transgenic science: altering a life form in the ways facilitated by transnational capital can have manifold effects on biodiversity and on economic and social relations. This is what I mean by saying that globalization and environmental change interpenetrate or that, to put the same thing another way, globalization is a more-than-human process.[81] The global environment is collaboratively created and recreated by both nonhuman and anthropogenic forces. Moreover, not all humans equally affect the global environment, meaning we need to look at power differentials structured by globalization in order to understand planetary problems.

Debates over GMOs exemplify how agro-food systems become central to the politics of globalization and environment. Small farmers occupy a complex position in these debates, with both biotech corporations and anti-GM activists (many of whom are well-off urbanites) claiming "the farmer" as the beneficiary of their efforts. On all sides of GM debates, this "poorly-defined category of 'farmer'" is imbued with political meanings that can be quite untethered from small farmers' own agencies, priorities, and lives.[82] This politicization of "the farmer" inflects not only GM debates but also another tangle of ideas about how globalized capitalism and environmental problems meet: the discourse on farmer suicides.

The Figure of the Farmer Suicide

An economic catastrophe forced India to restructure its economy in 1991. "Pledg[ing] its gold reserves as collateral to gain international loans from its former colonizer," India transferred forty-seven tons of gold to the Bank of England and accepted structural adjustments as conditions for an International Monetary Fund (IMF) bailout.[83] Twelve years later, when India hit US$100 billion in foreign exchange reserves, news reports hailed a "reversal of India's fortunes."[84] In a compelling reading of the "India Shining" megapublicity campaign from the latter moment (2003–2004), Ravinder Kaur locates a reconfigured politics of Indian citizenship epitomized by the "investor-citizen": an idealized figure "whose belonging to the nation is authenticated primarily through a capacity to invest and grow."[85] This new national ideal transcends the shame of the 1991 economic crisis by sidelining the poor. Kaur's analysis echoes criticisms of neoliberal ideology in Indian cultural texts such as Aravind Adiga's 2008 Man Booker–winning novel *The White Tiger*, which satirizes the "entrepreneur" as a moribund ideal that whitewashes exploitation and stokes violence. I suggest that the investor-citizen or entrepreneur is haunted by another figure, paradigmatic of unfulfilled desires to consume and to belong: the farmer suicide. This figure of the farmer suicide emerges as a sign for what is repressed or excluded from a neoliberal narrative of Indian citizenship based on investment and conspicuous consumption. Tellingly, small farmers are elided from the "investor-citizen" ideal. Consider an India Shining ad analyzed by Kaur that features three young, smiling, cis-female-presenting college students on bicycles. This text appears:

By taking a loan for my education,
I share the burden with my parents. . . .
By specializing in bio-genetics,
I gain wisdom for our rice fields.
By learning how to enhance our harvests,
I strengthen the backbone of my nation.
By being a partner in nation's progress,
I make my India shine.
I am India Shining.[86]

As Kaur points out, this ad makes the "claim of being ordinary" but features extraordinary subjects: in a gendered sense, because the ad situates women as "innovators and entrepreneurs in the fields of science and technology" despite India's "marked preference for sons, gender-based violence, and low human development indicators . . . [for] female citizens"; in a classed sense because poverty is elided to render middle-class experience "ordinary."[87] I would add that agriculture is framed as "the backbone of [the] nation," without any agriculturalists. The farmer is eclipsed by the biogeneticist, extolling an "enhanced" agriculture and ignoring the statistically significant number of Indians who depend on smallholder farming. This is a shift from a narrative in which *farmers* were the "backbone of the nation" to one in which they are peripheral. If belonging by investing and consuming is the new national imaginary on offer, then farmers are pressured to renarrate themselves as consumers and investors, losing their identities as food producers.[88] This shift from producer to consumer is material as well as symbolic, in that farming now entails buying expensive seeds and other inputs. Other types of consumerist aspirations, meanwhile, are all too often beyond the means of farmers, as I discuss in the coming pages. Excluded from the investor-citizen narrative, the farmer wells up as a return of the (national) repressed in the spectral figure of the farmer suicide, which manifests exclusion from neoliberal nationhood as shame and death.

Farmer suicides have become a constant presence in Indian media, also featuring in novels such as Neel Mukherjee's 2014 *The Lives of Others,* Kota Neelima's 2013 *Shoes of the Dead,* and Sonora Jha's 2013 *Foreign.* Indeed, in Akhil Gupta's view, the omnipresent farmer suicide has become "an arbitrary signifier used by different interest groups to push their own political agendas," much like the "farmer" in GM debates.[89] My analysis is focused not on the material phenomenon of farmer suicides, but on cultural narratives about that reality. But of course, this thinking can occur only in dialogue with acknowledging the very real phenomenon of premature deaths among indebted agriculturalists. In 2012 it was reported that an average of eighteen thousand Indian farmers committed suicide every year for the preceding sixteen years. These deaths have been concentrated in six of India's 640 districts, with the most notorious region being Vidarbha in Maharashtra.[90] This epidemic has been left unresolved by government, notwithstanding measures to help the families of suicides by financially compensating their loss. Compensation usually means a cash payment of about fifty thousand rupees (or US$800) and forgiveness of loans. But when compensation policies create budget problems, local officials have been ordered to stop classifying peasants' deaths as suicides. Concerns have also been raised that the payments could incentivize suicide.[91]

Indebted farmers commit suicide for a complex and contested set of reasons. The relevance of economic versus psychological factors—and indeed, the relevance of a category of "farmer suicide"—has become a politicized debate. Whereas government reports have pinned farmer suicides on individual psychology and alcoholism, activists argue that neoliberal policies and corporations pushing GM seeds lead to debt that motivates suicide.[92] While it is beyond the scope of this chapter to fully map these debates, I will discuss how farmer suicides are narrated in three social-scientific accounts. Anthropologists and sociologists have bolstered and nuanced activist explanations of the link between debt and suicide, highlighting how economics interact with environmental factors such as

drought (amplified by climate change) and with social/affective factors including shame, expectations of masculinity, familial conflict, and attitudes
toward consumption.

Gupta notes that, while agrarian debt is not uniquely caused by transgenic seeds, those seeds are involved in a larger "conjuncture of environmental change and neoliberalism in producing precarity."[93] Farming has
become "speculative": small farmers have to take out loans to begin, meaning they are "gambling on the weather and on global commodity prices."[94]
If the rains and the market are good, they may profit; if not, farmers will
get insufficient returns to pay back loans and will sink further into debt.
Cycles of debt are rendered likelier by liberalization, which has left farmers vulnerable to global price fluctuations, and by pressure to buy expensive GM seeds annually because of patent regulations. Gupta also cites
two environmental factors. First, soils are becoming depleted and contaminated by chemical fertilizers and pesticides as a result of monocrop
agriculture, which also encourages pests and erosion. Second, climate
change has made rainfall unpredictable, intensifying the vulnerability of
rain-fed agriculture (which is the majority of agriculture in India, and
most economically available to small farmers).[95] Gupta's analysis echoes
the environmental outlooks of both *Hansuli Turn* and "new famine thinking," in which "natural" events can be factors in a disaster but do not in-
dependently produce a disaster; instead, decisions about economic policy
combine with nonhuman forces to produce agrarian precarity. Moreover,
the environmental issues mentioned by Gupta are themselves results of
globalized capitalism, which fuels climate change and the depletion of soils
through carbon-intensive approaches to food production and distribution. Farmer suicides echo impacts from earlier processes of capitalization
and farmer exploitation, but also, following Gupta, are a regionally specific
response to how climate change interacts with neoliberal globalization.

Complementing Gupta's account of intersecting economic and environmental pressures, Nilotpal Kumar and B. B. Mohanty both highlight
the role in farmer suicides of frustrated aspirations to the consumption
that neoliberal ideology promised. From fieldwork in Vidarbha, Mohanty
observes that economic precarity does not determine suicides directly, but
interacts with feelings of disappointment that neoliberalism has not im-
proved standards of living (and with other social/affective factors including isolation, familial conflicts, and feelings of worthlessness).[96] Similarly,

Kumar's informants in southern Andhra Pradesh are pressured not only by debt and drought, but by regional masculinities that demand performative conspicuous consumption. (The "typical" farmer suicide is cis-male, although as Kumar notes, there are also suicides by female farmers.) Consumption patterns are locally dichotomized as *class* or *mass* (using the English words): "consuming *class*" is regarded as urban, as modern, and as a way of "moving upward from *mass* cultural practices," which are associated with a "'vulgar' agrarian lifestyle."[97] Frequently facilitated by going into debt, *class* consumption means buying TVs, motorbikes, and cell phones; building new houses; and performing a range of gastronomic behaviors and rhetorics. According to Kumar, "to aggressively emulate each other in consuming commodities" expresses "a unique kind of regional masculinity" that blends locally-defined masculinity (*paurusham*) with "consuming global icons such as Nokia, Honda, or Samsung."[98] Failure to consume *class* can signify as failed masculinity, triggering shame and even suicide. Thus, while Kumar and Mohanty each argue against reductionist economic explanations for farmer suicides, they offer social and affective accounts of how global capitalism is experienced: globalized consumer expectations articulate with local codes to create new pressures.

The importance of gastronomy among Kumar's informants is exemplified by the signifier "eating rice." Relying on a Bourdieu-influenced sense of food and drink as a primary field of "distinction," Kumar explains that dry millets have been replaced in this region by rice, perceived as more modern. Villagers ask whether one has "eaten rice" in order to inquire whether one has eaten "contentedly," making eating rice a "local . . . shorthand for the desire of an equal and modern self."[99] Rice has become the staple across classes; however, class distinctions are "woven around rice varieties," with finer grades of rice marking gentility.[100] Outdoor lunches and dinners characterized by excessive consumption (called *enjay* parties) and dining at restaurants are also sought-after modes of performative consumption. Kumar describes an "epicurean" impulse in which "gastronomic novelty and pleasure [are] at the centre of local discourses" of fashioning selfhood, and "eating out and drinking in male company" are modes of performing cosmopolitan masculinity.[101]

Conspicuous consumption (enabled by high-risk loans) emerges as a way that marginalized agrarians attempt to climb the ladder of global society. Rather than gastronomic desire and performative eating being inherently bourgeois, Kumar describes an "emulative consumption": *class* eating and purchasing behaviors are, for the rural lower classes, a mode of aspiration (much as Karali's refusal of leftovers in *Hansuli Turn* constitutes a bid for better status in a caste hierarchy intersecting with global capital). If humanists in the U.S. academy have tended to analyze cuisine and gastronomic rhetoric separately from "agricultural production and agrarian discourse" (as Carruth has suggested), both Tarashankar's novel and Kumar's ethnography refuse that separation.[102] Each evokes the centrality of gastronomic desire to the subjectivities of agriculturalists, noting an appetite for upward mobility expressed in ideas about eating. In chapter 3, I trace a similar preoccupation with "classy" dining among poor characters in Zakes Mda's early-2000s South African fiction, suggesting the importance of attempted gastronomic distinction across multiple marginalized populations confronting liberalization. The suicide controversy in India is a flashpoint in broader struggles around how the conjuncture of environmental degradation and neoliberalism affects the poor in the global South, resonating with other scenarios in which neoliberal ideology promised improvements in social and economic status that it never delivered, including opportunities to consume.

Building on Mohanty and Kumar's arguments that farmer suicides emerge from dashed aspirations to consume, I suggest that neoliberalism does not merely dictate a set of economic policies: by falsely promising prosperity, it also creates structures of feeling. As Gupta puts it, "poor peasants see richer peasants and urban people profiting from a neoliberal economy. They aspire to it, and it lures them into risky endeavors, which in turn delivers them not to a middle-class life, but instead exposes them to social death, the loss of face, and eventually, to death."[103] Along these lines, neoliberalism also needs to be understood in its broader entanglement with environmental shifts: neoliberalism is both the latest iteration of the consumptive capitalism that has caused an uneven climate crisis and also prone to interact with nonhuman factors in ways that intensify desperation, as when a cash-strapped farmer confronts a drought. What becomes visible in these sociological and anthropological accounts of farmer suicides, then, is a narrative of neoliberal-era globalization as a combined social, affective, economic, and environmental phenomenon that stratifies consumption and precarity.

Casualties of the Farmer Suicide Idea in *Peepli Live*

Kumar uses the term "FS thesis" to name the idea that self-inflicted deaths by farmers constitute a distinct etiological category from other suicides, differentiated by farming-related motives and statistically significant enough to demonstrate an agrarian crisis.[104] Skeptical of this FS thesis, Kumar diagnoses how the category "farmer suicide" has been imbued with cultural, political, and economic significance in ways that can gloss over complex rural circumstances. This is an important point, although I hesitate when Kumar schematizes "genuine" versus "fake" farmer suicides.[105] It is not, however, my expertise to debate the extent to which different factors contribute to rural suicides. Instead, I would explore the power that the *figure* of the farmer suicide has acquired in contemporary culture, a development contingent on yet in excess of real farmers' lives and deaths.

Indeed, the central tension in Anusha Rizvi's 2010 Hindi-language film *Peepli Live* is the relationship between the farmer suicide as figure and the actual deaths of agriculturalists. A darkly comedic satire of contemporary rural life, *Peepli Live* begins with brothers Natha and Budhia returning to their village, Peepli, after visiting the bank.[106] These small farmers have learned that, if they don't repay a loan, their land will be auctioned off. When Natha and Budhia approach local politician Bhai Thakur for help, he and his cronies jeer that the brothers should just kill themselves, because a new government program will compensate them 1 lakh (one hundred thousand) rupees. Taking this idea seriously, Budhia manipulates Natha into agreeing to be the suicide. But before any suicide can take place, a local journalist named Rakesh prints Budhia and Natha's story and it gets picked up by a TV channel. A media frenzy ensues, prompting Rakesh to question his own journalistic ethics. State and federal politicians campaigning for reelection spar over blame for the plight of farmers. Journalists scramble over each other to sensationalize the still-living farmer suicide, including a memorable scene in which one station films Natha's fresh turd. This chaos culminates in a fire and, it seems, Natha's accidental death. The film's denouement finds the village quiet after the media's departure, and Natha's family still indigent: Natha's death by accident (rather than the much-advertised suicide) means they will get no compensation.

The origins of Natha and Budhia's debts are not specified, leading reviewer M. K. Raghavendra to claim that *Peepli Live* depoliticizes indebtedness as a "'human' concern rather than an economic one" by obscuring its causes.[107] However, an early scene in which the brothers converse with neighboring farmers (Figure 1) does name the global forces at work, if perhaps glossing over responsible parties closer to home. "What good is farming?," asks one of Budhia and Natha's neighbors. "American seeds, American fertilizers. Pay for it, then pray for rain. They are shoving farming up our asses."[108] The neighbor flags the hegemony of U.S. agrochemical companies unleashed by liberalization. This moment also underscores the concatenation of political/economic factors with environmental circumstances: seeds that require a lot of water cannot produce an effective yield with insufficient precipitation, unless irrigated, which these farmers can't afford; debt deepens when farmers have already taken loans for expensive seeds and then their harvest fails. Natha and Budhia are not the only farmers struggling in Peepli.

Indeed, Natha's prospective death—spectacularized while he remains visibly alive, then immediately irrelevant to politicians and news cycles—is twinned by the actual death of another villager, Hori Mahato. Initially peripheral to the film's plot, the emaciated and exhausted Hori appears as part of the landscape in several scenes, digging earth to sell because his farm has been auctioned off (Figure 2). He is eventually found dead

Figure 1. Budhia and Natha converse with neighboring farmers (screen grab from early in *Peepli Live* [12:43]).

in his grave-like digging pit, bringing him to the center of Rakesh's attention. In a crisis of conscience, Rakesh asks TV newscaster Nandita: "Why is Natha so important to us? . . . There are other farmers too in this village. Aren't they equally important?" Rakesh explains that Hori "died of hunger" and repeats: "Is this not important?"[109] Nandita dismisses Rakesh's concern: "We're journalists, and this is what we do. If you can't handle this, then you're in the wrong profession."[110] She explains that viewers are interested only in Natha, because he is "the original live suicide. Do you have any idea how big this is?"[111] The codified narrative of the farmer suicide, the film suggests, has eclipsed the possibility of death by starvation. As demonstrated by the sensational "farmer suicide" stories spewed by TV journalists within *Peepli Live,* to take only surface-level interest in the plight of farmers is to turn an agriculturalist's life or death into meaningless verbiage.

Peepli Live also offers an explanatory concept distinct from that of the "farmer suicide": urbanization. The film moves toward conclusion with the camera reversing away from Natha's still-destitute family, initiating a series of rollicking shots that suggest an accelerated drive from village to city. This montage moves from dirt roads in Peepli, to a rural paved road, to a toll plaza and a busy highway, and finally to urban high-rises, including a condominium under construction behind a billboard advertising

Figure 2. Hori Mahato digs earth to sell, while Rakesh, pictured on a motorbike in the background, is about to rudely ask Hori for directions (screen grab from *Peepli Live* [30:06]).

"More Space. More Luxury."[112] The film began with the brothers traveling by bus and foot to the city and back to their village; now we have a return to the city, bookending the film's rural setting to highlight regional dynamics. And in the city, as the camera slows, we find Natha: still alive, sitting with a tool in hand amid a crowd of construction workers. Just before the ending credits, a statistic from India's 2001 census report appears: "8 million farmers / quit farming in India / between 1991 to 2001."[113] This statistic invites viewers to read the film as documenting a demise of agricultural livelihoods, which may leave former farmers stuck in limbo, incorporated into a precarious urban underclass, or simply dead, not unlike the subaltern characters of Tarashankar's novel sixty-odd years earlier. Urbanization entails ever-more migrants leaving impoverished rural areas and moving to cities in search of work, expanding informal settlements and urban poverty (a thread I take up in chapter 5).

The first Indian film to screen at Sundance and India's Oscars entry for 2010, *Peepli Live* has been praised by some reviewers for its astute "political farce" and "stinging critique of the disregard for India's dispossessed."[114] Others have been less enthused: Raghavendra charges superstar producer Aamir Khan with remaining "non-committal" about corporate causes of rural poverty to avoid upsetting potential funders.[115] A Vidarbha farmers' group urged the government of Maharashtra to ban the film on grounds that it "trivializes" farmer suicides, a response that reveals the risks of satire: the film's critique of how farmer suicides have been *represented* can seem to dismiss actual agriculturalists' deaths.[116] And admittedly, *Peepli Live*'s examination of rural masculinity hinges on suspect portrayals of women: Natha's wife and aged mother are shrewish burdens on him; Nandita is career-driven to the point of narcissism. Nonetheless, with its caricature of political and media discourse, and with Rakesh's insistence that rural people beyond Natha are "important," *Peepli Live* illuminates how "farmer suicide" has become a (potentially reductive) shorthand for a tangle of problems intensified by liberalization: poverty, hunger, drought, the urban–rural divide, a continued caste hierarchy, gendered pressures, and neoliberal structures of feeling that create aspirations to conspicuous consumption. Also relevant here are GM patenting and climate, but the problems of rural India, like such problems globally, cannot be reduced simply to GMOs, nor to farmer suicides, nor even to climate change. Instead, precarity emerges from a complex synthesis of environmental, political, economic, cultural, and affective factors, meriting sustained attention and nuanced narratives.

Conclusion: Agrarian Precarity and Beyond

In this chapter, I have argued that representations of Indian agriculturalists exemplify how ideas about food—including the labor, pleasure, social status, and basic needs attached to food—explain precarity as a synthesis of social, economic, and environmental disruptions. Putting GM debates and the figure of the farmer suicide in conversation with accounts of the 1943 famine, I have illustrated the persistence of hunger and agrarian crisis as concerns in Indian narratives (provoked by iterable intensifications of global capitalism in conjuncture with environmental forces). By beginning with 1943, I would situate this book's consideration of neoliberal-era environmental discourse in relation to longer processes of capitalist globalization and environmental change. In this way, I begin the book's argument that global South discourses around food and eating have become key cultural resources for parsing the intersections of globalization and environment.

Peepli Live satirizes the farmer-suicide sensation to critique bombastic performances of attention to rural India (by media and politicians). In this way, the film cautions against instrumentalizing or oversimplifying farmer suicides. But more nuanced representations of farmer suicides can engage a panoply of intersecting concerns. *Peepli Live* itself testifies to the cultural resonance of the farmer suicide as a figure for thinking through contemporary India's problems, and the global problems of a neoliberal consensus put into the pressure-cooker of climate change. The farmer-suicide figure demonstrates that ideas about agriculture, food-producing labor, starvation, and gastronomy have become central to a cultural reckoning with liberalization and precarity.

As I argue throughout *Precarious Eating*, cultural representations of eating and hunger function to highlight global injustice occurring at the intersection of the environmental, political, economic, and social. Food-focused narratives can invite a beyond-human understanding of globalization, showing how human and nonhuman forces intertwine to cause precarity in ways shaped by the power dynamics of an unevenly connected globe. Such representations also connect the intimate with the global: a metonymic logic invites readers to make sense of enormous and heterogenous systems by starting with something particular, whether molasses-making or Bt cotton. I'll be suggesting throughout this book that abalone, bananas, peaches, meat, and figures such as the butcher or the vegan appear in novels with a function similar to molasses-making in *Hansuli Turn*: as points of entry, giving readers purchase on problems that otherwise seem too large or multifaceted to contemplate. Climate change in particular has been described by influential thinkers such as Amitav Ghosh as too big for novels to represent. In the next chapter, I put Ghosh's recent nonfictional works into dialogue with his canonical environmental novel *The Hungry Tide,* to consider how depictions of consumption might transcend such supposed limits to novelistic representability.

2

Nutmeg and Disordered Eating

Reframing Climate Change

> Taking a nutmeg out of its fruit is like unearthing a tiny planet.
>
> Like a planet, the nutmeg is encased within a series of expanding spheres. There is, first of all, the fruit's matte-brown skin, a kind of exosphere. Then there is the pale, perfumed flesh, . . . like a planet's outer atmosphere. . . . Stripping off the mace reveals yet another casing . . . like a protective troposphere. Only when this shell is cracked open do you have the nut in your palm. . . .
>
> Like a planet, a nutmeg too can never be seen in its entirety. . . . A nutmeg has two hemispheres; . . . for one to be seen by the human eye, the other must be hidden.
>
> —AMITAV GHOSH, *The Nutmeg's Curse: Parables for a Planet in Crisis*

A planet is impossible to picture in all its complexity. There are too many environments and experiences on the earth to see all at once, making it difficult to narrate or even conceptualize planet-scaled problems. In his 2021 essay collection *The Nutmeg's Curse,* Indian novelist and public intellectual Amitav Ghosh raises and answers this representational challenge: he models a method of narrating planetary problems through nutmeg. Ghosh notes that one side of a sphere always "must be hidden" to the eye, expressing representational limits.[1] Yet nutmeg—which Ghosh compares to "a tiny planet"—somehow makes it possible to transcend these limits, to compose a sprawling and heterogeneous crisis into a narrative.[2] To accomplish this, Ghosh pivots from describing how the layers of a nutmeg resemble the layers of a planet to narrating planetary history by tracing the circulation of nutmeg.

71

The Nutmeg's Curse begins with a reconstructed account of colonial violence in the Banda Islands, an archipelago seized by the Dutch amidst the
spice trade because it was home to trees that produce nutmegs and mace.
This history exemplifies how European appetites have motivated imperial
expansion, genocide, enslavement, economic globalization, and environmental disruption. Planet-scaled problems can be narrated through this
single commodity (nutmeg) because it possesses several different linking
functions. One is historical: "Before the eighteenth century, every single
nutmeg and every shred of mace originated in, or around, the Bandas.
So it follows that any mention of nutmeg or mace in any text, anywhere,
before the 1700s automatically establishes a link with the Bandas."[3] Ghosh
implies that tracing nutmeg offers a methodological approach, a way of
focusing research to show how patterns of globalization and ecological
exchange link back to originary acts of colonial violence. In addition to
nutmeg establishing such historical links, references to nutmeg create
stylistic and thematic links across *The Nutmeg's Curse*. Ghosh proceeds
from the history of the Bandas to a set of loosely connected essays on
various problems all over the world, but he returns repeatedly to nutmeg.
Nutmeg functions as a narrative center, enabling *The Nutmeg's Curse* to
connect refugeeism, the importance of the Amazon, opioids, the fossil
fuel economy, Covid-19, climate change, and more. Such seemingly disparate crises are linked through the extractive processes of empire, as
nutmeg encapsulates. *The Nutmeg's Curse* exemplifies how references to
food commodities can be a stylistic strategy by which writers express
often-overlooked modes of global connectivity.

Nutmeg is not the only commodity that could anchor a narrative about
far-reaching processes of empire, globalization, and environmental destruction. Anthropologists, historians, and popular authors have written
similar books on sugar, tea, and salt.[4] Ghosh himself maps the opium
trade in order to retell transcontinental histories in his Ibis trilogy, while
The Nutmeg's Curse connects tea, opium, and spices: the Dutch initiated
large-scale opium trading in the seventeenth century "to pay for spices
from the Malabar Coast and the East Indies," then the British rescaled
"the cultivation of opium in India to industrial dimensions, . . . using it
to pay for the East India Company's tea purchases in China" until they
established tea plantations in Assam.[5] Julia Adeney Thomas clarifies the
environmental import of Ghosh's attention to commodity circulations,

suggesting that his novel *Flood of Fire* connects the linked trades in opium and tea to climate change, ocean acidification, and extinctions as a mode of illustrating that "in the global distribution of commodities lies the world's destruction."[6] Environmental crisis is indexed, in both fictions and nonfictions by Ghosh, as an effect of commodity extraction in a globalized economy structured by power differentials. Appetites for spices and other commodities motivated European expansion, with the extraction of lucrative foodstuffs and energy sources facilitating Europe's growing wealth and industrialization, leading in turn to the fossil-fuel guzzling that is a primary driver of climate change (and central to industrial food production). Comestibles from nutmegs to opium, then, can offer organizing logics to stories that sprawl across continents and time. These stories are essential to understanding how today's global environmental crisis came into being, and how it continues to spiral via energy-intensive consumption habits.

Tracing nutmeg is an approach to environmental crisis quite different from that demanded by Ghosh's 2016 nonfiction work, *The Great Derangement: Climate Change and the Unthinkable,* which charges novels with failing to represent climate change. To introduce this argument, Ghosh describes witnessing a tornado in 1978 in New Delhi (where such storms were unprecedented). If "novelists inevitably mine their own experience," this "encounter . . . should have been a mother lode . . . to be mined to the last little nugget," and so Ghosh wonders why no tornado occurs in his fiction.[7] He could not novelize this storm, he concludes, because, had he encountered an event of such "extreme improbability" in another writer's novel, his "response would be one of incredulity."[8] For Ghosh, literary fiction is the realm of the probable: the occasional unlikely event must not overshadow the ambiance of the "everyday."[9] Climate change is altering the everyday, making formerly hundred-year storms arise more frequently, morphing inconceivable disasters into mundane headlines. Yet such storms *feel* improbable, Ghosh asserts, preventing climate change from featuring in literary fiction. And whereas epic form "embraces the inconceivably large," in a novel "no one will speak of how the continents were created; nor will they refer to the passage of thousands of years: connections and events on this scale appear not just unlikely but also absurd."[10] Climate change is both too wild and too big for the novel, says Ghosh.

Since 2016, Ghosh's claim that "serious" novels fail to represent climate change has become an almost-obligatory citation in criticism on environmental fiction, and in many interdisciplinary conversations about planetary imaginaries. *The Great Derangement* may be invoked to underscore the representational and epistemic challenges of climate change, or to debunk Ghosh's pessimism about fiction, which strikes some (myself included) as overstated. I am tempted to suggest that, while Ghosh's claims resonate with climate-concerned scholars across many disciplines, they make the least sense to scholars of the novel.[11]

Yet, despite the seeming boldness with which Ghosh dismisses fiction's capacities, *The Great Derangement* is rife with qualifications. Though Ghosh initially frames his argument as about the novel genre and even the cultural imagination, it transpires that he is discussing a limited set of novels—those "regarded as serious fiction," meaning elite literary realism—and defining engagement with climate change narrowly (as the direct representation of catastrophic events or planet-scaled changes).[12] Ghosh argues that, since an inward "turn" in the twentieth century, "serious fiction" has specialized in the interior life of individual characters (what a novel theorist might call individuation or depth psychology).[13] Ghosh sees this focus as symptomatic of "a dominant [Western] culture in which the idea of the collective has been exiled from politics, economics, and literature alike."[14] This story of the novel is familiar.[15] But Ghosh's corollary claim that fiction is therefore missing an opportunity to represent climate change seems strange amidst today's robust critical conversation about "climate fiction," "cli-fi," or "Anthropocene fiction."[16] Ghosh is not alone in suggesting that climate change poses a challenge to the novel: Adam Trexler, for example, argues that "Anthropocene fictions" must reckon with a literary canon that privileges "self-reflexivity over reference to the material world."[17] But Trexler asserts that "landscapes, animals, devices, vehicles, geological formations, and buildings are formally constructive entities" in novels nonetheless, and that fiction has already innovated to represent climate change: "Melting ice caps, global climate models, rising sea levels, and tipping points have altered the formal possibilities of the novel."[18] Similarly, Stephanie LeMenager suggests that cli-fi "indicts the privatization of human experience even as it participates in" the novel genre's methods of "making social worlds by modeling individual consciousness in relationship with imaginary but possible worlds."[19] If Ghosh does not think there is "serious" climate fiction out there, others certainly do.[20] The strongest version of his claim, which is that the mere "mention" of climate change leads to "banishment from the preserves of serious fiction," falls apart in this context.[21]

Much of this cli-fi conversation, however, has centered American and British texts.[22] Popularly cited examples of "climate fiction" tend to be novels from the global North that thematize future disruptions to the current world order.[23] Rather than addressing this problem by "including" fictions from the global South, it is worth considering whether "climate fiction" might not be the most apt term to capture their environmental politics. This is not to suggest that texts from the global South have no relevance to climate change, but rather that their approaches may elude a popular genre category developed to suit Northern texts.

Many environmental fictions from South Africa and India do not take climate change as a primary theme or plot driver. Climate change might instead feature as one of a variety of disruptions instigated by colonization and exacerbated by postcolonial inequality. Ghosh's own novel *The Hungry Tide* mentions climate change as a factor that amplifies other challenges: in a diary entry about refugeeism and conflicts over land use in the Sundarbans region of India, for example, the character Nirmal enumerates among the region's challenges that "the land was being reclaimed by the sea."[24] While Ghosh has stated that research for *The Hungry Tide* sparked his interest in climate change, he laments that the "subject [of climate change] figures only obliquely" in the novel itself.[25] However, moments such as Nirmal's aside perform important work: Nirmal implies that climate impacts such as sea level rise matter in how they intensify existing conflicts. Such oblique engagement with climate change is not disregard. Indeed, novels may be well-suited to addressing climate change precisely because they can "obliquely" approach phenomena that are too large or heterogeneous to encompass head-on. This oblique method can retain attentions to historical contingency and local complexity that may disappear in more direct attempts to model climate change. Such fictions invite readers (especially those in the North) to reconsider expectations about how climate change ought to be represented.[26] What might become visible when other frameworks are primary?

In this chapter, I take *The Hungry Tide* as exemplary of how a novel can address environmental shifts not in terms of abstract universals,

Western science, or sudden ruptures, but in terms of the power dynamics of globalization as they register in everyday experiences such as eating, obtaining food, or being hungry. I do not search Ghosh's novel for a direct and catastrophic representation of climate change (as *The Great Derangement* would seem to demand). Instead, following the logics of *The Nutmeg's Curse,* I look to the understandings of interconnected planetary crisis—including but not limited to climate change—that emerge from a focus on commodities and consumption. To this end, I trace depictions of individual eating, food commodities, and structurally produced hunger in *The Hungry Tide.* This gastronomic reading shows that the individuation of character, far from preventing engagement with grander scales, can be a technique for foregrounding uneven effects of planetary problems. Individuating representations of eating, fishing, and going hungry can move environmental rhetorics out of the register of the catastrophic, and into the register of the everyday where realist novels excel, underscoring how environmental precarity inheres not only in exposure to disastrous storms but also in subtler changes to quotidian activities. In this way, I am suggesting something akin to what LeMenager calls the "everyday Anthropocene": a representational attention to daily lived experiences of environmental shift, as distinguished from epochal narratives.[27] Focusing on consumption draws out *The Hungry Tide*'s indirect approach to climate change, keeping the reader's attention not on the aggregate but on the unevenness of environmental disruption and its continuities with imperialist dispossession and global capitalism.

To read *The Hungry Tide* as a consumption fiction, I will first situate Ghosh's work in relation to postcolonial inquiries into globalization, identity, and the meanings of food. To this end, the next section establishes several received ideas about food in perceptions of Indian and diasporic South Asian literature and culture. After that, I sketch the conservation politics and history of violence that provide *The Hungry Tide*'s backdrop and motivate its canonization in postcolonial ecocriticism. Finally, I offer a food-focused reading of *The Hungry Tide,* ending by considering the affordances of this reading method for conversations about representability and what *The Nutmeg's Curse* calls "planetary crisis."

Chai and Chutnification: Considering Food in Indian Narrative

Food has a peculiar power in stories about India. Global Northerners often overidentify India with cuisine, enthusiastically embracing "Indian" restaurants and cookbooks, if not always Indian people.[28] Introducing her canonical 1985 cookbook *A Taste of India,* chef and actress Madhur Jaffrey writes that "an Indian is exposed to more combinations of flavours and seasonings than perhaps anyone else in the world," with characteristic spices such as "asafetida, whose earthy aroma tends to startle Westerners."[29] While elsewhere "food is eaten to fill stomachs," instead "in India . . . [we] eat to keep our bodies finely tuned, physically and spiritually."[30] To entice Western cooks, Jaffrey accords India both a national identity and an exotic mystique by virtue of its cuisine. This narrative is gendered and potentially sexualized via the cis-heteronormative "ideology of the [Indian] wife being the preparer of meals" for her husband, in which female cooking in the domestic space reproduces what Anita Mannur has called "culinary nationalism."[31] The cover of the 1986 Atheneum edition of *A Taste of India,* for example, pictures Jaffrey reclining in a red sari with a spread of cinnamon, garlic, ginger, coconuts, limes, nuts, and prepared food. This display suggests the plentiful availability of Indian cuisine for foreigners, offered by an ideal figure of domestic femininity. Jaffrey's phenomenal success speaks to the deliciousness of her recipes and her aptitude at translating them for Northern consumers, but also to her role in constructing such national narratives. Her career has been fundamental to the "invention of Indian food as a national cuisine in India and in the West," making Jaffrey an exemplary figure of both Indian nationhood and India's place in a globalized order as imagined via cuisine.[32]

Particular food products matter not only to Western attitudes, but also to the construction of national identity within India. Chai, for example, is now widely regarded as India's national drink, but it was not always. Although tea grows naturally in what is now India's northeastern state of Assam and has long been consumed there by the Singpho people, industrial production began only in the 1830s, spurred by British imperialists eager to reduce dependence on China. The British ignored Singpho sovereignty over the tea lands and converted Assam into a network of export-oriented plantations.[33] As Jayeeta Sharma has documented, this transformation "reordered Assam's natural environment," replacing "forested, riverine, and commons lands," including the rice fields of Assamese peasants, with monocultures.[34] Imperial stakeholders envisioned this as an "Edenic transformation . . . of a jungle into a garden."[35] Assam's rationalization exemplifies what Ghosh calls "terraforming": the imperial project of altering physical landscapes to create "neo-Europes."[36] As Kyle Powys Whyte elaborates in the context of North America, such ecological disturbances are not an accident but a tactic, establishing rule by disrupting Indigenous food systems.[37] Alterations to Assam's landscape were interwoven with a reinvention of local racial and ethnic categories, catalyzed by British importation of laborers from distant parts of India, who had "little option but to stay and toil"—even as tea plantations borrowed methods of coercion and bodily punishment from the cotton and sugar plantations of the Americas.[38] In Assam today, the "tea tribes" (descended from laborers brought by the British) continue to face exploitative working conditions and are campaigning for recognition as Scheduled Tribes.[39] Sharma argues that the "racialized creation of the tea labourer was the catalyst for a larger South Asian project of cultural redefinition," integral to constructing a "modern Indian political space."[40]

Tea's own meaning has shifted across this process of creating a "modern Indian political space." In part because of campaigns to expose abuses on plantations, Indian tea-drinking in the nineteenth century was limited to the *bhadralok* (the Anglophile elite employed by British firms) and viewed as "an index of [W]estern cultural mores."[41] Anticolonial nationalist movements positioned tea as a British imposition to be rejected. In a 1920s essay called "Tea or Poison," chemist and nationalist Prafulla Chandra Ray deplored tea as an unhealthy drink whose consumption displaced nutritious Bengali beverages and profited European capitalists.[42] As part of the Swadeshi Movement that urged Indians to reject British goods, Mohandas Gandhi similarly characterized tea as unhealthy, critiquing the use of indentured labor. Yet aggressive marketing by the Indian Tea Market Expansion Board (ITMEB) succeeded in spreading tea-drinking across classes, castes, and religions by reframing tea as India's national drink, "100% Swadeshi." Commercial artists such as Annada Munshi (1905–1985) utilized symbols such as the spinning wheel to align tea-drinking with Gandhian nationalism. Housewives feature in such ads as emblems of the Indian nation.[43] Related ads show Indians of all religious backgrounds sipping tea, such as the billboard pictured in Figure 3, which identifies a Sikh, a Muslim, and a Brahmin by their attire (turban, fez, and sacred thread). They are captioned "Wealth," "Health," and "Happiness," suggesting these values as part of a multiculturalist narrative of the Indian nation grounded in the act of tea consumption.[44] Such marketing

Figure 3. This commercial-art billboard pictures three figures—a Sikh, a Muslim, and a Brahmin—all drinking tea. Courtesy of the Centre for Studies in Social Sciences, Calcutta.

elides labor exploitation and the influence of British rule in order to produce commercial value from a particular narrative of national identity, an
idea of unity in diversity anchored by the gendered and classed image of
the housewife. Chai thus represents the ideological production of national
culture. The idea of tea as essentially Indian is inseparable from the
assertion of tea as essentially English, itself a form of "strategic amnesia"
about the provenance of "English" products.[45]

The reification of Indianness as Indian food has also shaped literature.
The best-known South Asian novel outside South Asia, Salman Rushdie's
1981 *Midnight's Children,* ties Indian identity to pickles and chutneys,
as its narrator extols the "symbolic value of the pickling process: all the
six hundred million eggs which gave birth to the population of India
could fit inside a single, standard-sized pickle-jar. . . . Every pickle-jar . . .
contains, therefore, . . . the feasibility of the chutnification of history; the
grand hope of the pickling of time!"[46] "Chutnification" names the creation of national memory in this hypercanonical text, miring the English-
language Indian novel in national allegory and ethnic identity at the first
mention of food. Rushdie frames a cohesive Indian identity as a "grand
hope" rather than a reality; nonetheless, his career has both encouraged
the overidentification of India with cuisine and influenced stylistic expectations for Indian writing in English. Pankaj Mishra quips that numerous Indian novelists suffer from "Rushdie-itis," a "literary condition" in
which "Midnight's Grandchildren" are produced: "sprawling shapeless
narratives where all the traditional ingredients of the novel—irony, style,
sense of economy and structure—have been abandoned in an effort to
arrive at spicier concoctions."[47] While Mishra describes Rushdie-itis as a
phenomenon of literary style, his own gastronomic metaphor implies an
intimacy between formal expectations and the appetite for depictions
of food. Literary gastronomy and a kind of stylistic overindulgence are
apparently the perfect pairing for Indian authors seeking global acclaim.
Rushdie, meanwhile, has also become representative of the imperiled
right to freedom of creative expression since 1989, when Iranian leader
Ayatollah Ruhollah Khomeini issued a *fatwa* demanding Rushdie's death
in response to his fictionalization of the Prophet Mohammad in *The
Satanic Verses.* This threat sent Rushdie into hiding; after returning to
public life, he suffered a brutal attack onstage in August 2022.[48]

Rushdie's career points to the politicization of ethnic, religious, and national identities that many postcolonial and diasporic writers investigate through gastronomic metaphors. Spices are "a favored trope for filtering questions of national and diasporic belonging and affiliation," while disordered eating can signify discomfort and anxiety around postcolonial nationhood.[49] Chutney's allegorical stickiness extends beyond the novel for Tamil American poet Divya Victor, whose prose poem "C is for Comorin and not Chutney" opens, "I am not allowed to talk about chutney here because . . . well-mannered Indian writers don't let their origins hang out like some prolapsed hem. . . . We are of the opinion that when we say chutney, you think of 'chutney' and you are *veryvery* wrong in doing so."[50] Victor wryly evokes a literary culture exhausted by allegorical interpretations by "you" the Northern reader, desperate for chutney to refer simply to a condiment. Yet Indian authors may also use gastronomic language to capitalize on orientalist fantasy, marketing books to a mostly white public in the global North via what Mannur notes as "palatable multiculturalism."[51] Authors such as Rushdie and Arundhati Roy also use culinary metaphors to self-consciously ironize the packaging of India as a delicacy; according to Mannur, the "culinary register can deliberately and strategically disrupt the notion that cultural identity is always readily available for consumption and commodification and always already conjoined to culinary practices."[52] And even as cooking can entrench normative gender roles, the culinary can also be reworked as a space for "inhabiting queerness," as Mannur argues vis-à-vis *Bodies in Motion* by Sri Lankan American novelist Mary Anne Mohanraj.[53] (I'll take up a South African example of the kitchen's queer potential in chapter 4.) Literary gastronomy can reaffirm gendered nationalist ideologies and the exoticism surrounding both postcolonial and diasporic subjects, yet can also subvert orientalist and cis-heteronormative fantasies through a wider array of significations.

But when and how might eating, cuisine, and food systems appear in Indian literature not just as metaphors, but as ethical and environmental concerns in their own right? Even if overshadowed by multiculturalist celebrations of Indianness as Indian food, concerns about foodways, food access, famine, and agricultural labor have long mattered to Indian fiction. Consider, for example, canonical mid-century novels such as Gopinath Mohanty's 1954 *Paraja,* Bhabani Bhattacharya's 1954 *He Who Rides a Tiger,* and Tarashankar Bandyopadhyay's 1946–1951 *Hansuli Banker Upakathā* (discussed in chapter 1). Nor are such serious issues obstructed by a gastronomic register concerned with cooking and eating, in my view. Transferring these concerns to contemporary literature, I believe we can learn more by examining the potent metaphorics of food in conjunction with food's material importance, integrating conversations about "chutnification" with those about hunger and environmental changes. With food access and agro-food systems as pressing global concerns in this era of climate injustice, I contend that the role of eating in many "serious" Anglophone cultural texts converges with their approaches to the global environment. An attention to food in environmental fiction can also help reevaluate claims about fiction's supposed inattention to climate change, by approaching climate from an oblique angle.

Environmentalism and the Poor; or *The Hungry Tide* Take 1

Ghosh's own novel *The Hungry Tide* takes place in the Sundarbans, a tidal mangrove forest home to the iconic Bengal tiger. Project Tiger, a conservation program of India's national government supported by the World Wildlife Fund (WWF), has attracted censure by displacing islanders and refugees from tiger-reserve lands in this region. Project Tiger epitomizes an antihuman style of wildlife conservation modeled on practices from the global North, according to Michael L. Lewis, who argues that Indian environmental policy has been swayed by conservation biology as it developed in the late 1960s at Harvard University. (India's present approaches to conservation also echo longer histories of European experimentation in the colonies documented by Richard Grove.[54]) Since the Wildlife Protection Act of 1972, India has undertaken aggressive policies focused on creating enormous nature parks—"some are thousands of square kilometers"—that by law are supposed to be free of human inhabitants.[55] This strategy, encouraged by Northern organizations such as the WWF and the International Union for the Conservation of Nature, has displaced thousands of people. According to Lewis's study, many Indians feel that conservation would be better pursued by establishing smaller parks in dialogue with human communities.[56]

These dynamics reached an extreme when Indian police massacred a group of refugees squatting on Morichjhāpi, an island in the Sundarbans designated for tiger conservation.[57] My understanding of this event relies on articles by Annu Jalais and Ross Mallick, two of the few detailed accounts available.[58] The settlers at Morichjhāpi were post-Partition refugees from Bangladesh, a group that has suffered violence and discrimination. Low-caste and poor refugees were dispersed to camps in various Indian states, settled on infertile land, and treated like serfs. In 1975, some of these refugees organized to resettle in West Bengal. A group relocated to Morichjhāpi and set up tube wells, saltpans, schools, and a fishing industry. When local journalists noted their successes, the West Bengal government censored the press.[59] An economic blockade was set up, followed by a forcible eviction. Thirty police boats surrounded the island to cut off food and water. Police deployed tear gas, destroyed homes and infrastructure, sexually assaulted refugees, and on January 31, 1979, gunned down thirty-six people. The precise death toll is unclear, as bodies were dumped in the river, preventing exhumation.[60] No charges were brought against the police or politicians involved.

After the massacre, according to Jalais, locals from the Sundarbans began to narrate their own marginalization in ways informed by the mistreatment of the refugees. An important component of this narrative is how the government prioritized tigers over people, creating a context in which "taste" becomes violent:

> The villagers explained that tigers, annoyed at the . . . violence in the forest had started attacking people and . . . ended up getting a taste for human flesh. Others argued that it was the corpses of killed refugees . . . that had given them the taste. Morichjhanpi was a turning point after which maneating became part of the tiger's "nature" or "behavior." . . . The government was happy as long as the tigers thrived. . . . Whether the islanders lived or died, as had been the case for the refugees, made no difference, because they were just "tiger-food."[61]

Endangered but also dangerous, Bengal tigers kill an average of forty to sixty humans per year in the Sundarbans.[62] Jalais's interviewees position this conflict not as innate, but as sparked by changes in "taste" resulting from governmental betrayal of refugees and islanders. Forced competition for scarce land and resources has harmed both subaltern humans and tigers. Whereas Mallick sets "environmentalists" and "poor people" in opposition, Jalais's interviews suggest that subaltern groups in the Sundarbans are not opposed to conservation, but simply to a hierarchy in which their own lives are disposable.[63]

Influenced by Jalais's research, *The Hungry Tide* scrutinizes antihuman conservation practices and asks readers to rethink what constitutes environmentalism.[64] The massacre at Morichjhãpi haunts the novel's narrative present, with journal entries by the deceased character Nirmal recounting these 1970s events. The novel opens, however, in the early 2000s, with the cetologist Piya Roy arriving in the Sundarbans to study Gangetic and Irrawaddy dolphins (or Orcaella). The American child of emigrants from Bengal, Piya has a commitment to animal conservation and little knowledge of human lives in the Sundarbans. She is not wealthy by American standards, but privileged by citizenship and education. Piya meets Kanai Dutt, an arrogant Bengali businessman visiting his aunt Nilima. Attracted to Piya, Kanai invites her to stay at Nilima's guesthouse. But when the two part company, Piya gets into trouble with two corrupt officers from the forest department. She is rescued by a fisherman named Fokir and escapes on his boat. (Readers later learn that Fokir is the son of Kusum, a refugee killed at Morichjhãpi.)

Piya is delighted when Fokir takes her to a pool where Orcaella gather. She later realizes that Fokir knows this pool because of his livelihood, fishing and crabbing. As a cetologist and animal-lover, Piya regards nonhuman animals with a combination of scientific curiosity and reverence. Fokir is also a detailed observer of animal behavior, aware of the migratory patterns of dolphins, but because tracking these animals (who themselves eat fish and crustaceans) supports his foodways. Fokir must be resource-conscious because, as a fisherman, he depends on local ecosystems. Piya and Fokir thus have incommensurable worldviews: Piya sees the Sundarbans primarily as dolphin and tiger habitat, whereas for Fokir the immediate environment represents a primary food source.

While Piya initially finds an easy symbiosis between her research and Fokir's fishing, things become complicated when Piya hires Fokir to take her out on a second boat trip, accompanied by Kanai as translator. Conflicts between these three characters—diasporic conservationist, subaltern fisherman, and postcolonial elite—peak over prioritizing the lives of impoverished humans versus endangered animals: Fokir dismays Piya by helping villagers kill a trapped tiger that, as Kanai points out, had killed several people from the village. The tiger-killing scene would suggest that conflicts between subaltern needs and Northern environmentalism are not always easy, or even possible, to resolve. Yet this sense of irresolution threatens to collapse into a didactic harmonization in the novel's abrupt ending, when Piya suddenly learns to reconcile her own priorities with subaltern concerns. First, Fokir dies while shielding Piya from a storm with his body. Piya is narrated as traumatized by this event, but processes this trauma off-stage: the narrative speeds forward to Piya returning to the Sundarbans after a recovery period. Fokir's grieving family, meanwhile, is barely mentioned as the aftermath of his death is glossed over in a two-page chapter plus a short epilogue. The epilogue focuses on Piya's acceptance that environmentalism must take forms that do not harm the poor. Announcing that conservation groups have offered to fund her research, Piya pledges to "share the funding" with an antipoverty nongovernmental organization (NGO) so that "the local fishermen would be involved," because she no longer wants to do "work that places the burden of conservation on those who can least afford it" (327).

With this ending, in which the American learns to rethink her conservation strategies, Ghosh's novel scans as an educational tale about what Ramachandra Guha and Joan Martinez-Alier call "the environmentalism of the poor."[65] *The Hungry Tide* may elude reception as "climate fiction" because its references to climate impacts (such as rising water levels) are subtle. However, problems with Northern conservationism feature loudly, making the novel a happy "fit" for postcolonial ecocriticism. As Pheng Cheah puts it, "*The Hungry Tide* is a favored text of ecocriticism because it does not shy away from the critique of environmentalism," or rather critique of the *antipoor* variant of environmentalism practiced by many bourgeois Northerners, transnational NGOs, and postcolonial governments.[66] Scholars tend to share Cheah's focus on how *The Hungry Tide* excavates the polarization of human rights and animal rights and displaces the "full-stomach environmentalism" of bourgeois subjects in favor of an environmentalist orientation that acknowledges subaltern resource needs.[67]

But, if we read *The Hungry Tide* simply as a parable about the environmentalism of the poor, the ending is problematic. The speedy conversion of a Northern scientist and animal lover seems to present wildlife conservation and subaltern access to resources as easy priorities to reconcile: a facile "lesson" whose condition of possibility is the quickly forgotten death of the subaltern character, Fokir. However, the confluence of social and environmental concerns in *The Hungry Tide* can be differently mapped in terms of food and eating, in ways that complicate this ending. Reading with a focus on disordered eating, hunger, and culinary commodities maintains a sense of irresolution: at the novel's end, privileged characters and subalterns remain differently embedded in a global food regime, differentiating their experiences of environmental precarity. This sense of context-specific embeddedness in the food regime provides the multiscalar thinking needed in order to conceptualize a changing global environment while attending to questions of power. Climate change, in this novel, constitutes one among a range of societal and environmental disruptions caused by imperialism, postcolonial governance, and globalized capitalism, as expressed through references to food.

Culinary Commodities and Disordered Eating, or The Hungry Tide Take 2

Throughout *The Hungry Tide*, Piya's anxieties manifest in her inability to stomach Bengali food. This element of Piya's psychology, which I read as disordered eating, commands substantial space in the narrative. For Ghosh, it is because of such obsessions with the "individual psyche" that novels fail to engage environmental issues at the planetary scale.[68] Yet I choose to read Piya's eating as disordered not in order to pathologize her as an individual, but rather in order to situate her as a narrative device that illuminates structural violence. In my view, *The Hungry Tide* purposes depth psychology toward exploring global dynamics: Piya's disordered eating symptomatizes the harms wrought by industrial food production and food globalization. Her eating habits offer a way to understand how individual engagements with such larger systems are infracted by race, caste, class, citizenship, and gender, and how environmental precarity links to imperialistic modes of producing and circulating food commodities. If we read Piya's eating as disordered, then her characterization denaturalizes a food regime damaging to both society and environment.

After the tiger-killing incident, Kanai admonishes Piya to stop pigeonholing Fokir as "some kind of grass-roots ecologist" (245). Kanai insists that "there [isn't . . .] anything in common between you. . . . Nothing. He's a fisherman and you're a scientist. What you see as fauna he sees as food. He's never sat in a chair, for heaven's sake" (222). Perceiving "fauna" and perceiving "food" are, Kanai suggests, two fundamentally different ways of thinking about the nonhuman world. Of course, Kanai's commentary is laced with classist scorn: he positions environmentalism as an orientation available only to the Western-educated, suggesting that concerns about "food" are unsophisticated to exclude them from environmentalism's purview. Yet, if read against his grain, Kanai's comment intimates that "food," not just "fauna," could be taken seriously as an organizing framework in this environmental novel.

This idea of two different perceptual modes—seeing fauna versus seeing food—is reiterated at *The Hungry Tide*'s closing when Piya remarks that "home is where the Orcaella are" and Nilima replies: "That's the difference between us. For me, home is wherever I can brew a pot of good tea" (329). Nilima's closing platitude reduces her to a figure of perfect Indian domesticity, associated with home comforts such as sipping chai. On the surface, this is a cheesy narrative closure; however, it is possible to read against this grain of resolution. Recall the figuration of the housewife sipping chai in campaigns to foment national identity and tea sales while eliding tea's associations with worker exploitation and imperialism. Read in dialogue with this history, Nilima's tea-drinking signals the entanglement of domestic comforts with labor exploitation, environmental transformation, and geopolitical power. When reading such moments in relation to the material and cultural histories of the foodstuffs invoked, the numerous references to food in *The Hungry Tide* invite critiques of the power imbalances inherent to colonialism, postcolonial nationalism, neoliberal globalization, and individual acts of consumption.

References to bananas, for example, signal how asymmetrical power relations color everyday interactions between Ghosh's characters. Bananas are one of Piya's few preferred foods, as Fokir's son Tutul remembers on the day of his father's wake: "Tutul appeared beside her. He placed a couple of bananas on her lap and sat with her, holding her hand, patient and unmoving" (323). Tutul's gesture perhaps reassures Piya that Tutul does not blame her for his father's death, positioning the banana as a gesture of goodwill. However, material and cultural histories grant the banana a wider range of possible meanings. Likely first domesticated in southeast

Asia, bananas were a prime object of trade in the "Monsoon Exchange" between South Asia and the Horn of Africa as early as the first millennium BCE. Banana species diversified over centuries in the Lake Victoria highlands and rainforests of Central and West Africa, where they were propagated and domesticated. The banana became a staple food on island colonies in the Atlantic.[69] Scholarship influenced by Alfred Crosby's "Columbian exchange" thesis tends to credit Iberian actors with transferring the banana and plantain to the Americas; however, Judith A. Carney and Richard Nicholas Rosomoff argue that enslaved Africans likely brought these plants.[70] By the mid-twentieth century, the banana's intimacy with exploited labor took new forms: the agricultural giant United Fruit controlled vast "Banana Republics" across Latin America and the Caribbean, rife with both worker exploitation and interference by the U.S. government. Banana workers continue to face exploitation and pesticide poisoning, and have repeatedly organized to resist.[71] Bananas, then, recall violence and labor exploitation across several phases of globalization. They accordingly have a sinister valence in global literature and film: Latin American writers such as Gabriel García Márquez have drawn attention to the histories of brutal worker exploitation, land appropriation, forest clearing, and political violence surrounding banana exportation from Latin America and the Caribbean, while Franck Bieleu's 2011 film *The Big Banana* documents such problems in Cameroon.[72] The banana's significance in a global novel such as *The Hungry Tide* is conditioned not only by the commodity's material and cultural history in South Asia, but also by its meaning in such stories from elsewhere of global capitalist monocultures.[73]

In my reading, bananas in *The Hungry Tide* signal social transactions rendered unequal by Piya's status as a privileged American consumer. Whereas India grows its own bananas for domestic consumption, most bananas in American stores come from Central and South America.[74] Susan Willis suggests in a 1987 article that, for Americans, bananas once represented "the exotic, the tropical," but in the late twentieth century became "commonplace everyday-in-the-lunchbox fruits," refiguring the global South as "a cornucopia spilling out a steady supply of ordinary foodstuffs for North America's supermarkets."[75] Thinking about Piya as an American consumer, her predilection for bananas could connote carefree food habits undertaken at other people's expense. Piya is described as if she were the primary mourner at Fokir's wake, comforted by the "patient" Tutul bringing her bananas. This is a bizarre reversal, given that Tutul has lost his father. It makes sense that Piya is traumatized, yet there is a narcissism in her feelings taking priority. Indeed, Piya's feelings are frequently prioritized through the efforts of other characters to satisfy her fastidious tastes. Piya repeatedly refuses the cooking of her hosts; at Nilima's guesthouse she is eventually served "plain mashed potatoes and two bananas," rather than "the usual fare of rice and fish curry," to accommodate her special "eating preferences" (187). Piya's eating marks the ethical ambiguity surrounding her role as simultaneously a person of Bengali heritage and an outsider, a well-meaning conservationist with limited local context, whose privileged participation in the food regime (and in global mobility) shapes the complex ethics of her "return" to Bengal.

More complicated still, Piya's eating habits scan as disordered, suggesting her own trauma even while food preferences are an arena in which she asserts primacy over other people. At one level, Piya's alimentary avoidances express her troubled diasporic identity, as she specifically refuses to eat Bengali food. This behavior stems from Piya's childhood in Seattle, when she "discovered, from pointed jokes and chance playground comments, that the odors" of her mother's Bengali cooking "followed her everywhere" (81). Food smells breed shame because they reify cultural and racial difference; Piya's playground experience is typical of narratives in which "food odors . . . serve to negatively racialize South Asian bodies."[76] Her "response was to fight back . . . against [the odors] and against her mother, shutting them away with closed doors, sealing them into the kitchen" (81). When Fokir cooks onboard his boat, the "acrid odor of burning chilies" brings Piya's childhood "phantoms . . . alive again, clawing at her throat and her eyes, attacking her as though she were an enemy who had crossed over undetected. She retreated to the bow and when [Fokir] followed her there, with a plateful of rice and cooked crab, she fended him off with her protein bars and her bottled water" (81). With the reference to "phantoms" and Piya's interpretation of Fokir's generosity as an assault to "fend off," her behavior signals not simple rudeness, but anxiety. Piya's avoidance of Bengali food indicates an ambivalence rooted in the difficulties of diaspora: her backstory is one of childhood isolation, stuck at home with a mother who suffered from depression until dying of cervical cancer. As an adult, Piya self-isolates:

she travels constantly for work and stops seeking relationships after being mistreated by a boyfriend. Yet, even as these details render Piya sympathetic, her food habits become markers of American self-indulgence when they accompany her to Bengal. Ghosh's characterization of Piya as an anxious eater illustrates how the violent trajectories of food capitalism land unevenly on different populations: Piya is simultaneously a person with childhood trauma that manifests as disordered eating and a privileged American who puts her needs before those of Sundarbans residents through her food preferences.

Ironically, the only "Indian" food that Piya likes is Ovaltine, a malted chocolate milk powder trademarked by Associated British Foods. Piya describes drinking Ovaltine as "a habit my parents brought over.... They used to buy their groceries in Indian stores. I like it now because it's easy to carry and convenient when you're out on the water" (187). Piya's inherited predilection is for a mass-produced residue of British rule, pointing to how histories of colonization tend to hybridize eating patterns. That Piya advertises Ovaltine as "convenient" suggests her immersion in consumer-capitalist ideology. Similarly, when traveling, Piya carries nutrition bars in order to avoid local cuisine, rarely eating "anything not from a can, a jar or a package" (80). Of course, on a literal level, this is practical: Piya is traveling where potable water may be scarce, and trying to avoid waterborne illnesses. However, Ghosh's repeated references to the anxiety that Piya attaches to eating—particularly to Bengali food—invite a symbolic reading in which Piya's choices index both psychological harm and structural inequality. Nutrition bars, like Ovaltine, link Piya to the industrialized food system, of which she is both victim and agent. Rejecting Bengali home cooking in favor of mass-produced and packaged foods, Piya is embedded in the global food regime to the exclusion of participating in local foodways, and thus functions as a figure for the alienated consumer. By describing Piya's diet of nutrition bars, Ovaltine, bananas, mashed potatoes, and bottled water as disordered eating, I would also put pressure on the normalization of diets constructed around processed, packaged, mass-produced food. What is "disordered" about Piya's eating is that she takes participation in the industrial food system to an extreme; this characterization denaturalizes complicity with industrialized foodways. Piya's cathexis to industrial food products becomes symptomatic of global power hierarchies, underscoring that the current food regime impedes environmentally, culturally, and physically healthy eating.

Piya's eating habits, then, exceed the function of developing the individual character's subjectivity. Her preferred foods are metonyms for the globalized food regime. When Piya's relations with food clash with Fokir's eating patterns, her eating habits allegorize neoliberal disruptions to local foodways. On one occasion, Piya offers to share her "carefully hoarded stock of nutrition bars" with Fokir and Tutul (115). They have stopped Fokir's boat near the pool where Orcaella congregate, but Piya worries that Fokir will want to depart before she can observe the dolphins through a full tidal cycle. She suspects that Fokir and Tutul are low on food, but nonetheless hopes they will stay overnight. For this reason, she offers the nutrition bars. (Tutul accepts, but not Fokir.) By offering to share, Piya would justify obstructing Fokir and Tutul's normal fishing patterns. (Ironically, by the end of the scene, Piya's concern seems unnecessary, as Fokir and Tutul were only waiting to move the boat a small ways in order to fish for their dinner.) Piya's behavior allegorizes the global North's imposition of food products on the South: she offers to replace functional local foodways (fishing and crabbing) with a mass-produced commodity (the nutrition bar). Piya's relations to commodities not only particularize her viewpoint but also invite readers to situate global networks of food distribution as a mode of imperialistic disruption to local livelihoods and environmental understandings. In this way, individuation can paradoxically avoid stymieing the novel at the scale of the individual, instead facilitating multiscalar conceptualizations of the individual's embeddedness within global environmental politics and power structures.

In considering how Ghosh's portrayal of individual psychology might enable structural critique of an environmentally, societally, *and* psychologically damaging food regime, a key interpretive question is whether Piya's disordered eating functions as a metaphor for anxiety about her diasporic identity, or as a symptom. Instrumentalizing disordered eating as a metaphor could raise ethical concerns (as does metaphorizing environmental irresponsibility as "derangement"). As Susan Sontag has famously written, using illness as metaphor is a way of stigmatizing ill individuals: "Nothing is more punitive than to give a disease a [moralistic] meaning. . . . In the last two centuries, the diseases most often used as metaphors for evil were syphilis, tuberculosis, and cancer—all diseases imagined to be, preeminently, the diseases of individuals," unlike conta-gious plagues seen as affecting whole communities.[77] If we were to read Piya's disordered eating as a metaphor, Ghosh's characterization of Piya would emblematize the problematic features that Ghosh himself attri-butes to the modern novel: individualizing to a fault, inhibiting attention to larger structures (societal, ecological, economic). Reading moralizing meanings into disease is differently problematic when it is not individual-izing, as when discourses around contagion are used to scapegoat entire populations, much as Donald Trump's "China virus" rhetoric coincided with spikes in anti-Asian hate crimes in the United States early in the Covid-19 pandemic. All these examples suggest the troubling potency of discourses that attribute moralistic meanings to disability or disease.

But what if Piya's disordered eating is not a metaphor, but rather a symptom of structural impacts related to racialization, displacement, and expectations about eating in a globalized world? While disordered eating might seem more individual than contagious disease, Susan Bordo and others argue that medicalized accounts of eating disorders need to be tempered by attention to structural factors, such as racist body norms and the targeting of low-income populations by the fast food industry.[78] According to V. G. Julie Rajan, South Asian femininity is doubly bur-dened: by colonial ideologies of racial difference that inform both North-ern and postcolonial gender norms, and by patriarchal expectations in which the female body becomes the proving ground for ideologies of national and diasporic identity enforced through "shame and honor."[79] Citing studies that show Western beauty standards have spawned eating disorders among Japanese and Zulu women, Rajan contends that "India is missing from the list of countries most affected by eating disorders" only because of an "absence of research."[80] Rajan finds eating disorders prevalent on "even a random questioning of South Asian American women."[81] As Sunita Puri notes in a personal illness narrative, it becomes harder for women of color to find treatment when "the dominant medi-cal and psychological discourse on anorexia focuses almost exclusively on white upper-class girls."[82] Given how reluctance to report a problem or seek help can skew quantitative data, it matters to consider more im-pressionistic and qualitative accounts, such as Puri's personal narrative, Rajan's informal interviews, and even Ghosh's portrayal of the fictional character Piya. As these three narratives of South Asian American women with eating disorders all emphasize, the psychology of disordered eating cannot be understood apart from racialized gender expectations. Reading Piya's eating as disordered is a way to shift definitions of pathology out of the medical realm and into the sociostructural. Piya's characterization challenges stereotypes that eating disorders affect only "privileged, heterosexual white girls" and suggests that disordered eating can be a manifestation of trauma related to racism and xenophobia as well as gender.[83] At the same time, to characterize avid participation in an industrialized food regime as disordered eating is a way to denaturalize that regime, flagging its imbrication with the geopolitical patterns of colonization and racialization that harm Piya as a South Asian American woman yet give her power over residents of the Sundarbans. Given the resource intensity of industrial foods such as nutrition bars and bottled water, Piya's association with these products also reveals limitations of her megafauna-focused conservation ethic: Piya's conservationism does not mitigate the social or environmental damage with which she is complicit as a food consumer.

Structures of Hunger

Aptly named, *The Hungry Tide* encourages readers to see such connections between individual eaters and global problems by highlighting the mediating meso-scale: the socioeconomic and ecopolitical structures of hunger. In the Morichjhāpi massacre, withholding food functioned as a weapon: some refugees were killed at gunpoint while others were starved out. As Kanai's deceased uncle Nirmal recounts in his journal, refugees were trapped on the island by police, with no one allowed to leave or to bring them supplies. Soon, "despite careful rationing, food had run out and the settlers had been reduced to eating grass. The police had destroyed the tube wells and there was no potable water left" (215). Nirmal records that, when he managed to bring supplies, one of the refugees—Fokir's mother Kusum—bemoaned that

> the worst part was not the hunger or the thirst. It was to . . . listen to the policeman . . . say that our lives, our existence, were worth less than dirt or dust. "This island has to be saved for . . . its animals, . . . it belongs to a project to save tigers, which is paid for by people from all around the world." Every day, sitting here with hunger gnawing at our bellies, we

would listen to these words over and over again. Who are these people, I wondered, who love animals so much that they are willing to kill us for them? (216–17)

Tiger conservation has become an excuse for the forced starvation of subaltern humans, a situation whose ethical bankruptcy Kusum would underscore. Kusum interrupts the neoliberal consensus on environmentalism, in which iconic animals are prioritized over marginalized humans, by repeatedly invoking hunger. This passage situates dominant conservation strategies as inseparable from value judgments about who deserves to eat, which are in turn laden with racial, class, and caste bias.

In addition to exposing antihuman conservation practices, *The Hungry Tide* attends to environmental shifts that impact food access for the poor. For example, the prawn industry has imperiled fishing because of new nylon nets "so fine that they catch the eggs of all the other fish" (112). As Fokir's wife Moyna explains, the local NGO could not get the nets banned because "there's a lot of money in prawns and the traders had paid off the politicians. What do they care? . . . . It's people like us who're going to suffer" (112). Fish are a key part of local ecosystems, but they lack the iconic status of tigers, meaning internationally funded conservation projects are unlikely to address the commercial overfishing that disrupts subaltern foodways.[84] Dangerous food gathering, meanwhile, is a "way of life" in the Sundarbans, where "hunger drove [the islanders] to hunting and fishing, and the results were often disastrous. . . . Thousands risked death in order to collect meager quantities of honey, wax, firewood and . . . sour fruit. . . . No day seemed to pass without news of someone being killed by a tiger, a snake or a crocodile" (67). These islanders are "ecosystem people": they depend "for their survival on the seasonal cycles of adjoining ecosystems," exposing them to precarity when those ecosystems are threatened, and to the dangers of the ecosystem itself.[85] In this context, a socially responsible environmentalism would protect resources for local use, rather than exclude subaltern populations from tracts of land when their foodways are already precarious.

If Piya's food "preferences" are simply contrasted to this landscape of subaltern hunger, they smack of American privilege. Eating processed food creates a perceived distance from the use of the environment, obscuring the labor and sourcing practices behind commodities; this is a sense of distance that "ecosystem people" cannot afford. However, Piya's eating patterns are not mere "preferences," but rather symptoms of racialization and incorporation into globalized capitalism's oppressive structures. Her disordered eating and subaltern hunger are two facets of the same food regime. Juxtaposing Piya's disordered eating to descriptions of local and regional patterns of foraging, fisheries, and hunger, *The Hungry Tide* illustrates how structural factors such as socioeconomic status, race, and citizenship condition each person's incorporation into the global food system, which metes out food unevenly alongside cultural and emotional loss.

When we track not just fauna but also edible commodities, disordered eating, and hunger, *The Hungry Tide* does not resolve tension between bourgeois and subaltern environmentalisms so much as illustrate unresolved difficulties in how environmental changes intertwine with the politics of eating. Ghosh offers the subjectivity of a character with whom privileged readers may identify, fulfilling an expectation for literary realism. However, he also imbricates Piya's psychology in the material dynamics of the global food regime, integrated with the structural production of subaltern hunger and environmental precarity. Rather than individuation entailing a retreat from larger scales, Piya's relations with food situate her within the material structures of global capitalism, inviting scrutiny of this system that produces environmental crisis. *The Hungry Tide* exemplifies the capacity of consumption fictions to knit together polyscalar portraits of globalization and environmental politics, informed equally by local and larger contexts.

Conclusion: From Climate Change to Planetary Crisis

Alongside hunger, another key expression of precarity on this changing planet is refugeeism. Ghosh's recounting of the Morichjhāpi story in *The Hungry Tide* illustrates how refugeeism can be caused by tension around national borders, religion, and caste, and then rendered more precarious by environmental politics. In his later research for *The Nutmeg's Curse*, Ghosh turns to the "refugee crisis" in Europe that began in 2015 to consider how climate change plays into such problems. Learning that large numbers of Bangladeshis were undertaking dangerous Mediterranean crossings, Ghosh first hypothesizes that many could be "climate migrants," as "scientists have long predicted that flooding and saltwater intrusion will displace millions more from the low-lying plains of the Bengal Delta."[86] Speaking with a Bangladeshi refugee named Khokon in Italy, Ghosh learns that intensified flooding, droughts, and hailstorms had destabilized the rice harvest of this young man's family: "As the environmental disruptions accelerated, the political situation also began to deteriorate," with members of a ruling party seizing the family's land.[87] Learning these details, Ghosh notes his own surprise that Khokon, and many others in similar circumstances, rejected the "climate migration" descriptor: "No, he insisted, there were many other reasons for his departure: political violence, the employment situation, family disagreements, and aspirations to a higher standard of living."[88] Ghosh describes a gradual change in his own reactions to this:

> I was tempted to assume that these migrants were unwilling . . . to acknowledge the reality of their predicament. . . . It seemed beyond dispute to me that these men were climate migrants, whether they knew it or not; I persuaded myself that I understood their stories better than they did themselves, because I had access to more authoritative information.
>
> It was not till much later that I began to understand that the difference between the migrants' thinking and mine was that for them climate change was not a thing apart, a phenomenon that could be isolated. . . . Rather, their experience was formed by sudden and catastrophic intersections of many different factors. . . .
>
> Viewed from this perspective, climate change is but one aspect of a much broader *planetary crisis*: it is not the prime cause of dislocation, but rather a cognate phenomenon. . . . Climate change, mass dislocations, pollution, environmental degradation, political breakdown, and the Covid-19 pandemic are all cognate effects of the ever-increasing acceleration of the last three decades . . . driven by the dynamics of global power.[89]

The refusal of refugees to frame their stories as "climate migration" helps Ghosh see a different framing, in which climate change cannot be isolated from other factors. The term "planetary crisis," which Ghosh uses throughout *The Nutmeg's Curse* (rather than focus on "climate change" as he did in *The Great Derangement*), points to this concatenation of factors: forever wars, geopolitical and domestic inequalities, refugeeism, Covid-19, racial violence, climate change, and more. In the subaltern framing received from Ghosh's migrant interviewees, climate change is an important part of the story, yet there is no reason to promote it above other factors. To fixate on climate change would be to ignore the refugees' own perspectives in favor of a ready-made framework of understanding imported from the global North and more influenced by "scientists" than by refugees themselves.

There is a similar risk, I think, in looking for texts from the global South to fit the Northern rubric of "climate fiction." Rather than assuming that texts centered on climate change are the most urgent for contemporary environmental politics, one can begin by asking what frameworks environmental narratives from the global South themselves present as important. It is possible also to consider oblique engagements with climate change as having a specific political thrust: they can acknowledge climate change as one of many intersecting factors, rather than as an overriding explanatory concept. While Ghosh attributes this lesson to interviewing migrants for his *Nutmeg's Curse* research, readers can already see such subtle differences in framing in *The Hungry Tide,* a novel that, by refusing to place climate change at the center, instead evokes a planetary crisis in which various environmental disruptions can be traced back to relations of power exemplified by the global food regime. To pursue climate justice, it is necessary to resituate climate change as just one part of a larger planetary crisis that has been shaped by globalization and empire, as is keenly expressed through Ghosh's references to eating, globalized food commodities, and hunger.

Analyzing *The Hungry Tide* as a consumption fiction (rather than as "cli-fi" or a parable about the environmentalism of the poor) can open literary-critical imaginations toward the ways in which novels may decenter climate change in order to recenter the asymmetrical cultural, economic, and political processes that drive a multifaceted planetary crisis. Rather than focus on climate change, *The Hungry Tide* maps the fossil-fueled movements of edible commodities, people, capital, and ideas that determine so much about climate change, *and* about the economic and social injustices that in turn shape exposure to environmental precarity. What Ghosh describes in *The Great Derangement* as a failure to engage climate change more than "obliquely," then, I would reframe as a strength of consumption fictions. By refusing to take climate change as their primary lens, such narratives highlight the continuities of contemporary environmental crisis—including but not limited to climate change—with globalization and imperial dispossession. In the next chapter, I'll discuss how the idiom of hunger and taste can also support pro-poor environmental politics in contexts where other environmental rhetorics are overdetermined by neoliberal policies. To this end, I consider eco/food politics in postapartheid South Africa and in the fiction of Zakes Mda.

PART II

Environmental Politics of Consumerism and Cuisine in South Africa

3

Hunger versus Taste

Fishing and Foraging in a Tourism Economy

Since 1991, a "whale crier" has wandered the seaside cliffs of Hermanus in South Africa's Western Cape, blowing a kelp horn to help tourists spot whales. Promoting Hermanus's reputation for whale-watching, this "much loved tradition" also invites questions about capitalist relations with nonhuman life, as raised in Zakes Mda's 2005 satirical novel *The Whale Caller*.[1] Whereas the whale crier guides tourists to the whales, Mda's titular character uses a kelp horn to call "whales to himself . . . so as to have intimate moments with them. He was not a showman, but a lover."[2] Likely inspired by a real-life resident, Mda's Whale Caller contrasts the whale crier in ways that denaturalize the commodification of whales for the tourist economy, resituating whales as potential love objects. Drawing a love triangle among the Whale Caller, his favorite whale Sharisha, and his human girlfriend Saluni, Mda's novel foregrounds how conflicting ideas about the nonhuman are inflected by neoliberal capitalism. Indeed, the environmental politics of *The Whale Caller* are not just about whales, but spill into a range of commentaries on resource consumption in a liberalized and tourist-facing South Africa. Preoccupied with ecotourism but also with fisheries, restaurants, and supermarkets, *The Whale Caller* addresses how the neoliberal economy both commodifies nonhuman life and drives disparities in resource access for humans.

Commodification and disparity animate Mda's depiction of the informal trade in abalone, an endangered mollusk (*perlemoen* in Afrikaans; the scientific name for the species most common in South Africa is *Haliotis midae*). When the Whale Caller and Saluni find a sack filled with abalone, the Whale Caller pronounces the sack's owner a "poacher," citing regulations that govern subsistence fishing: "The law allows you only four perlemoens a day for the pot" (190). Himself poor, the Whale Caller ventriloquizes a bourgeois conservation perspective that takes into account only nonhuman life. The owner of the sack, called the "puny man," protests that these fishery regulations condemn the poorest: "Big companies are making money out of these perlemoens. The government gives them quotas. What about us, sir? . . . How are we expected to survive?" (191). The puny man has been cast outside the legal trade, meaning "poaching" is hardly a choice. Conservation policies that disregard socioeconomics can be blamed for the "woes" of the puny man's village, "where the whole economy depends on poaching" (191). Organized crime syndicates dictate the informal market's "established racial hierarchies," as delineated in the puny man's free indirect discourse: "Coloured folk sell their harvest to white men who pay about two hundred rands a kilogram. The white men sell to the Chinese men for about a thousand rands. . . . The Chinese ship the abalone to the Far East where they get about two thousand five hundred. . . . The puny man . . . is at the very bottom of the food chain" (192). The "food chain," usually an ecological metaphor for how different species consume one another, here indexes how food systems create hierarchies among humans. The informal abalone market encourages a racialized stratification of wealth, maintaining the poverty of most people identified as "coloured."[3] South Africa's ballooning income gap manifests in the puny man's description of "double-storey houses" rising from the "dusty townships," which belong to a few "well-known poachers [who] have become rich" (191). Mda is telling a situated story about conditions in this village. Yet, at the same time, Mda is tracing transnational movements of capital, organic material, and food. Scaling from local to global, the informal abalone trade offers an (extralegal) example of how postapartheid South Africa participates in a globalized food system on terms that exacerbate both inequality and environmental precarity.

Abalone "poaching" is common in the Western Cape, where it became a site of intense conflict in the 1990s. During apartheid, five white-owned companies had dominated the abalone industry. Informal trade spiked when high prices for abalone in China, Hong Kong, Taiwan, Singapore, and Japan coincided with disappointment in postapartheid fishery reform.[4] Traditional fishers in communities such as Hawston (adjacent to

Hermanus) began protesting how the rights allocation process ignored their historical relationship to this resource. (Fishing and harvesting from the ocean are important aspects of indigenous foodways at the Cape, and often traditional occupations passed down from enslaved ancestors.[5]) Some began "protest fishing" without permits and selling on the informal market. However, this informal market morphed into an organized crime network.[6] Violent conflicts arose in 1994–1996, described in newspapers as the "abalone war."[7] In 1998, the Marine Living Resources Act codified a quota system, criminalized noncompliance, and defined three categories of fishers—commercial, recreational, and subsistence—with the expectation that "subsistence" fishers would not sell their catch. Those trying to make a living as independent small fishers were categorized as noncompliant "subsistence" fishers, and therefore criminalized as poachers.[8] This entrenched disruptions to coastal livelihoods, leaving many fishers with no choice other than participation in the crime syndicates of the informal economy. Threatened by overfishing and increased lobster predation, *Haliotis midae* became so unstable that South Africa banned commercial abalone fishing in 2008; the ban was ineffective and was rescinded in 2010.[9] Meanwhile, after nine years of activism critiquing the 1998 law, a successful court challenge in 2007 led to an "'interim relief measure' quota [for] a new category of 'artisanal fishers,'" which then translated into draft legislation as the Marine Living Resources Amendment Bill of 2013.[10] Lesley Green details how ongoing events have provided some opportunities for small fishers, such as through an app called Abalobi that allows them to share information and sell their catch directly to restaurants, but also how the hearings regarding the draft legislation in 2013 tended to reframe a "fight for a commons" as "a right to corporate personhood," leaving many future challenges for small fishing cooperatives and for equitable management of oceans.[11] Failed fishery reform has threatened both abalone populations and coastal communities such as Hawston, whilst Hawston's whiter and wealthier neighbor Hermanus enjoys a lucrative tourism industry.

Published in the early 2000s and invoking the abalone war, *The Whale Caller* highlights how food inequality and environmental regulation entangle in neoliberal South Africa. Tensions around abalone symptomatize a larger conflict between the appetites of corporations and the needs of residents: while industries such as tourism and mining are booming, the gap between rich and poor has widened since the end of apartheid.[12] Criminality needs to be understood in relation to this wealth inequality. The mismanagement of abalone fisheries also exemplifies "greenwashing," or disguising injustice behind conservationist rhetoric. Twenty-six percent of South Africans suffer from hunger, industrial agriculture and extraction are devastating the land, and electricity shut-offs ("load-shedding") are increasingly severe.[13] Yet South Africa is marketed to foreigners as both an ecotourism destination and a "foodie" capital. As in India, then, environmental and food politics in South Africa are intertwined with divergent narratives of picturesque abundance and of widespread poverty, hunger, displacement, and energy shortages.

Invocations of hunger and taste in South African literature cut to the heart of these contradictions, revealing key tensions of neoliberal-era environmental politics. Mda's puny man critiques both conservation policies and the stratified informal market by invoking hunger: "We have got to eat, sir. . . . We have got to feed our children" (191). Much like Kusum in Amitav Ghosh's *The Hungry Tide,* the puny man invokes hunger to interrupt a neoliberal conservationism that protects animals at the peril of marginalized humans. In a nation with a long history of greenwashing, the language of conservation has been appropriated by apartheid and then postapartheid governments. Hunger offers an alternate idiom, enabling a subaltern critique of neoliberal approaches to economy and environment while opening space for a different kind of environmental discourse.

Thanks to Rob Nixon's 2011 monograph *Slow Violence and the Environmentalism of the Poor,* Ramachandra Guha and Joan Martinez-Alier's term "the environmentalism of the poor" has circulated widely in the environmental humanities. However, Guha and Martinez-Alier also use "'empty-belly' environmentalism" as a synonymous term for global South mobilizations that emphasize resource access for the marginalized. In contrast, the "'full-stomach' environmentalism" of the leisure classes focuses on majestic animals (such as whales) and iconic landscapes.[14] It is no coincidence that Guha and Martinez-Alier describe these differing environmentalist modes through metaphors of hunger and satiation. For starters, "empty-belly environmentalism" emphasizes literal access to food, with examples such as the Penan people's resistance to logging that disrupts their foraging, or Thai rice farmers mobilizing against eucalyptus monocultures.[15] Beyond the material importance of food itself, Guha and Martinez-Alier's terminology exemplifies how eating and being hungry serve as potent metonyms for patterns of uneven resource consumption— making them common foci in South African environmental novels.

Contemplating hunger, taste, and tourism in South Africa's Western and Eastern Cape provinces, this chapter attends to how social inequality is produced, critiqued, and aestheticized at the intersection of environmental politics with what I call "neoliberal consumption culture": expectations about food and eating in a neoliberal society. Narratives of hunger can engender counterimaginaries of resource management and human– nonhuman relations that would operate on different terms. This chapter traces how both neoliberal consumption culture and such counterimaginaries manifest in recent gastronomic trends and grassroots movements, and in Mda's fiction. First, I sketch out a landscape of environmental commodification and alternative food in postapartheid South Africa. By "alternative food," I mean any set of foodways proclaimed (defensibly or not) as an alternative to the globally dominant industrialized agro-food regime. "Alternative food" is therefore a capacious and capricious category, as I show by juxtaposing the grassroots movement for food sovereignty to trends in the neoliberal service economy, including culinary tourism, ecotourism, and the incorporation of "indigenous foods" into gourmet cuisine. As I scrutinize through the 2014 cookbook *Strandveldfood,* some so-called "alternatives" extend the commodifying logic and unequal access of the neoliberal agro-food regime, even when making "environmental" gains, while others work creatively at the edges of neoliberalism to support subaltern (as well as nonhuman) flourishing.

Turning to Mda, I argue that a focus on eating and female characters reveals his environmentalist critique of unequal consumption, but also showcases how alternative food practices unfold in tangles with neoliberalism and with gendered ideologies. *The Whale Caller* and Mda's 2000 *The Heart of Redness* both explore impacts of globalizing South Africa's economy, including how tourism changes foodways and local environments. Although *The Heart of Redness* seems to privilege ecotourism as alternative to neoliberal development, I argue that a subordinated narrative of food sovereignty disenchants the masculinist, predatory politics of ecotouristic ventures and offers a better alternative: an environmental politics guided by Xhosa and Khoena women, whose feminist food sovereignty practices combine culinary traditions with adaptations to the tourist economy. In *The Whale Caller,* playful portraits of ritualized dining and grocery shopping censure a consumption culture that fixates on "taste" (the aesthetics and spectacle of food) while sidelining hunger. Consumerism tempts even neoliberalism's staunchest critics, such as the female protagonist Saluni, whose characterization as obsessive consumer sharpens Mda's critique but bleeds into misogyny and ableism. Taking these two novels together, I argue that Mda offers environmentalist and pro-poor critiques of both neoliberal consumption culture and illusory "alternatives," variably with a feminist or misogynistic gloss. Mda's satires illustrate that, if we would address either structural inequality or environmental crisis, we must first disrupt a consumerist structure of feeling.

Tourism, Indigenous Foods, and Food Sovereignty Activism

The end of apartheid enabled South Africa's reintegration into the global economy after economic isolation; however, the transition compromised many socialist commitments of anti-apartheid movements. The negotiated settlement did not redistribute wealth or land, nor divest from a carbon-intensive, extractive minerals economy. Instead, under pressure from financial institutions, the African National Congress (ANC) government embraced neoliberalism, leaving a swelling income gap that remains racialized (despite the emergence of a black middle class). Foodie culture coexists with widespread food insecurity, while biodiversity and natural beauty are optimized for tourists rather than local use.

Ecotourism, an important source of capital in South Africa, enjoys a reputation among sustainability-oriented economists and policymakers as a "holy grail" reconciling the priorities of equitable development and conservation.[16] But in practice, locals and the poor often benefit little. Ecotourism aligns "postcolonial economic development projects and global capitalism" with "the biocentric idea of natural wilderness," a suspect Western environmentalist mode.[17] This "wilderness" ideology has underwritten the doctrine of *terra nullius* and the expulsion of native peoples to form national parks whose flora and fauna are then enjoyed by wealthier citizens and foreigners. An iconic example is the case of the Makuleke people, who own the northernmost section of Kruger National Park after a successful land claim. The ANC has represented this as a "tribal" and state collaboration, yet the Makuleke are "not taken seriously" in conversations regarding the park's future.[18] Because setting aside parks and protecting endangered species have been used to justify exclusion and violence, environmentalism can seem at odds with improvements for low-income populations. To redress this heritage of antihuman conservation, ecotourism would need to transcend its current model, which is "set to benefit . . . (overwhelmingly white) market leaders" and "black political elites."[19]

Culinary tourism, meaning travel motivated by food or drink, has also surged in the new South Africa, especially in the "gastronomic hub" of the Western Cape.[20] International travel columnists rave about Cape Town's gourmet restaurants and the wineries of Constantia, Stellenbosch, Franschhoek, and Hermanus, which are popular with both foodies and tourists interested in sustainability.[21] Craft beer tourism is also on the rise since the early 2000s.[22] Hermanus, part of the Overstrand municipality, is touted for its "farm to table" and "sea to table" restaurants, as well as its scenic wine route. In 2020, Overstrand Hermanus was the only African city to make the UNESCO "Creative City of Gastronomy" list. As part of this designation, Hermanus promised to set up numerous new festivals, a Junior Master Chef competition, and also a food bank—a laudable but likely insufficient intervention to improve food access.[23]

Like ecotourism, culinary tourism and foodie culture entangle with neoliberal approaches to environmentalism and economic growth, often perpetuating racial and class inequality. These tensions are obvious in the wine industry, which was built on enslaved labor. After slavery became illegal at the Cape, the *dopstelsel* or "dop/tot" system (in which workers were partly paid in wine) created a legacy of alcoholism, domestic violence, fetal alcohol syndrome, and endemic tuberculosis. The dop/tot system has been outlawed since 1962, although some reports suggest that certain estates continue the practice. Many wineries today are ameliorating their labor practices in response to political pressure, economic opportunities through Fairtrade branding, and perhaps "moral obligation."[24] Yet maintaining profitability in an export-driven market has meant "neoliberal moves towards more casual and contract labour," increasing the gap between skilled workers with stable jobs and the precariously employed rural poor.[25] Closely tied to the wine industry, culinary tourism epitomizes the uneven opportunities offered by postapartheid economic growth.

Both ecotourism and culinary tourism flourish against the backdrop of South Africa's liberalized agro-food system, in which apartheid legacies collide with neoliberal policies to intensify food inequality. In 1994, a vast majority of agricultural land (80 percent) was controlled by only sixty thousand commercial farmers, while two million subsistence farmers were crowded onto 13 percent of the land.[26] Postapartheid land reform has been minimal (although in 2020 the government announced a plan to redistribute seven hundred thousand hectares of state-owned land).[27] Legislation deregulating agriculture has concentrated profit from the food system into a few hands and intensified food insecurity.[28] Smallholders remain vulnerable to losing their land, and the number of midsized farms has dwindled before a concentration of large, white-owned agribusiness farms.[29] Vertical integration is also growing: supermarket chains and large-scale processors control the food system from cultivation to retail. Despite grassroots efforts to link smallholders to supply chains, supermarkets generally source from agribusiness farms and disseminate a Western diet high in sugar, fat, and animal protein, which has increased malnutrition.[30] And while chains such as ShopRite Checkers and Pick n Pay dominate retail, the encroachment of supermarkets into poor areas may threaten informal vendors without offering better options for low-income consumers. The urban poor purchase most groceries from *spazas* (shops run out of homes) and hawkers, who may be reselling the same produce from supermarkets, but offer options such as small quantities, credit, and locations along transit routes. These informal businesses are precarious: most go under within a few years, and meanwhile struggle with theft and spoilage.[31] Between the vulnerability of smallholder agriculture and the instability of urban foodways, only 46 percent of households are "food secure," even though South Africa's constitution guarantees the right to food.[32]

A range of eco/food social movements and food-sourcing trends have arisen as supposed alternatives to the industrialized and liberalized agro-food system, some more successful than others at addressing food justice. As one example, restauranteurs in the Western Cape have taken an interest in foraging "indigenous foods" such as dune spinach, *soutslaai* (ice plant), and oysters. Such native species are important to protect for their biodiversity value and their ecosystem services; for example, dune spinach helps to maintain the fragile dunes at places such as Boulders Beach in Cape Town, where dune protection projects also support efforts to conserve African penguins (Figure 4).[33] And in theory, indigenous ingredients can inspire innovative and healthy dishes while supporting small-scale, environmentally friendly farmers, fishers, and foragers through "farm to fork" connections.[34] To the extent that restaurants pursue such goals, the indigenous foods trend is an aspiration to "eco-gastronomy," or "food production focused on the stewardship of ecosystems and social justice."[35] Serving indigenous foods can also celebrate repressed cultural histories, according to chef and food writer Nompumelelo Mqwebu, for whom a national food history has been "either misconstrued or really lacking . . . because of a failure of acknowledgement of the various cultural groups that are indigenous to South Africa," as well as disinterest in native plants.[36] Noting a "lack of available authentic South African cuisine in our South African restaurants," Mqwebu has responded by featuring indigenous crops and precolonial cooking techniques in her cookbook *Through the Eyes of an African Chef.*[37]

However, the indigenous foods trend can stray into cultural appropriation when practiced by non-indigenous chefs and marketed to wealthy, primarily white customers. Arguably the most famous forager of "indigenous" South African foods is Kobus van der Merwe, proprietor of the

Figure 4. Dune spinach growing at Boulders Beach, Cape Town. This edible native plant helps keep the dunes stable. Photo by the author, October 2, 2022.

internationally renowned restaurant Wolfgat. Housed in a former fishing cottage in the village of Paternoster, Wolfgat serves fished, hunted, and foraged *strandveldfood* (Figure 5). *Strandveld,* literally "beach field," refers in this case to the Saldanha Strandveld, a "specialty limestone and granite Fynbos region" on South Africa's West Coast north of Cape Town.[38] (*Fynbos,* literally "fine bush" or "fine plants," is an umbrella term for the broad diversity of shrub species characteristic of the Cape floral kingdom.) As van der Merwe describes in his cookbook *Strandveldfood,* he sought to develop a cuisine that conveyed this region's "special sense of place" by asking himself "what kind of diet would the first inhabitants of this region have lived on?"[39] Offering recipes that combine limpets and *bokkom* (salted and air-dried fish) with foraged plants, *Strandveldfood* is replete with praise for the Saldanha Strandveld's "breathtaking landscapes, incredible plant life, . . . unique architectural style, . . . inhabitants with their typical turn of phrase and, of course, its distinctive delicacies."[40] This description positions West Coast "inhabitants" as part of the landscape, mere background to the activities of the chef. In the cookbook's foreword, Renata Coetzee describes van der Merwe as "a unique modern-day hunter-food-gatherer who . . . daily traverses the same dunes and shores where the Khoi-Khoin and San, the first humans on planet Earth, collected food for the pot some 100,000 years ago."[41] Coetzee rhetorically positions van der Merwe as *replacing* indigenous people, a maneuver that idealizes the history of colonization by invisibilizing actual descendants of original inhabitants. Van der Merwe himself writes: "In South Africa we are a nation of heritage foragers."[42] This "we" claims foraging "heritage" as belonging equally to every South African, eliding that European settlers disrupted Khoena, San, and Xhosa foodways. Van der Merwe adds that "a large percentage of the population still relies on wild food as a part of their daily diet," but without acknowledging that a gourmet restaurant like Wolfgat benefits from and participates in Paternoster's ongoing conversion from fishing village to tourist destination—a pattern that threatens local foodways.[43]

Paternoster's reconfiguration speaks to the broader expansion of touristic and service industries in postapartheid South Africa, changes that perpetuate apartheid-era exclusions in a new form. During apartheid, removals of residents of color from Paternoster were proposed to create an area for white vacationers; a 1981 column in the *Cape Times* compares

Figure 5. Limpet and heerenbone bobotie with dune spinach and peach chutney at Oep ve Koep, Kobus van der Merwe's first restaurant in Paternoster, South Africa, which continues to serve gourmet *strandveldfood* under different management. Photo by the author, September 30, 2022.

this "plight of Paternoster" to the infamous demolishment of Cape Town's District Six (see Introduction).[44] A common pattern during apartheid was that fishing communities were displaced (in places such as Oude-kraal, Skipskop, and Clifton) to make way for luxury residences and hotels, where prices have skyrocketed in the new millennium. National parks too are often part of this pattern: south of Paternoster, the Lange-baan Lagoon in West Coast National Park is an area where traditional fishers have protested quota restrictions and unfair competition from commercial and sport fishers.[45] Paternoster experienced a transition in the early 2000s to a tourism-based economy as "fishing became less lucra-tive and legislation around small-scale fishing rights became more com-plex," leaving the fishing community "largely excluded from the benefits of development."[46]

In addition to providing an alibi for such displacements, the gour-met indigenous foods trend can threaten the biodiversity it would cele-brate. In a telling anecdote from 2016, one chef "collected and discarded kilograms of plant material from a fragile section of coast without any knowledge of indigenous plants."[47] Unlike that chef, van der Merwe is careful to flag environmental concerns and offer guidance on sustainability. He suggests that many indigenous plants can be grown in pots to prevent overforaging, and notes that, because overfishing threatens "fishermen, consumers and mother nature" alike, aspiring foragers should pluck abundant creatures such as the delicious but invasive Mediterranean mussel (*Mytilus galloprovincialis*).[48] However, this attention to sustainability starts to seem more like greenwashing in Coetzee's foreword: "The Khoi-Khoin . . . collected only enough for their needs so as to ensure future growth and supply of foods. . . . Kobus has the same knowledge of the seasons and of nature, and holds to the principle of collecting only enough for the day."[49] By attributing expertise in sustainability to van der Merwe, Coetzee shores up the rhetorical maneuver of replacing indigenous people.

While purveyors of indigenous foods will vary in their cultural politics and environmental practices, incorporating such foods into expensive restaurants certainly cannot address the negative impacts of the industrial food system at scale. A restaurant like Wolfgat, which seats twenty and serves a seven-course tasting menu for 1050 rand (about US$67) per person, can cater to only a narrow slice of South Africans and foreign tourists.[50] This focus on rarefied, unscalable food pathways is a common problem with foodie culture: trends such as foraging and "farm to fork" claim to be alternatives to industrial food, but often perpetuate classed and racialized disparities in access to good food.

Indigenous foods are also invoked, however, in a very different alternative to industrialized food: food sovereignty, a global movement that has inspired a new coalition in South Africa. The transnational farmer-activist organization La Via Campesina defines "food sovereignty" as "the right of peoples to healthy and culturally appropriate food produced through sustainable methods and their right to define their own food and agriculture systems."[51] Food sovereignty should not be confused with "food security," a concept associated with the United Nations Food and Agriculture Organization (FAO) and considered hegemonic by activists. Whereas food security means "physical and economic access to sufficient, safe and nutritious food," food sovereignty demands "democratic control over the food system."[52] The South African Food Sovereignty

Campaign (SAFSC) wrote in 2015: "We are not simply calling for technical solutions for households to access food," but rather "for the deep transformation of our food system by breaking the control of food corporations, repositioning the state to realise the Constitutional right to food and . . . creating . . . space for the emergence of food sovereignty alternatives from below."[53] Where ecogastronomic restaurants enact small-scale shifts in food sourcing, food sovereignty offers a holistic critique of the neoliberal agro-food regime and supports community-based alternatives. Similar efforts come from aligned organizations such as the World Forum of Fisher Peoples (WFFP), founded in India in 1997, which met in Cape Town in 2014 to assert the rights of indigenous and traditional fishing communities to continue their livelihoods and to protest quota systems that benefit large-scale commercial fishing in the name of conservation.[54]

Food sovereignty functions as a "movement of movements," a broad umbrella sheltering grassroots organizations from around the world.[55] South Africa's food sovereignty movement illustrates on a national scale this convergence among diverse groups. The SAFSC launched in 2015 to create a "unifying national campaign" across more than fifty preexisting organizations, including environmental justice groups, seed-saving initiatives, the landless peoples movement, farming cooperatives, the solidarity economy, and trade unions.[56] Framing climate justice and food sovereignty as interrelated, the SAFSC underscores how climate shocks such as amplified drought and flooding impact the food system. The SAFSC has demanded a food sovereignty act that would guarantee a basic income, affordable prices for staple food, a renewable energy transition, protections for indigenous seeds, solutions to farmworker exploitation, a halt to farmland being converted to mining or "game farms for the rich," and community-based water management.[57] Beyond creating political pressure toward this visionary trajectory, the SAFSC also seeks to address community needs and build knowledge commons in areas such as agroecology, seed saving, community/cooperative finance, nutrition, and even indigenous foods. Early in the Covid-19 pandemic, the SAFSC created a mapping project to highlight water-stressed communities, published Covid-19 safety guidelines for food growers in ten languages, and called on supermarkets and the government to establish "people's pantries" for vulnerable communities.[58] The last of these reveals how activists against the neoliberal food regime must partially rely on it while other foodways are coming into being. For Vishwas Satgar and Jane Cherry, the SAFSC exemplifies a politics "beyond reform (managing the system) or revolution (violently destroying the system)." Food sovereignty instead means "build[ing] a new popular imagination" and concrete steps toward a different food system, while improving food access in the meantime via existing pathways.[59]

The SAFSC also affirms women's rights to land, acknowledging women as "the people who produce most of the world's food."[60] Tabara Ndiaye and Mariamé Ouattara, consultants of the New Field Foundation microgrant organization in West Africa, argue that, because women perform 70 percent of food production and processing in Africa, food sovereignty necessitates women's leadership.[61] Many postcolonial governments approach rural women only "in the form of instruction, . . . [arriving] in a village with new seeds, chemicals, and fertilizers and tell[ing] women farmers what they must do."[62] Such practices dismiss rural women's extensive agricultural knowledge and leave food production lands (which women often work but do not own) vulnerable to sale.[63] For Ndiaye and Ouattara, "the most effective method of achieving thriving food systems . . . is to support rural women to bring it about themselves, . . . [giving] their organizations enough leeway to decide what they will produce and how."[64] Stronger food systems cannot be instituted top-down, but must arrive through feminist food sovereignty, as scholars such as Elaine Salo have also argued in the South African context.[65] Interweaving gender equity with goals such as ecologically sound foodways and land rights for marginalized peoples, the emergence of the SAFSC underscores the salience of food sovereignty mobilization as a strategy to negotiate neoliberal South Africa's challenging environmental politics and food inequalities.

Ecotourism versus Feminist Food Sovereignty in *The Heart of Redness*

Imbalanced resource access is a key concern in Mda's writing, notwithstanding his own status as a postcolonial elite.[66] And eating is frequently an associated trope: after Mda gained literary prominence with anti-apartheid plays in the 1970s, he became a commentator on postapartheid problems through works such as his 2002 *The Mother of All Eating*, which leverages eating as a euphemism for political corruption. The idiom of eating likewise animates Mda's environmental politics and his critique of neoliberalism in *The Heart of Redness* and *The Whale Caller*. Both novels have enjoyed warm ecocritical reception, but food and eating make few appearances in this scholarship, despite Mda's many pages on fishing, dining, supermarkets, and the aphrodisiacal properties of oysters.[67] Instead, critics read *The Heart of Redness* as a parable advocating ecotourism or subaltern environmentalism, while *The Whale Caller* attracts approaches focused on human–cetacean relations.[68] But Mda's references to food do not gel into comforting morals about the "right" way to respect the subaltern or protect the nonhuman; nor does his satirical approach to characterization or his gender politics. Often, Mda attributes greedy appetites to precisely those characters whom we might associate with alternatives to neoliberal conservationism.

What if we read *The Heart of Redness* and *The Whale Caller* not as ecojustice parables, but as satirical consumption fictions? Satire, and comedy more broadly, can be an important tool for unsettling "ethical, political, and scientific orthodoxies" in environmental thought, as Allison Carruth has explored in American and Canadian literature.[69] While Mda provides stinging critiques of neoliberal consumption culture, his novels also contend with how neoliberal ideologies infiltrate even potential "alternatives," debunking simplistic dichotomies. I argue that *The Heart of Redness* offers a problematic (and problematized) alternative to extractive development in the form of ecotourism, but also a subordinated narrative of food sovereignty that evokes a rural feminist ecopolitics.

In *The Heart of Redness,* a black South African named Camagu returns from exile in the United States only to be disenchanted by postapartheid corruption. Unable to find work in Johannesburg, Camagu impulsively pursues a beautiful stranger to Qolorha, a Xhosa village in the Eastern Cape. Two factions, the Believers and Unbelievers, are debating proposals to build a casino that would reinvent Qolorha's modest tourism industry. Mda interweaves this postapartheid story with a narrative set during the nineteenth-century Xhosa cattle killing, a genuine historical event. In 1856, amidst European military incursions and the bio-ecological assault of lung sickness on the amaXhosa's cattle, a young woman named Nongqawuse reported receiving a prophecy: if the amaXhosa killed their cattle and burnt their crops, ancestors would rise to bring new cattle and expel the Europeans. Riven between those who believed this prophecy and those who did not, the amaXhosa were overswept. Europeans seized their lands and reduced fifty thousand famished people to wage laborers, while forty thousand starved.[70] The 1990s conflict in Mda's novel recasts these tensions around nineteenth-century colonization and hunger, now invoking conservation and postapartheid "development." Bhonco, leader of the Unbelievers, asserts that the casino will bring jobs and "civiliza-tion."[71] The Believers, led by Zim, insist the plan will destroy Qolorha's natural resources for the pleasure of tourists, enriching only developers.

Instead of the casino (or the "cultural village" created by a local white man, which stereotypes Xhosa customs), Camagu proposes an ecotour-istic alternative: a backpackers' hostel for "communing with unspoiled nature," advocating "the kind of tourism that will benefit the people, that will not destroy indigenous forests, that will not bring hordes of people who will pollute the rivers and drive away the birds" (201). At first glance, Camagu's plan seems to harmonize environmentalism with equitable development. But Camagu's idea relies on an outmoded and politically suspect concept of "unspoiled nature." Describing Qolorha as untouched wilderness ignores how Qolorhans use their environment, and even sub-sumes the humans themselves into the category of "nature" that ecotourists might like to see.[72] Moreover, Camagu's scheme is self-interested, provid-ing him with both income and personal satisfaction. Like the casino plan, the backpackers' hostel profits an outsider; for locals, it could do more harm than good.

Ending with the backpackers' hostel coming to fruition, Mda's novel may appear to idealize ecotourism—but only if we collapse the novel's perspective with that of Camagu. The novel, however, repeatedly de-stabilizes Camagu's authority, particularly in subplots concerning food and local women. While Camagu occupies the most narrative space, a secondary narrative explores women characters' food gathering prac-tices and environmentalist discourses. Early in the novel, a young Khoe woman named Qukezwa critiques the casino plans, while Camagu ini-tially supports the casino, asking Qukezwa why her father Zim is "against progress" (102). Camagu queries Zim's views rather than supposing that Qukezwa's own opinion might be of interest, one of many details ex-posing Camagu's masculinism. Qukezwa's response does not parrot her father's ideas, but rather shows her own investment: the casino would impoverish local people, because "this whole sea will belong to tourists and their boats and their water sports. . . . Women will no longer harvest the sea for their own food and to sell" (103). This conversation sways Camagu to Qukezwa's view. Prioritizing use of the environment by local women gathering food, Qukezwa rather than Camagu scrutinizes "development" from a perspective invested in local economics, foodways, and environmental concerns.

Camagu, however, steals credit for Qukezwa's ideas by monopolizing space both in Qolorha's public fora and in Mda's narrative. Qolorhans challenge Camagu's right to public space in several instances. At a village fundraiser, Qukezwa compels Camagu to declare which woman from a crowd is most beautiful, subjecting his "cosmopolitan judiciousness to delightful mockery."[73] Similarly, when Camagu chides against the casino plan at a village meeting with the developers, Bhonco demands, "Is he circumcised? Are we going to listen to uncircumcised boys here?" (202). For the amaXhosa and other southern African groups, circumcision ceremonializes the transition into manhood, a tradition Camagu dismisses: "Facts are facts, whether they come from somebody who is circumcised or not" (202). He would use a Western rationalist discourse of objectivity to make identity irrelevant to his right to speak. But Zim concurs with his nemesis Bhonco here: "Yes, it does matter. . . . Of course, if this son of Cesane is uncircumcised we shall not deal with him." This passage checks Camagu's authority and complicates the account of his male privilege: Camagu is reduced to a "boy" because he is an outsider, making masculine authority culturally contingent.

The circumcision passage also complicates any identification of Camagu as "closely associated with the author."[74] Mda and Camagu do share biographical similarities, such as having a Western education. But the novel questions, rather than endorses, the tendency of the Western-educated cis-male to claim discursive space. Camagu bluffs his way out of the circumcision question, challenging Bhonco "to come and inspect [him] here in public to see if [he] ha[s] a foreskin" because "he knows that no one will dare take up that challenge. And if . . . they did, they would not find any foreskin. He was circumcised, albeit in the most unrespectable manner, at the hospital" (202). To assert his authority, Camagu would evacuate Xhosa circumcision of its meaning and attendant ceremonies, substituting an anatomical status for the cultural production of manhood. This disrespect renders his occupation of space in Qolorha a usurpation.

Rather than Mda endorsing antifeminism on Camagu's part, he prob-
lematizes Camagu's claims to public space. This invites questions about
the similarly outsized role of Camagu's development ideas in narrative
space, rendering ambiguous the novel's tones toward both Camagu and
ecotourism.

If we focus not on Camagu but on women characters, a feminist ecopolitics begins to emerge, built from a fusion of Xhosa and Khoena culinary traditions, local botanical knowledge, and democratic nationalist
discourse. Men on Qolorha's council want to withhold the right to speak
not only from Camagu but also from Qukezwa, who stands trial for violating the Xhosa law against felling trees. When Qukezwa explains that
she cuts down "foreign trees" that use too much water and kill indigenous
species, her knowledge of ecosystem stewardship inspires the respect of
elders who "nod their agreement" (215–16). Nonetheless, Chief Xikixa
insists that Qukezwa's father be tried in her place because she is unmarried, and therefore a minor. Qukezwa protests that unmarried women
being tried as minors comes from "the old law . . . that weighed heavily on
our shoulders during the sufferings of the Middle Generations. In the new
South Africa where there is no discrimination, it does not work" (213).
The "Middle Generations" designate amaXhosa who came between the
1850s cattle crisis and 1994, spanning colonial, segregationist, and apartheid periods. "Old law" refers not to an indigenous tradition, but to "customary law," a colonial divide-and-rule tactic.[75] Of course, that "there is
no discrimination" after apartheid is not true. Qukezwa's comment may
sound naïve, but I read it as strategic: she recombines democratic nationalist discourse, Xhosa tradition, and knowledge of local ecosystems in
service of a feminist environmentalism.

Indeed, Qolorhan women have an environmentally friendly adaptation to the encroachments of tourism that predates Camagu's arrival,
contesting the primacy of Camagu's development solutions. Qukezwa and
the minor characters MamCirha and NoGiant practice food sovereignty
by harvesting mollusks both for familial consumption and for sale to the
local hotel. Rather than operate in isolation from economic globalization,
this practice combines subsistence food harvesting with tapping into the
tourism economy; the fisherwomen insulate themselves from full incorporation into wage or gig work while still deriving some benefit from tourism. For Qukezwa, MamCirha, and NoGiant, food sovereignty is not only

an ideology of transcending neoliberal food systems, but a praxis of working adaptively at neoliberalism's edges.

Yet the growing tourism economy threatens mollusk harvesting when the casino developers plan to privatize the sea. Camagu also encroaches on the women's business for his own gastronomic and financial gain. When he first encounters Qukezwa, MamCirha, and NoGiant harvesting mussels and oysters, "Camagu is curious.... He ... was not aware that the amaXhosa of the wild coast eat the slimy creatures from the sea" (101). These mollusks are in fact a storied part of Xhosa cuisine, as Mqwebu describes in her cookbook: her recipe for "Mussels—the Xhosa way" simply instructs readers to light a fire on the beach and cook the mussels in seawater. In the framing text, Mqwebu describes a long history of Xhosa women harvesting and boiling mussels (*imbaza*). She also situates gathering mollusks as an interface between the amaXhosa and Khoena.[76] Though unaware of such culinary traditions, Camagu becomes invested for gastronomic reasons: "It all started with oysters and mussels that he ate at Zim's. He was sold on the taste" (138). The phrase "sold on the taste" invites us to think about the relation between "taste"—an aesthetic preference that might seem innocuous—and money.

Camagu's gastronomic interest becomes an interest in profit. Lacking a job, he decides "to learn to harvest the sea himself. But [MamCirha and NoGiant] would not teach him. He was good as a customer and not as a competitor" (138). Undeterred, Camagu learns from Qukezwa. While "NoGiant and MamCirha were not happy that he was no longer buying their seafood," Camagu "made up his mind to catch oysters and mussels, keep them in sea water as he was taught by the women, take them in his car, and sell them to hotels in East London" (138). Rather than "compete with the women," Camagu attempts to structure this as "a cooperative society" selling all their catch, which "is not as lucrative as they might wish. It is struggling on. But Camagu, for the first time after many years, is a very fulfilled man" (139). Camagu is "fulfilled," indicating his emotional stake in feeling useful, but MamCirha and NoGiant benefit little from the cooperative society; it is Camagu who needs their knowledge. The novel frames this in gendered terms, repeatedly referring to MamCirha and NoGiant as "the women," while linking Camagu's satisfaction to him being a "man." While Camagu declines to view himself as an encroaching outsider, his cooperative society is a false solution to the threats posed by the casino plan: it is another outside incursion, which does not substantially improve local women's material circumstances ("It is not as lucrative as they might wish").

Camagu co-opts space from Qolorha's women, both in harvesting the sea and in the narrative space of the novel. But when read within the framework of feminist food sovereignty, perhaps reading against Mda's grain, the women playfully reclaim this space. Oysters (*imbhatyisa*) are locally known as an aphrodisiac, offering the women an opportunity to "burst out laughing" when Camagu enthuses about them; they tease Camagu that "[a] man needs all the strength he can get" and leave him "a bit embarrassed" (102). This detail also invites us to read Camagu's "fulfilled" feeling in a bawdier way. Oysters are linked to Camagu's lustful middle-aged masculinity, cultivating a mocking tone to destabilize Camagu's self-assertion. MamCirha, NoGiant, and Qukezwa are confident foragers and entrepreneurs who are alternately generous, annoyed, and amused with a somewhat silly Camagu.

By giving Camagu and his development strategies so much room in the narrative, Mda does reify a focus on ecosocial cure-alls that we can associate with a masculinist and Westernized politics of expertise imposed on the rural global South. (Notably, Camagu's cooperative society also suggests another biographical similarity to Mda, who established a beekeeping project with rural women in the Eastern Cape in 2000.[77]) Yet we can also read around this thread, attending to moments of satirical play against Camagu and to the understated narrative of food sovereignty. As an alternative ecopolitics that exists in an uncomfortable but ongoing dialogue with tourism, food sovereignty here emerges from local eating culture and foodways managed by savvy Khoena and Xhosa women. Feminist environmentalism comes into focus when we interpret *The Heart of Redness* not as a parable that reconciles conservation priorities and subaltern needs via ecotourism, but instead as a satire that ridicules quick fixes for sustainable development. Cosmopolitan author that he is, Mda would nonetheless have us laugh at outsiders' development strategies, and at Western-educated cis-men who take themselves a bit too seriously.

Looking versus Eating in *The Whale Caller*

So far I have traced a minor narrative of food sovereignty in *The Heart of Redness,* which offers a feminist alternative to externally imposed eco-development. *The Whale Caller* poses different challenges to feminist reading: Mda portrays the central female character, Saluni, as an acerbic drunk whose pro-poor critiques of neoliberal society are dogged by her hatred for animals and her voracious consumer desire. Discomfort with Mda's representation of this subaltern woman as a material girl may be one reason why readings of *The Whale Caller* have focused on the non-human.[78] I instead delve into Saluni's unsettling craving to consume, which satirizes the pervasive consumerist spirit that ecotourism and ethical eating would greenwash.

Mda's satire of neoliberal development operates at the conjuncture of environmental attitudes with consumer culture, and thus finds its paradigmatic expression in the process that literalizes the "consumption" of resources: eating. His depictions of appetite, while seemingly less "environmental" than passages about whales or fishing quotas, are indispensable to my reading of *The Whale Caller* as an environmentalist satire of neoliberal consumption culture. By contrasting looking to eating, I argue, Mda critiques the tourism economy, supermarkets, and foodie culture for prioritizing aesthetics ("taste") over food access. Optical motifs— blindness, eyes, simulacra, simulation, and windows—situate this image-focused consumption culture as emblematic of the neoliberal era, underscoring that we cannot achieve environmental or social justice goals until we dismantle a consumerist structure of feeling. However, the novel portrays consumerism as a feminine addiction to food and shopping, problematically linking Mda's critique of neoliberal ideology to a misogynistic and ableist characterization.

The Whale Caller, the novel's conservationist, equates legality with morality when he endorses conservation policies without questioning whether they are fair, such as when he reminds the abalone "poacher" of "the law," or gets upset if "an angler does something unseemly, such as use a piece of lead to sink the hook. Although it is illegal to do since it pollutes the water, selfish people do it all the time" (190, 166). The Whale Caller condemns "illegal" behavior without considering that poor fishers may be using any materials available. The rhetoric of legality suggests that, while the Whale Caller is himself poor, he represents a capitulation to antipoor environmental ideology. This is partly a matter of genre: though characters in *The Whale Caller* display some of the individuation typical of realist novels, they function more as mouthpieces for ideologies that Mda would satirize. The Whale Caller character operates as a sketch of "full-stomach environmentalism," fixated on charismatic megafauna in ways that become fetishistic: "He blows his horn even harder, and the whale . . . performs the tail-slapping dance that is part of the mating ritual . . . making loud smacking sounds that leave the Whale Caller breathing more and more heavily. . . . He is drenched in sweat as his horn ejaculates sounds," and ends the night "wet and sticky from the seed of life" (41, 66). Readers might share the embarrassment expressed by Saluni, who shouts: "You have shamed yourself—and me!" (66). By satirizing the Whale Caller's sexual love for the whale Sharisha, Mda questions forms of animal appreciation that would fetishize nonhumans. The Whale Caller character anchors Mda's satire of Western-style environmental policies that idolize megafauna and sideline the poor.

Saluni's wrathful responses, however, exhibit an ugly speciesism. Saluni curses at and moons Sharisha. When the Whale Caller worries that fishing "hooks and tackle in the sea will kill many innocent fish and other sea creatures," Saluni retorts, "we are catching them here, man. They are going to die in any case. . . . What's the difference?" (166). Saluni is heartless toward nonhuman animals. She is also an alcoholic, and her "obsessive" behaviors, such as checking the lock on the door five times, suggest obsessive-compulsive disorder; however, her disabilities are represented with little understanding or sympathy (99). Readers are instead invited to sympathize with the Whale Caller's thankless struggle to get Saluni to stop drinking, whilst Saluni manipulates and even abuses him. Mda thus makes Saluni a "cackling" shrew who beleaguers her boyfriend and hates nature (114). This misogynistic and ableist characterization raises the gendered stakes of Mda's choice to represent Saluni as voracious consumer, as I'll discuss momentarily. With Saluni as the only woman character of any significance, *The Whale Caller* lacks an analogue to the subaltern feminists of *The Heart of Redness*.

Although nasty to animals, Saluni indicts the Whale Caller for obscuring human needs such as those of Lunga Tubu, a boy from Zwelihle township who sings for tips on Hermanus's waterfront. The Whale Caller cannot hear Lunga Tubu's singing, to Saluni's outrage: "You can hear your whales a hundred miles away but you cannot hear a boy only a few meters below us? . . . He is here at least twice a week. But you never see him because you only see whales" (84–85). Saluni condemns single-species environmentalism (as embodied in the Whale Caller) for its inattention to poverty. The Whale Caller does not see or hear the boy, literally, yet this works as a metaphor for his lack of awareness about social inequality: the Whale Caller's obsession with megafauna "blinds" and "deafens" him. Indeed, sight and blindness encode social and environmental consciousness and unconsciousness throughout this novel. These motifs instrumentalize disability, a problematic tactic but one with a range of resonances in postcolonial literature; the relationship between metaphorical and literal blindness thickens later in the novel, when Saluni blinds herself in order to monopolize the Whale Caller's caring labor.[79] For now, Saluni upbraids the Whale Caller for his inattention to Lunga Tubu and denounces income disparities:

> Saluni explains . . . that Lunga Tubu's presence here destabilises the serenity of Hermanus—a sanctified playground of the rich . . . [who] would rather forget: that only a few kilometres away there is . . . a whole festering world of the disillusioned, those who have no stake in the much-talked-about black economic empowerment, which is really the issue of the black middle class. . . . While the town of Hermanus is raking in fortunes from tourism, the mothers and fathers of Zwelihle are unemployed. . . . They have seen politicians and trade union leaders become overnight millionaires. . . . Only tiny crumbs trickle down to what used to be called "the masses." (86)

As Saluni narrates, mass public campaigns against apartheid have given way to closed-door politics, with the formation of a black elite and continuation of white privilege at the expense of the majority. In voicing this widely held view, Saluni articulates a canny concern for the poor, whereas the Whale Caller is too fixated on whales for the good of humans. The contrast between the Whale Caller and Saluni allegorizes a disarticulation between conservationist and social justice discourses, which must be reconciled to support environmental justice.

But, lest the novel slip into moralism, Saluni's characterization underscores how rhetorics of social justice can remain entangled with consumer tastes complicit with neoliberalism. Saluni critiques economic injustice yet epitomizes a consumerist ethos, lusting after fancy foods and other luxury goods. I build here upon Deborah Posel's definition of postapartheid consumerism as participation in capitalist market relations wherein

"aspirations to consume . . . are closely linked to the making and performance of selfhood."[80] Saluni's income level never really changes, yet she
redefines her selfhood through schemes to indulge increasingly extrava-
gant consumer desires. Saluni's "rent-a-fish" scheme, for example, begins
when she proposes that the Whale Caller start fishing "so that we can
raise our standard of living" in preparation for what Saluni believes is her
future trajectory toward fame as a singer (170, 161). The phrase "standard
of living" comes from early-twentieth-century American middle-class
ideology, referring to a "quality of life" that "increasingly became defined
through consumer goods."[81] By linking Saluni's aspirations to this structure of feeling, Mda critiques the proliferation of consumerist ideologies
that accompanied South Africa's liberalization. Saluni initially plans to eat
the Whale Caller's catch and sell any surplus to generate a small income
(not unlike Qukezwa, MamCirha, and NoGiant). However, these modest goals evaporate when the Whale Caller catches a huge *kabeljou* and
Saluni charges tourists for pictures with this fish. This "rent-a-fish" business replaces selling or eating the fish itself. The value of fish as food is
thus displaced by the aesthetic value of a simulacrum (the photo, which
tourists use to pretend they caught the fish). In some ways, Saluni's rent-
a-fish concept subverts the capitalist pecking order: it sidesteps state-
imposed quotas that restrict small fishers' catch, and generates income
for the poor by tricking the friends and family of tourists (the potential
photo viewers). Yet, in allowing the spoilage of what could have been
food, Saluni's "new venture" also stinks, figuratively and literally (169).
The *kabeljou* starts to reek after two days; Saluni clings to it until "people
begin to complain" that the fish "fills the whole area with its stench" (170).
While the Whale Caller and Saluni continue the rent-a-fish business with
new fish, the incident brings home that something is rotten: consumerist
obsessions with image obscure basic needs, such as fish to eat.

Of course, those of us who enjoy middle-class lifestyles should hesitate
to critique consumer desire on the part of the disenfranchised. Although
Mda does attribute greed to poor characters who eke small profits from
tourism, he does not castigate individuals who aspire to material comfort so much as critique a consumerist structure of feeling. Saluni is not
so much a realistic "person" as a contradictory placeholder in the novel,
enabling Mda to insert both leftist critiques of neoliberalism (which he

seems to endorse) and consumerist attitudes that he would satirize. In this way, the novel suggests that consumerism is pervasive even among critics of neoliberalism. Still, it is troubling that Mda makes the emblem for such consumerist attitudes a woman of color who is both poor and disabled. While redeeming gender politics can be found in the second-ary narratives of *The Heart of Redness,* a critical feminist reading of *The Whale Caller* requires reading the story thoroughly against the grain of its implied misogyny, ableism, and problematic class politics.

It is possible to acknowledge both how the characterization of Saluni as would-be greedy consumer is problematic and also how it enables critique. It is crucial that Saluni can never satisfy her consumerist appe-tite, exposing the discrepancy between neoliberal capitalism's promises and its realities. This crystallizes in "civilised living," Saluni's name for her ritual of simulating bourgeois eating: she acts out the patterns of luxury dining, instructing the Whale Caller to "sit down . . . with a white tablecloth, flowers and a candle" for dinner "in a number of courses—the same macaroni and cheese served as a starter, entrée and dessert" (71). Whereas the Whale Caller thinks eating should be a pragmatic matter of "fill[ing] his stomach," Saluni insists that the Whale Caller learn "how to eat a meal of many courses, which she says they are destined to do one day. . . . 'We were born for better things. At least I was'" (71). Considering fine dining a destiny, Saluni also espouses the belief that individuals become "better" by climbing the social ladder. "Civilised living" thus paro-dies the European "civilizing" mission, combining a capitalist-Protestant ideology of work, competition, and social mobility with the notion that some individuals deserve better lives than do others. Saluni is unable to attain the class status that these narratives promise and is left eating macaroni and cheese, exposing colonialist and neoliberal ideologies as excuses for differentiated privilege.

The motif of civilized living satirizes the unfair expectation that poor South Africans should accept bourgeois ideology without getting middle-class stuff. Saluni and the Whale Caller are imitating fine dining while living in a Wendy house (a playhouse for children), thus "play-acting" a middle-class lifestyle that they are denied. They likewise go to the super-market to act out the delectation of foods that they cannot buy, trolling the aisles for "food they like, and then eating it with their eyes. . . . Saluni stops in front of a shelf containing cans of beef stew. . . . She swallows hard as she eats the stew with her eyes. . . . Food fit for a queen. She gormandises it all with her greedy eyes" (71–72). Mda satirizes the food regime's big lie: that, with packaged, industrialized food delivered globally via supermarkets, everyone will eat like "a queen." Saluni, who cannot afford this food, can only "eat with her . . . greedy eyes," underscoring the distance between alimentation and the aesthetics of food (associated here with the "eyes"). Even while extending the misogynistic portrayal of Saluni as avaricious, this visual simulation of eating presents the fact that South Africa's poor have yet to obtain the goodies promised with democracy and liberalization. Saluni may have middle-class desires, but poverty bars her from eating middle-class food: "By the time they walk out of the supermarket they have satisfied their *tastes,* now they go back home to satisfy their *hunger* with macaroni and cheese" (72; emphasis mine). "Taste," connoting a bourgeois aesthetic to which Saluni aspires, is bifurcated from "hunger," an embodied experience of poverty. By separating the aesthetics of eating from sustenance, Mda underscores the gulf between neoliberal capitalism's idealized imaging and its material delivery.

The Whale Caller also uses a lexicon of windows and likenesses to explore the roles of visual perception and image in perpetuating inequality. Saluni calls her ritual in the supermarket "window shopping," which caricatures the idea of observing goods without buying as a leisure activity (71). Like the rent-a-fish sequence, the window shopping scene opposes simulacra to sustenance. Not only are Saluni and the Whale Caller looking rather than eating; they are not even ogling food itself, but the pictures on cans: Saluni pretends to eat "the pieces of meat, tomatoes, carrots and potatoes swimming in brown onion gravy on the label" of canned beef stew (71). This detail satirizes the normalization of processed, packaged foods and questions the aesthetic logic under which we desire an image rather than a material good. This image-driven logic is central to supermarket culture, according to scholar/activist Raj Patel: "We're tricked by the simulacrum, mistaking the dead green 'Certified Organic' packaging for a living connection" because we have never "experienced a direct connection to the people who grow our food. . . . When you shop in a supermarket, you're already inside the label."[82] The aesthetics of the label cannot be separated from material effects, as the idolization of images further alienates consumers from food production.

Thus querying why images of food become coveted aesthetic objects in ways that supplant nutritional value, *The Whale Caller* scrutinizes a consumption culture that prioritizes aesthetics and images over access to food. This culminates in a sequence on fine dining, inviting readers to look askance at foodie culture. To supplement window shopping with "window eat[ing]," Saluni and the Whale Caller dress up and stroll through Hermanus's restaurant district, staring into windows to watch people eat (111). First passing "American-type fast food franchises," they desire something "classier" and continue down "a street that prides itself on its restaurants," each of which "boldly advertises some foreign cuisine, ranging from Indian and Chinese to French and Italian" (112–14). This description speaks to the crescendo of upscale "global" cuisine in the tourist-friendly Western Cape, and to how culinary globalization informs consumer expectations and thus shapes local foodscapes. Cuisines from all over the world are celebrated but local cuisine is sidelined, with our characters finding only one restaurant "that unashamedly boasts of specialising in South African cuisine" (115). Like chef Mqwebu, Mda evinces his suspicion of a "local" foodie culture that prioritizes cuisines from elsewhere. At the same time, he acknowledges that globalization is dynamic but not new, and that Cape traditions are hybrid: the single "South African" restaurant serves "Cape Malay food," the cuisine "of the melting cultures of Indonesia, India, Malaysia, Khoikhoi, and Dutch" (115; see also chapter 4 of the present book). Mda also presents upscale world restaurants as the other side of the coin from fast food, critiquing both the up-market "tastes" that a globalized food regime encourages and the low-quality, insufficient fare that the same system metes out to the poor.

To underscore how the aesthetics of food sideline hunger, Mda presents fine dining as a spectacle for which the Whale Caller and Saluni are the hungry audience. They gaze into a sushi restaurant at "patrons sitting on . . . mats on the floor like a congregation of some New Age religion, eating delicate oval-shaped balls of rice rolled in fish. . . . Other worshippers are . . . drinking some whitish sacramental drink" (113). Exoticizing Japanese cuisine as part of the rarefied culinary globalization that accompanies an influx of tourists, Mda's mock-religious rhetoric positions foodie culture as characterized by excessive ceremony. Sushi-eating made South African headlines in the fall of 2016, when business mogul Kenny Kunene tweeted that politician Julius Malema had practiced *nyotaimori*: eating sushi off the bodies of naked women.[83] The ensuing scandal underscores how (in this case gendered) power differentials capacitate gourmet cuisine. Similarly, at the Cape Malay restaurant, Saluni and the Whale Caller "have to press their faces against the panes in order to have a good look" at the diners inside (115). The importance of the window in "window shopping" and "window eating" is literalized as the restaurant window becomes a screen, separating Saluni and the Whale Caller from the food while making them the audience to a spectacle of consumption.

At the same time, window metaphorics reverse the tendency for poverty, hunger, and racialized bodies to be rendered as consumable images. There is a long history of Europeans subjecting colonized and racialized Others to the gaze: an infamous example is the story of Sarah (Saartjie) Baartman, a Khoe woman mythologized as the "Hottentot Venus," whose body was exhibited in Europe in both life and death. In contemporary South Africa, poverty and African cultures are differently distilled into consumable images through mainstays of the tourism industry such as the "township tour" and "cultural village."[84] In *The Whale Caller*'s fine-dining sequence, the privileged classes are finally the ones behind the glass. Beyond critiquing the tendency to aestheticize food, Mda also shifts the emphasis so that the spectacle becomes not the food itself but greedy eaters: "boerewors-roll-chomping tourists, mustard and ketchup dripping from their fingers and chins;" and food "worshippers" from Hermanus's upper crust, including "youthful upwardly mobile lovers" and "retired millionaires" (19, 115–16). Both tourists and locals are ridiculed for flaunting money in acts of literalized conspicuous consumption.

The Whale Caller provides a much-needed (if crude) counter to this consumption culture obsessed with spectacle. He notes that the "worshipping of food [is] obscene" because the food "will be digested and will surely become stools. Then it will be scorned and despised. People forget that only a few hours back they were venerating it" (116). Refusing to aestheticize goods that are basic to bodily functions, the Whale Caller offers a plea to regard food as a basic need. While sustenance is the essential purpose of food, the Whale Caller and Saluni are put in the position of simply looking at foods they cannot eat. Thus juxtaposing eating to looking, Mda critiques the aestheticization of food in South Africa's tourism economy. This critique of gastronomy resonates on several scales, applying to foodie dining culture, to a touristic economy in which South Africa is packaged for display, and to the cult of conspicuous consumption that undergirds neoliberal ideology.

Of course, the Whale Caller's scatological scorn does not redistribute power. Those who resist the dynamics of the global food system are still interpellated in them, as becomes clear when Saluni and the Whale Caller tangle with a maître d'. He invites them in; when Saluni insists that "they would rather enjoy his decorative delicacies with their eyes," the maître d' banishes them: "You make my customers nervous watching them like that. Please go and be spectators somewhere else" (113–14). Even though the foods are aesthetic objects ("decorative delicacies"), it is reprehensible to spectate just "with their eyes"—as if Saluni and the Whale Caller had any choice. The poor are punished for looking at the indulgences of the rich, even as conspicuous consumption begs for attention. With the absurdity of Saluni's "window eating," Mda satirizes the real absurdity: that social inequality can be aestheticized. As Julie Guthman puts it, "privileged eating is intrinsically tied to impoverished eating" in that "what allows an aesthetic of food is disparity."[85] Beautiful foods accessible only to elites are symptoms of an ugly food system.

Mda's depictions of the Hermanus restaurant scene and of Saluni (who critiques neoliberalism yet has foodie desires) invite those on the left to consider when and how we remain embedded within neoliberalism's material and affective structures, even when we are critiquing the neoliberal agro-food regime. With her own consumerism as playacting, Saluni functions as an ironized archetype of the acquisitive consumer. Her simulations of middle-class behavior draw our attention to the gap between neoliberalism's promises and its results, but also underscore that consumerism is itself performative, producing spectacles of indulgence. Foodie aesthetics offer an apt metonym for the broader commodification of appearances in neoliberal cultures of environment and consumption, helping us consider how a focus on image guides mainstream discourses of environmentalism and ethical eating that may displace the real work of addressing inequality and environmental damage. When read as a consumption fiction, *The Whale Caller* castigates this structure of feeling where image takes precedent over material need. In drawing our attention to the visual and performative aspects of tourist-facing restaurants,

The Whale Caller confronts the greenwashing prevalent in foodie culture and neoliberal environmentalism, even as it runs the risks of instrumentalizing disability and gendering consumer desire as feminine.

Conclusion: Consumer-Citizen or Plain Consumer?

The Heart of Redness and *The Whale Caller* emphasize the roles of both ecotourism and foodie culture in sanitizing neoliberalism. Scenes in which eating becomes a spectacle literalize "conspicuous consumption," disenchanting foodie ideology while ripping away neoliberalism's façade of growing the wealth for all and greening the economy. By admitting foreign dollars and culinary globalization on terms that exacerbate the gap between the hungry and the well-fed, South Africa may have enabled a food scene reminiscent of, say, consumption culture in the United States, which pairs performatively "green" high-end foods with labor exploitation and food insecurity. As Guthman seminally argued, pursuing alternative food via a market-based framework will replicate many of the social harms of industrial food: California's organic movement, for example, devolved from a radical critique into the "gentrification of organic food" in part "thanks to chef-led advocacy of organics" by celebrities such as Alice Waters.[86] Scholars such as Susie O'Brien have made related arguments that an individualizing, consumerist logic circumvents social change in North American local food movements.[87] Might something similar be happening in South Africa's Western Cape, as chefs incorporate foraged indigenous foods into trendy new menus for tourists? Categories such as "local," "farm-to-fork," "ecogastronomy," and "indigenous" can become little more than buzzwords.

With a similar skepticism of green marketing and individualist logic, Jennifer Wenzel has characterized our era in terms of "postconsumerism," or the "structure of feeling evoked by discourses of enlightened consumerism that promise to help the poor or save the planet by buying things."[88] This ethos disavows collective mobilization by encouraging people to take action by spending money, as individual consumers. With this "atomizing withdrawal from the public/planetary demands of environmental citizenship," postconsumerism "collapses the rights and responsibilities of the citizen into a matter of consumer 'choice' (or the ruse of choice)," generating only mild (or illusory) mitigation to destructive capitalism.[89] Mda exposes the shallowness of postconsumerism in depicting ecotourism, which repackages conservation in ways still dictated by masculinist outsiders (in *The Heart of Redness*) and fails to protect either whales or subaltern humans (in *The Whale Caller*). Together, these novels draw our attention to how ecotourism remains part and parcel of a neoliberal logic in which environmentalism and environmental justice become mere aesthetics, rather than avenues of genuine social change. People are interpellated as consumers whose individual "tastes" might be suited by these trends, rather than as potential participants in collective action.

But Mda also draws our attention to gastronomic spectacles that make no claims to be green or ethical. Whereas postconsumerism appears in the sustainability discourse of restaurants serving indigenous food and in the ecotourism hostel suggested by Camagu, the restaurant culture depicted in *The Whale Caller* reeks of straightforward consumerism. Apartheid history, in which "blackness was produced as in part a restricted regime of consumption," enabled a scenario in which overconsumption itself could be construed as participation in the long-sought-after democracy, according to Posel.[90] If overconsumption equals democracy, then a consumer practice does not need to clean up its image in order to be glorified. This is another postapartheid ethos that Mda satirizes, pointing to how readily conspicuous consumption—epitomized by eating-as-spectacle—overlaps with the postconsumerist logic of ecotourism and ecogastronomy. Gourmet food doesn't need to package itself as "green" or "ethical" if consumers already feel that capitalism is good and consumption is virtuous. Mda's novels underscore, then, that little social progress can be made beyond a modality of overconsumption until the equation of citizenship with consuming is disrupted.

Mda's consumption fictions demand social change far beyond extending the delights of consumerism to more people or "greening" the neoliberal economy. By making aestheticized eating the metonym for what's wrong in globalized culture, Mda brings home that to meaningfully address environmental crisis requires tackling the neoliberal structure of feeling that would equate equity or joy with consuming more and more. Still, "taste" and food-related ceremonies are not always odious. Saluni's ritualized simulations of bourgeois consumption not only betray her consumerist desire, but also offer performative resistance to being (like the puny man) "at the very bottom of the food chain." And in *The Heart of*

Redness, the mollusk-gathering activities of Qolorhan women offer not only an environmentally friendly mode of surviving, but also a celebration of Xhosa and Khoena gastronomic traditions in a space of economic precarity. When juxtaposed with the neoliberal consumption culture that dominates in *The Whale Caller,* the good "taste" of oysters and mussels in *The Heart of Redness* serves as a reminder that foodways can be otherwise, even though this "otherwise" must continually fight for space on the margins of the neoliberal agro-food regime. In the next chapter, I turn to vegan trends, queer politics, and Zoë Wicomb's fiction to consider how performative and parodic engagements with consumerism and meat-eating can enable creative resistance to racial and gendered oppression, resistance that rethinks, rather than avoids, suspect foods such as supermarket products and meat.

4

Queer/Vegan Reading

Consumption and Complicity from Supermarket to Butcher Shop

"South Africa's Western Cape is barely Africa," announces a 2016 travel review in the British newspaper *The Telegraph*. "It is more like a mix of California and the Mediterranean than the southern end of a turbulent continent."[1] In likening the Western Cape to Euroamerica, this review echoes some South Africans who critique Cape Town and its surrounding region for looking toward Europe rather than toward Africa. *The Telegraph*, however, intends to praise the Western Cape (while disparaging the "turbulent continent") and encourage culinary tourism: "Over the past decade there has been a gastronomic revolution that would suggest Cape cuisine is up there with the best in the world."[2] While *The Telegraph* celebrates "the past decade," culinary fusion at the Cape reflects centuries of often-violent globalization and cultural intermingling. Curries, samoosas, and rooti, as well as bobotie and tomato bredie—characteristic of Cape Malay cuisine and Cape food more generally—reflect the influences of people from South and Southeast Asia, East Africa, and the Arab world, many of whom arrived as enslaved or indentured laborers.[3] Such histories may be forgotten, sanitized, or sensationalized in efforts to render the Cape palatable for foreigners.[4]

Harder-to-digest accounts of eating and cuisine, however, can exemplify how both reconfigured oppression and new modalities of agency manifest in neoliberal-era culinary attitudes and practices. This chapter investigates discordant significations of Cape cuisine, supermarkets, and meat-eating/veganism in postliberalization South Africa. I examine controversies around vegan advocacy, vegan/vegetarian restaurant culture in Cape Town, and the commodification of queer identities in dialogue with the writing of Zoë Wicomb. A major South African writer who lives in Scotland, Wicomb epitomizes the Cape "cosmopolitan" or "translocal" for many critics; her fictions link "coloured" and diasporic experiences to material circulations of capital, commodities, botanical matter, and bodies (human and nonhuman).[5] Such translocal connections and conflicted identities frequently register in Wicomb's writing via interactions with food, as several scholars have begun to explore.[6] Wicomb has also been received as a font of "queer energy" by scholars such as Andrew van der Vlies, who attributes this force to characters that "disrupt normative expectations of them in relation to gender, ethnicity, or behavior" whether or not they identify as queer in sexual orientation.[7] Bringing together these several angles, I explore how Wicomb uses depictions of food-shopping, cooking, eating, and butchery to destabilize identity categories and temporalities normative to neoliberal-era consumerism.

To this end, I examine Wicomb's novels *Playing in the Light* (2006) and *October* (2014) in relation to queerness and veganism, both of which are multivalent and racialized signifiers in postapartheid culture. In my usage, queerness bridges from an identitarian category affixed to non-cis-heterosexual people to a methodological orientation that reveals how formations of racialized sexuality and gender are constructed via consumption patterns. Contemplating a postapartheid context where "queer" is positioned to demarcate difference, I address how disarticulations from normative cis-heterosexual whiteness sometimes align with (and sometimes refuse) neoliberal consumerism. Veganism similarly operates both as a nonnormative dietary category that can imply various racial, classed, gendered, and political identities and as a methodological category, as I develop a postcolonial vegan analytic. Queerness and veganism function in methodologically similar ways in this chapter to articulate how racialized gender and sexuality are expressed through consumption and cuisine.

In the chapter's first half, I consider how supermarket shopping and queerness manifest as vectors of performing whiteness or Western-style identity, but also sites for defying consumerist, cis-heteronormative, and white-centric temporalities of family life. Contextualizing my analysis in relation to queer studies, South African temporalities, and supermarket culture, I focus on the meanings of supermarkets and fruit that *Playing in the Light* activates to capture shifting ideas about identity and desire in the 1990s moment of South Africa's political transition. In the second half of the chapter, I extend preoccupations with consumerism and queer temporalities to engage meat-eating and veganism. I place controversies around vegan advocacy and field observations of vegan restaurants in dialogue with the scholar/activist field of vegan studies, and then consider the violent yet redemptive meanings of meat in *October*.

As I will show, relationships to supermarket shopping, queerness, and meat suggest complex performances of racialized gender and sexuality. Characters in both novels actualize their identities through consumer behaviors and culinary habits that often associate them with troubling formulations of racial supremacy, class bias, and/or speciesist violence. Yet Wicomb's characters also transgress racialized global capitalism, assaying nonnormative temporalities, connections, and identities, by reclaiming what I call "tainted foods": products metonymic of exploitation and violence, and thus on the wrong side of eco/food politics. Rather than there being a corresponding "right" side, Wicomb's novels suggest that violence is inescapable within globalized capitalism. Certain foods such as meat may seem especially tainted, but these significations are not transhistorically stable; instead, they are context-specific and subjective. *Playing in the Light* and *October* reckon with globalizing violence as foundational to cuisine, exploring how acts of consumption both link human bodies into this oppressive system and provide opportunities to experiment with embodied deviance from normative scripts of race, class, gender, and sexuality.

Queer after Apartheid: Neoliberalism, Temporality, and the Supermarket

In bridging identitarian and nonidentitarian definitions of queerness, I am interested in how certain rights for some queers became metonymic of the practice of democratic freedom in South Africa, shifting the terms of normativity to create a neoliberal South Africa still structured by exclusion, even though on different terms from the apartheid state. Queerness is interesting to study as a way to understand other shifting social relations (such as race and class) because identitarian queerness occupied a special symbolic role in South Africa's political transition. South Africa's 1996 constitution was the first in the world to ban discrimination based on sexual orientation, and the country legalized gay marriage in

2006; in postapartheid public culture, "gay rights" have been presented as "a key sign of the democratic values of the 'new' nation."[8] Contra the "homosexuality is un-African" discourse of some sub-Saharan African politicians, a narrative emerges of gay-friendliness as modern, evidence of readiness to enter global society with all its neoliberal trappings. So, while the transition from apartheid to neoliberalism decriminalized homosexuality, it enshrined versions of gay rights that reinforce Western identity categories (predicated on a "homo/hetero binary" and the idea that sexual behavior defines a category of personhood).[9] Also reinforced were neoliberal capitalist norms, via "homocapitalism": "the selective in-corporation [into consumer capitalism] of some race-, class- and gender-sanitized queers"—typically white, middle-class, cis-gendered gays—"and the disavowal of others through a liberal politics of recognition that obvi-ates the need for redistribution" of resources.[10] Homocapitalism can mani-fest in legal codifications that protect the "rights" of certain queers to be "citizen-consumer[s]," and in gay-themed commercial activity (so-called "pink/ rainbow capitalism"), as in Cape Town's tourist-friendly gay neigh-borhood De Waterkant.[11] A commercialized Western-style gay identity spreads in lockstep with neoliberal capitalism, even as queer-phobic vio-lence persists.[12]

Such complicities of "gay-friendliness" with neoliberal globalization can splinter privileged queers away from anticapitalist, antiracist, and other liberation struggles, and can be detrimental for many sexual minori-ties. In the American context, these problems are diagnosed by queer of color critique: scholars such as Roderick A. Ferguson trace how queer liberation was intertwined with struggles for racial, class, and gendered justice at the moment of Stonewall, but then "overtaken by single-issue formulations of queer politics . . . that would promote liberal capitalist ideologies" by "produc[ing] the respectable gay as one of the ideals of neoliberal capital and urbanization, an ideal embodied in whiteness."[13] In South Africa, the racial splintering of queer politics was seeded during the apartheid era. Apartheid policy included the repression of sexual and gender diversity and the insistence on rigid gender roles as well as racial categories; while gay organizations did exist, they tended to be racially segregated and reluctant to take a stance against apartheid. The mostly white Gay Organization of South Africa (GASA), for example, sought to remain "apolitical" and failed to support Simon Tseko Nkoli, a United

Democratic Front activist who was one of twenty-two people charged
with treason in the 1985 Delmas Treason Trial and who was ostracized by
comrades for coming out as gay.[14] Nkoli's activism, including cofound-
ing the Gay and Lesbian Organization of Witwatersrand (GLOW), was
notable for his insistence that apartheid and homophobia needed to be
contested together. After apartheid, the mainstreaming of gay rights discourses has not necessarily benefitted all gender and sexual minorities.
Brenna Munro suggests that, when "a Western-style gay identity" is understood "through the formula 'gay equals modernity equals capitalism,'"
this marginalizes "alternative, indigenous modes of sexual practice and
identity," and exposes queers in general to blame for the failures of neoliberalism.[15] A triumphal narrative about gay rights sidesteps ongoing
race- and class-based inequality. A question that follows queer characters in South African literature, then, is whether and how they might
become "figures of a desire for nonnormative utopian spaces that might
serve for queers as for *all* subjects of the precarious neoliberal present,"
yet simultaneously invoke "a critique of complicities between queer uni-
versalism and neoliberalism."[16]

Queer theorists have also explored ways in which nonnormative
queerness might challenge capitalism's hold over modern life by disrupting normative temporalities. "Chrononormativity" is Elizabeth Freeman's
term for how temporal regulation "organize[s] individual human bodies
toward maximum productivity" in a heteronormative capitalist system,
making "historically specific regimes of power" seem like "ordinary bodily
tempos and routines."[17] Yet there are always embodied tempos that exceed capitalist and nationalist regularization: for Freeman, working-class
American queer cultural productions link deviant bodies to "bad timing"
that can destabilize the norms of "patriarchal generationality and a mater-
nalized middle-class domesticity."[18] Chrononormativity resonates with
postcolonial theories of hegemonic temporality, such as Pheng Cheah's
formulation that "the hierarchical ordering and control of the world as
we know it is based on . . . Northern- and Eurocentric regimes of temporal measurement."[19] But the idea of queer temporalities (as those that
disrupt capitalist rhythms) must also negotiate with how participation in
capitalism has been racially coded. I build on Freeman's analysis but also
on queer of color critique and South Africanist scholarship to address
how sexuality and capitalism intertwine with race.

During apartheid, the rhythms of normative middle-class life described by Freeman would be unavailable for South Africans whose family life was disrupted by pass laws, removals, and migrant labor: black
families were restricted to living on "reserves" far from urban centers,
while many black men stayed in hostels isolated from family in order to
work. After apartheid, Deborah Posel has argued, "freedom" became codified as the purchasing and ostentatious display of luxury goods, and this
construction of freedom as "conspicuous consumption" elides the con-
tinuing unavailability of resources for the majority of South Africans.[20]
At the same time, attributions of "conspicuous consumption" also risk
homogenizing (and demonizing) South Africa's complex black middle
class. In this context, a queer politics of disrupting consumer-capitalist
temporalities could signify as a failure to participate in racial liberation
(constructed as conspicuous consumption), or as a critique that calls out
the limitations of that construction. My readings of *Playing in the Light*
and *October* consider how various kinds of deviant subjects—"queer" in
a broad sense—might enact alternatives to chrononormativity, and thence
to neoliberal-era capitalism and the racialized sexual/familial normativity that underwrites it.

The idea of a queer temporality disrupting chrononormativity also
intersects with narratives of South Africa's arrival into multiracial democracy as itself queerly timed. Late to the postcolonial party, still in transition, and ahead on gay rights, South Africa "has always seemed curiously
out of synchrony with the rest of the world" in the timings of colonization, racial governance, and postcoloniality.[21] Yet today, Rita Barnard
notes, there are striking "congruities between South African and global
structures of feeling, including . . . a pervasive feeling of disappointment
and diminished expectations, a sense of entrapment in the distracted
present of social media and consumption, and an intensification of rage
and impatience."[22] This makes South Africa an intriguing context in
which to explore the role of consumption (in the senses of consumerism
and media consumption implied by Barnard, and in the other registers
this book evokes) in creating that "feeling of disappointment" paradigmatic of the neoliberal era. Rather than regarding disappointment as
purely negative, van der Vlies argues that postapartheid fictions can turn
"bad feelings" of waiting, boredom, stasis, and disappointment with South
Africa's incomplete transition "into new appointments with the unfolding

experience of alternative lives and possible futures."[23] If bad feelings and bad timing can disrupt capitalism and signal new potentiality, I would explore how representations of bad food, what I'm calling "tainted food," might paradoxically become part of strategies to reinvigorate eco/food politics.

Taking queerness as a way to engage with shifting ideas of race and class in transitional South Africa, I will read *Playing in the Light* as articulating a nonprescriptive queerness that both is and isn't about sexual desire, and that disrupts the ways in which racial and class identities are temporally regimented through normative routines of family life, including shopping at the supermarket. The supermarket in Wicomb's novel dialogues with the real-world phenomenon of "supermarketization" or the "supermarket revolution": the spread of supermarket chains in the global South, driven by "the growth of disposable incomes and the need for diversifying" from an agricultural economy, which in South Africa are tied to the end of apartheid-era economic isolation.[24] Supermarketization shifts the terms of food access in class-specific ways, with wealthier neighborhoods often likelier to have convenient supermarket access. Informal retailers (such as *spazas* and fruit/veg or meat stalls) may remain crucial to food access even where supermarkets are available, since they offer options such as shopping on credit or buying a single egg.[25] In this context, supermarket shopping can signify as a racially inflected class performance: a middle-class behavior.

This signification especially attaches to Woolworths, an upscale supermarket and clothing retailer referenced in *Playing in the Light*. A South African company founded in 1931 and named after the American F. W. Woolworth Company, Woolworths Holdings Limited has at times been a locus of racial tensions.[26] In 2012, language on Woolworths's career site about hiring black, coloured, and Indian candidates provoked rightwing internet postings that accused the company of "anti-white racism" and declared a shopping boycott as part of a "white solidarity" campaign.[27] Individual employees rejected these claims, as did the company. Woolworths explained that it was complying with the Employment Equity Act by reserving "some positions (where there is under-representation)" for "Africans, coloureds, Indians, women and people with disability. . . . We appreciate . . . the need to contribute to levelling the playing fields for certain groups of South Africa's population. This is not a racist practice."[28]

The narrative of Woolworths's hiring practices as motivated by "anti-white racism" (when the company was seeking to address the *under-representation* of people of color, women, and disabled people) reflects a right-wing perception that Woolworths *ought* to belong to white people. While these may be the views of a small minority disgruntled with multiracial democracy, opponents of the white-supremacist campaign suggested on Facebook and Twitter that they too perceived Woolworths as white, and problematically so. One satirical post asked, "Is it not possible that Woolworths has no white staff because they would ruin the stores colonial mise-en-scène?," implying that Woolworths perpetuates a dynamic of people of color serving white customers. Another wrote, "White people boycotting Woolworths? It won't last. Once they see the queues we cause at Spar, they will forgive Woolies," implying that Woolworths is the "white" supermarket while people of color shop elsewhere.[29] Apparently "Woolies" has been coded as a white consumer space. Visiting Woolworths stores will reveal that people of many races both work and shop there, and yet these online debates suggest how Woolworths functions as a symbol of aesthetic or cultural whiteness, as I'll trace through *Playing in the Light.*

Supermarketization has arguably intensified the racialized ways in which food capitalism connects consumer to product via unequal trade relationships, industrialized production, and monocultural export economies, alienating consumers from cultivation and food sourcing. These spatial connections facilitate what I call "capitalist efficiencies": regularized intervals of normative middle-class life and industrial productivity that hide their true costs (both social and environmental). In *Playing in the Light*, I will argue, fruit from Woolworths connects race, class, and desire with the supermarket: patterns of purchasing fruit constitute performances of prescribed identity, reinforcing scripts of race and class. Supermarket fruit reminds the reader that consumerism functions as a technology for managing bodies and feelings, which are subjected to the regularized intervals of capitalist time. And yet, fruits also become messy signifiers for a less rigid racial identity and for queer desire. Eating fruit indexes a search for non-prescriptive modes of belonging.

Queering the Supermarket in *Playing in the Light*

Playing in the Light stories Marion Campbell, an aloof businesswoman in 1990s Cape Town who discovers that her parents were "play-whites":

persons once classified as "coloured" who "passed" as white during apartheid. Marion's investigation of her family brings her into a confusing intimacy with Brenda Mackay, a "coloured" employee at Marion's travel agency whose own class position is shifting. The novel thus probes the social construction of race as it intersects with class and desire in a neoliberalizing Cape Town. "Coloured," meaning multiracial, was originally an apartheid term to designate a broad spectrum of people whose ancestors included Khoena, San, and Xhosa groups indigenous to southern Africa; enslaved and indentured people from places such as India, Madagascar, Mozambique, St. Helena, and the East Indies; and European settlers.[30] Under apartheid, people classified as coloured experienced "a precarious fusion of selective privilege and oppression."[31] Anti-apartheid activists often rejected the term "coloured" in order to include the multiracial population within the black/African majority; Wicomb argues in a 1993 essay for instead acknowledging specificities of coloured experience, including marginality in Africanist organizations but also complicity with the oppression of Africans.[32] Since 1994, some progressives regard the term as "white-imposed, reactionary and indicative of new forms of racism; an apartheid relic best left behind,"[33] whereas critical race theorists such as Zimitri Erasmus argue that coloured identities are not just "apartheid labels imposed by whites," but a "creolized [social] formation shaped by South Africa's history of colonialism, slavery, segregation and apartheid."[34] "Coloured" remains in use both as an administrative category (e.g., in the census and equity policies) and as a cultural identity that is variously embraced, redefined, and "contested."[35] The term, with all its ambivalence, remains important to Wicomb's writing, which is why I use it.

I am interested in how Wicomb uses representations of food-shopping, cooking, and eating to situate coloured identities in relation to material inequalities and sexual norms reshaped by South Africa's postapartheid entrance into neoliberalism. *Playing in the Light* traces how modes of purchasing and eating food can ossify racial and class categorizations, or can instead disrupt normative identity categories. From the novel's outset, food and appetite broker relations among affect, habit, and material privilege in Marion's confrontation with racial identity. As Marion explores her family's past, she often "isn't hungry" and must convince herself to eat.[36] Failed appetite figures Marion's emotional struggle, even as it is a material privilege that Marion has ample food to eat when she

"isn't hungry." Readers are told over and over that Marion buys her groceries at Woolworths, which comes to constitute her performance of white,
middle-class identity. (I describe Marion's whiteness as a performance
not because her family was "passing," but because all social identities are
performances of conditioned behaviors—a point important to this novel
about the social construction of race.) Marion brings groceries to her
aging father, John, "unpacking a Woolworths bag of fruit into a cut-glass
bowl," but John "sulks and does not eat the slice of bread she has buttered
with margarine":

> How can butter from God's cattle be bad for one? . . .
>
> Marion says that she'll leave some prepared dinners from Woolworths
> in the fridge. You mustn't shop at Woolworths, he says, it's too expensive.
> She takes from her cooler bag a bottle of Zonnebloem, still cold. He . . .
> complains that he doesn't like wine; it's cheap stuff that bergies drink. . . .
>
> Cheap stuff? Marion repeats. She has admonished herself to be patient,
> but that commodity runs out without warning. . . . It's no good trying to
> civilise you. (11–12)

John rejects Marion's "expensive" tastes, yet sneers at "cheap" tastes attributed to "bergies" (a slur for Cape Town's houseless population, referring
to living on Tafelberg, or Table Mountain). Marion, meanwhile, has the
white-bread tastes of a middle-class supermarket shopper. She replaces
butter with margarine, appreciates the convenience of "prepared dinners,"
and associates expensive groceries with being "civilised," a word laden with
imperialist associations. Even her patience is a "commodity." Meanwhile,
"Zonnebloem" ("sunflower") is both an actual wine producer and the
name given to part of Cape Town's District Six during apartheid to re-
designate it as a "white" neighborhood; the mention of "Zonnebloem" gestures toward the idea of "whitening" coloured history and space, making
this consumer product (the wine) stand in for the construction of Marion
as white. Marion epitomizes consumer-capitalist ideologies and white
bourgeois positionality through her association with Woolworths.

This linking of Marion to the supermarket connotes the atomization
and inequality of life under racial capitalism, not unique to the neoliberal moment but rather intensified by the affective impacts of having
"passed" during apartheid. Not unlike Amitav Ghosh's character Piya (see
chapter 3 of the present book), Marion lives alone unhappily and thwarts

potential friends and boyfriends. The novel links this self-isolation to Marion's childhood of "endless rules and restrictions" and "closed doors that locked her out," stemming from the anxiousness to pass of Marion's mother Helen (60). "Alerted . . . to the many shades of whiteness" and determined to achieve the "brightest" (middle-class Englishness), Helen chopped family life into regularized intervals: "parcelled days" and "tightly wrapped days" (128, 60, 61). To pass, the novel suggests, entails a rigid management of temporality in order to enact "domestic time": "a particular heterogendered and class-inflected" expectation that women facilitate routines such as family dinnertime, complementing the masculinized temporality of capitalist "work" time.[37] By regulating time, Helen seeks to produce not only middle-classness, but also whiteness. She must appear effortless while exerting great effort: "Under the glaring spotlight of whiteness, [Helen and John] played diligently, assiduously," Marion later thinks to herself, making "play-whites" a "misnomer. . . . There was nothing playful about their condition" (123). Through Helen, Wicomb draws out how intersecting racial, class, and gendered identities are regimented in capitalist societies by the temporalities of the middle-class home. Gradations of whiteness emerge through the regularization of time into segments associated with the middle-class family. The regimentation of time and space in *Playing in the Light* evokes specific apartheid restrictions, yet also wide-reaching constraints to life under capitalism, which is part of why these structures do not vanish after apartheid ends.

A key image of capitalist efficiencies enforced by "passing" is a set of trays of apples, imagined by Marion. This vision links middle-class whiteness to the normalization of food via industrial agriculture and supermarkets:

> Secrets, lies and discomfiture—that was what her childhood had been wrapped in. Each day individually wrapped. . . . Before her an image arises: the past laid out in uniform trays of apples, wrapped in purple tissue paper. Marion loves apples; it is irksome that something she finds delicious should now be infected, a drop of poison hidden in the core, under the wholesome, glossy skin. (59–60)

The image of "uniform trays of apples" with "a drop of poison" borrows its power from anxieties about industrial food containing harmful substances. Industrial food is also tied to social inequalities that control who can eat what, who can own what. Linking such menaces to "skin," Wicomb's image connotes a class system buttressed by racial hierarchy: "delicious" for a white-identified child such as Marion, but toxic. Under the skin of the perfect packaged apple lies the "poison" of differentiated privilege. (In a different reading, the "glossy" apple "skin" concealing a poisonous "drop" might also be Marion's racist vision of her own body as contaminated by nonwhite "blood.")

The uniformity of the apple trays calls up the rationalization of shopping for food: the growth of supermarket chains in the global South synchronizes such shopping (for the middle-class consumer) with a standardized set of global foodways, even as local dynamics such as informal vending persist. Not only does the homogenization of produce offer a metaphor for austere racial norms, but supermarket shopping itself boxes middle-class consumers into particular patterns even as it excludes poorer consumers, expressing a formalization that constrains Marion yet marks her as privileged. Also key is the language of normalized time: "each day individually wrapped." The tightly packaged apples nod to how food access determines daily and weekly routines differentiated by race, class, and gender: consumption patterns produce the temporal regulation that creates taxonomies of identity. Food-shopping is the temporality in which race and class are lived.[38]

Yet fruit's significance expands beyond identity-regimentation: as Marion's white identity destabilizes, fruit-eating aligns with same-sex intimacy as a sign of exceeding rigid racial categories. Marion cajoles Brenda into joining her on a research trip, which culminates with the discovery that Marion's parents' "maid" Tokkie was Marion's grandmother, meaning her parents had been classified as coloured. The two women return late to Marion's flat, where Brenda is awakened by Marion having a nightmare:

> The woman thrashes, moans and weeps so pitifully . . . that Brenda goes . . . to soothe her, to try to wake her up. Marion . . . clings for dear life and shudders with sobs. . . . Brenda can do nothing but lie down . . . and . . . hold [Marion] tightly in her arms, stroke the shaking shoulders, rest her cheek on Marion's face to keep her from rising. . . . Marion clings to her, until the taut, arched body finally stops shaking and the breathing subsides. Helpless as a baby, her arms are tightly wrapped around Brenda; her head rests on Brenda's breast.

> Like lovers, they wake together. Still entwined . . . for seconds they lie
> stock-still, then Marion disentangles herself limb by limb. (99–100)

The image of Marion's body "taut" and "arched" until her "breathing sub-
sides" suggests an orgasm and its denouement; the women wake "like
lovers." But perhaps more important than the scene's queer eroticism
is its ambiguity. Brenda is cast not only as lover, but as maternal figure;
the women's surprising bodily intimacy could figure the convergence of
their racial identities as Marion tries to re-understand herself as coloured.
Thus, complicating what van der Vlies describes as a pattern of conversations about sexual identity "overshadowing" those about race and
class, this scene instead positions sexuality as racialized, and queer desire
as a way of rethinking racialized intimacy or affiliation.[39] Rather than
seeing concern with sexuality or with race as either/or, I read Marion
and Brenda's relationality as being both about same-sex intimacy and
about the social construction of race via consumption habits.

Queer erotics arise as a way to explore shifting race and class identifi-
cations in part because queer liberation was wrapped up in anti-apartheid
struggles, such that "the gay, lesbian, or bisexual person . . . became a
kind of stock minor character in the pageant of nationhood in the 1990s,
embodying the arrival of a radically new social order and symbolically
mediating conflicts over race and class."[40] But rather than Wicomb offering a flat gay, lesbian, or bisexual character, her characters engage with
queerness as a multivalent and ambiguous signifier, in ways that open up
racial and class categories as themselves multivalent and ambiguous. The
nature of the affinity between Marion and Brenda is undefined, hard to pin
down—and this is precisely the point. In the wake of apartheid's racial
taxonomies and amidst an ongoing regime of capitalist normalization,
queerness becomes a mode of demarcating the uncertainty or flux that
emerges out of Marion's unsureness as to whether she is now white or
coloured (or neither, or both).

This range of meanings unfurls as the two women move from the
bedroom to the kitchen, where they eat fruit from Woolworths:

> There is a bowl of peaches, which [Brenda] prods for ripeness. Dare I eat
> a peach? Brenda calls theatrically. . . . I never understood it, she says, the
> idea of being challenged by a peach, but it's simple, isn't it? Refined people

struggle with the possibility because of the juice that will dribble down
their chins. So the answer to Prufrock is to eat the fruit before it's ripe, or
to tackle it with a knife and fork.

... Nonsense, [Marion] says, it's about eating fruit when it looks perfect, before it's over the hill—firm, perfect shape, perfect colour.

Brenda snorts. The gospel according to Saint Woolworths: packed in
polystyrene and labelled ripe, when the rest of us know that ripeness
doesn't go with looking perfect. (100–101)

Marion is again associated with Woolworths, which for Brenda represents
prioritizing appearances, unlike "the rest of us," a phrase that identifies
Brenda with coloured and/or black working-class skepticism of white
bourgeois norms (even as "Dare I eat a peach?" invokes T. S. Eliot, marking Brenda as a university-educated person, as van der Vlies points out).[41]
Peaches from the supermarket thus index the difference in racialized
class attitudes between Brenda and Marion, with Marion's values linked
to sexist ideas about cis-feminine aging while Brenda suggests a less
superficial idea of embodied "ripeness." Thinking about race in relation
to fruit is more than a metaphorical connection; there has long been in
South Africa a "historically constitutive relationship between the work-
ings of race and regulation of consumption."[42] Under apartheid, race
was used to control buying power, but also defined and demonstrated by
class performance. Wicomb's novel witnesses the postapartheid shuffling
of these terms: an upwardly mobile coloured or black identity is possible
for Brenda, even as a racialized wealth gap widens nationally. Though
Marion's racial identity is in flux, buying fruit from Woolworths is a class
performance that reasserts her whiteness. Consumption in the sense of
eating thus epitomizes how consumption in a broader sense (purchasing)
constructs identity.

But even as buying fruit from Woolworths produces Marion's white
middle-classness, eating peaches loosens this identity, inviting the possibility of a shared racial identity and/or an erotic connection with Brenda.
Brenda suggests that Marion is now "coloured" and "free to be noisy,
free to eat a peach, a juicy ripe one, and free of the burdens of nation
and tradition" (102). She is suggesting that Marion can be absolved from
bourgeois white behavior expectations, offering messy peach-eating as
metonymic of freedom. Extending the erotics of the nightmare scene,

Brenda "dips a couple of peaches briefly into boiling water and slips off the skins. . . . I love the way it comes off, she says, holding the slippery, naked fruit between two fingertips before biting into it. She wipes the dribbling juice with the back of her hand" (101). This sensual moment suggests the possibility of romantic intimacy, which would be queer in its timing as well as its same-sex orientation: "ripeness" might be available to these women who are too old to be "looking perfect" by hegemonic standards, as Brenda's earlier comment implies (100). But in Marion's mind, the fruit transforms to represent failure: Marion "stares at her peach; she cannot bring herself to eat it. Naked, slippery—that's me, that's who I am, she thinks. Hurled into the world fully grown, without a skin" (101). Having no "skin" suggests Marion's disorientation about her race, which entails both convergence with and difference from Brenda, "who may or may not care for her, who waits for her to eat a peach" (101). An elusive and expansive relationality exists between Marion and Brenda, suggesting desire and shared experience then pulling them away. Peach-eating thus blurs erotic desire, homosocial affiliation, and racial identification, all constructed via consumption practices. The queer erotics of the peach introduce feelings of disorientation and loss, but also destabilize Marion's compulsion to racially "sort" and temporally regulate herself. An undefined queerness could be the sign or substance of Marion's capacity to exceed normative categories.

In *Playing in the Light,* then, supermarket fruit indexes the oppressiveness of consumer capitalism, rigid racial categorization, the normative family, and their expected time intervals, yet at the same time opens up queer possibilities. Fruit from the supermarket functions as a tainted food, representing the performance of middle-class cis-heterosexual whiteness through consumerism. And yet, fruit-eating suggests queer relations that would defy the identity categories, tempos, and cis-heterosexual romantic patterns imposed by globalized consumer capitalism. "Queer" can signal the cathexis through commodities to sanctioned Western modes of non-normativity, but can also indicate refusal of such commodifying identity logics. Invoking consumption in proximity to queerness, Wicomb's writing stretches beyond hegemonic definitions of queer identity, resituating food shopping and eating as potential sites to simultaneously refuse Western models for queer life *and* normative South African expectations of cis-heteronormative life and apartheid-freighted racial identities. *Playing in the Light* invites a queer reading of how race, gender, and desire can fit together in ways that transgress the neoliberal normalization of Western and consumerist (homo)sexuality.

Staying with relations to food that invoke and challenge racialized normativity, the next section turns from the supermarket to the kitchen and the butcher shop. I discuss the cultural politics of meat-eating and veganism in contemporary South Africa in dialogue with the scholar/ activist field of vegan studies. I then explore how *October* depicts inter-actions with meat as both reifying and destabilizing gendered, classed, and racialized power relations.

Thinking Meat and Vegan Studies

Ecofeminists have noted an alignment among meat-eating, animal abuse, and misogyny at least since Carol J. Adams's 1990 *The Sexual Politics of Meat,* which attributes the subordinations of nonhuman animals and women to a shared logic of domination. Nuancing this analysis, schol-ars in "vegan studies" are developing intersectional and transnational approaches to address racial, cultural, environmental, and economic complexities of meat-eating and veganism. In *The Vegan Studies Project,* Laura Wright argues that a perceived crisis of white heterosexual mascu-linity in contemporary America triggered a "backlash" against cis-male veganism, seen as signaling "weakness, emasculation, and un-American values"; vegans have even been vilified as terrorists.[43] A postcolonialist by training, Wright also endeavors "to extend . . . vegan studies beyond the West," developing a vegan approach to refugeeism.[44] By combining seemingly separate topics such as the Syrian refugee crisis, meat, and climate change, a vegan analytic can "illuminate underlying and invisi-ble linkages . . . overlooked in more traditional deconstructive analyses of power."[45] An intersectional vegan analysis should also address patterns of racialized labor. As A. Breeze Harper notes, many vegan products sold in the United States are produced by the exploited labor of Black and Brown people in other countries; regarding such products as "cruelty-free" masks "*cruelty* to thousands of *human beings.*"[46] Similarly, many vegan foods produced and consumed in South Africa are harvested in conditions where black farmworkers are exploited by white farm own-ers.[47] Even if vegans attempt a stance "oppositional and confrontational to the consumer mandates of capitalism" as Wright suggests, buying such products reinscribes vegans into these racialized dynamics of global capitalism.[48]

To note such problems is not to dismiss the moral or environmental value of vegan praxis; as Wright puts it, "adopting a vegan diet constitutes environmental activism, whether or not the vegan intends such activism," because plant-based diets can reduce food-related greenhouse gas emissions by 29–70 percent.[49] But, if race and labor are ignored, vegan and animal rights advocacy can undermine their anti-oppression logic, as illustrated by two controversies in postliberalization South Africa. The country leads the African continent in the consumption of beef, poultry, pork, mutton, and lamb, with meat consumption swelling since 1982 (accompanied by a 25 percent increase in problems such as obesity, hypertension, and stroke).[50] Yet cities such as Cape Town and Johannesburg are also sprouting vegan and vegetarian restaurants and events.[51] There is no precise data on the number of vegetarians or vegans in South Africa, but organizations such as the South African Vegan Society (initiated in 2007) attest to their growing presence.[52] Amidst this trend, four faculty members at the University of Cape Town (UCT) proposed at a 2015 meeting that animal products no longer be served at humanities-faculty events to avoid "suffering, cruelty and killing."[53] After acrimonious discussions, the proposal was voted down. Opposed faculty found the conduct of the proponents disrespectful, with some stating that the proposal was racist. Media flagged this as an exposure of "racial and colonial fault lines."[54] Similar divergences animated a 2007 controversy when South Africa's National Society for the Prevention of Cruelty to Animals (NSPCA) attempted legal action to halt the Zulu practice of *ukweshwama,* which entails killing a bull by hand. Sandile Memela, minister of arts and culture at the time, described the NSPCA's critique as "selective racism that condemns . . . African rituals."[55] Both incidents exemplify how veganism and animal advocacy can stoke conflict around cultural difference and racial injustice.

Comparing the two incidents, Michael Glover claims there is an important difference: the NSPCA was targeting a non-Western cultural practice, whereas when UCT serves meat, the animals are "killed in (Western) industrial processes"—seeing as South African meat comes primarily from American-style factory farms—and would be eaten by faculty from various backgrounds.[56] Yet both controversies involve complainants exhorting others to change their cultural practices. As Luis Cordeiro-Rodrigues suggests, the UCT proposal may have been alienating because it had nothing to say about the Rhodes Must Fall movement ongoing at the time. Rhodes Must Fall advocated for the removal of colonial symbols from campus and for additional antiracist changes, such as centering African thinkers in the curriculum. By presenting vegan advocacy as nonracialized, proponents of "animals-off-the-menu" assumed a posture of "racial innocence . . . during a black struggle context," and in so doing "ignore[d] that the proposal has, even inadvertently, the gaze and performative function of whites teaching blacks how to behave."[57] Animal advocacy has been racialized as an antiblack movement in South Africa: settlers frequently cited goals such as elephant conservation to justify displacing Africans from their land, and dogs have been instrumentalized to secure white property claims, such that the dog became a symbol of apartheid.[58] As Maneesha Deckha points out, racism and speciesism are mutually constructed through imperial histories: "Race was a species-dependent category, pivoting on indices of animality; different races were seen to be different species."[59] British colonizers regarded non-European practices toward animals as evidence that the colonized were "subhuman," ignoring "the astonishing levels of violence towards animals in Britain among the propertied classes."[60] Claims about the non-European treatment of animals became, not unlike claims about the non-European treatment of women, "a platform for imperialism."[61] A vegan proposal that fails to address such histories can smuggle in a racist agenda regardless of proponents' intentions.

But while these controversies may amplify vegan advocacy's reputation for "puritanical rhetoric and . . . 'all-or-nothing' approaches," this baggage comes with certain white/Western hegemonic incarnations rather than being inherent to veganism.[62] Indeed, Kenyan vegan scholar Evan Maina Mwangi argues that animal rights work is "misrepresented as the preserve of affluent white people and their elite black lackeys" because of "stereotypes circulating in African societies about animal rights activists as . . . white racists who pretend to love animals to assuage their guilt for hating fellow humans."[63] Such "stereotypes" may be an understandable product of racist and colonialist iterations of animal rights advocacy; nonetheless, Mwangi transcends these ideas by considering "human-animal studies from perspectives other than those of predominantly white authors," addressing how African literary texts weave together respect for oppressed humans, for nonhuman animals, and for the environment.[64] In the realm of activism, Cordeiro-Rodrigues argues that vegan and racial justice advocacies in South Africa could be integrated by tackling problems such as the proximity of factory farms to townships, where they disproportionately affect black people's health.[65] Addressing such environmental racism would constitute a postcolonial vegan advocacy.

A postcolonial vegan analysis could also examine meat-eating in white supremacist and masculinist incarnations of Afrikaner culture, a topic raised by both Wicomb and fellow South African writer Marlene van Niekerk. In a 1993 essay, Wicomb likens the *braaivleis* or *braai* (barbecue) to "necklacing," in which a rubber tire is placed around a victim's chest, filled with petrol, and set on fire. Necklacing was used both by the apartheid government against activists and by township residents to punish informants; more recently, the practice surfaces in xenophobic violence. For Wicomb, the *braaivleis* and necklacing both epitomize violence sprung from desperation: "Boers trekking from British domination relied on shooting buck and eating the roasted meat in the open veld; necklacing eliminates those who endanger the community."[66] The *braai* also features in van Niekerk's wry "typology" of Afrikaner eaters, which includes the "Old Sort": a racist patriarch who cherishes the *braai* as "time to bond with the men and with Castle Lager."[67] The Old Sort believes that "pasta, quiche, and green salad is food for gays. Vegetarians are even more alternative than gays, they must be lesbian. Sushi is quite beyond the pale."[68] Van Niekerk lampoons a white cis-heterosexual masculinity that feels equally threatened by nonnormative diets and sexual orientations. An "alternative," multiethnic cuisine (characterized as much by sushi as by a plant-based diet) is conflated with gay and lesbian identities. While invoked parodically by van Niekerk, this intimacy among sexual and gender identity, race, and eating habits points to the queer potential of intersectional veganism. In context-specific scenarios where meat-eating manifests as cis-heteronormative and white supremacist, resistance to meat-eating can become legible as a feminist, antiracist, decolonial, and queer praxis.

And notwithstanding the controversies discussed above, veganism in South Africa is a multiracial and multicultural trend. Popular start-ups such as Fry's Vegetarian and websites such as Vegan Review evidence that veganism "extends beyond the country's wealthy white minority."[69]

Certainly some vegan establishments in Cape Town operate at high price points and with a white or Western aesthetic, such as Nourish'd Café and Juicery (Figure 6) or Infinite Café, whose expensive menu options use European and American products such as Oatly and Miyoko's, and vegan products abound in high-end markets such as Wellness Warehouse. Yet other restaurants offer more affordability and Afrocentric vibes, such as Veganville in Long Street, which shares its premises with the African fashion emporium WAG. Seven Colours Eatery, though located in the tourist mecca of the V&A Waterfront, provides affordable vegetarian and vegan

Figure 6. Nourish'd Café and Juicery location in Observatory, Cape Town. The "We Are CASHLESS" sign—a common measure in Cape Town to discourage crime—implies that this vegan restaurant understands itself as catering to the city's wealthier side while seeking refuge against inequality-driven crime problems. Photo by the author, October 2022.

options as part of "Traditional South African Food"; a sign greets guests with *Molweni* ("hello" in Xhosa) and describes the culinary heritage of founder Chef Nolu. Prashad Café, a family-owned Indian food chain, capitalizes on the marketability and trendiness of plant-based food, declaring itself a "Vegetarian and Vegan Restaurant" at the top of the menu and featuring a neon pink, Instagram-ready "Namastay @ Prashad Café" sign (Figure 7).[70] These anecdotal observations suggest that the racial, cultural,

Figure 7. "Namastay @ Prashad Café" neon sign inside restaurant location in Kloof Street, Gardens, Cape Town. Photo by the author, October 2022.

and class politics of South African veganism are quite varied—if sometimes tense. Anesu Mbizvo, co-owner of a Johannesburg vegan café and
yoga studio, explains that one challenge for African vegans is the cultural
value of livestock: if livestock define familial wealth, then, "when you
slaughter an animal at a gathering, it's seen as you giving of yourself.
Whereas getting some vegetables from your veggie patch doesn't really
equate to the same amount of giving. . . . That's one of the barriers to veganism for people of African cultures."[71] Mbizvo's example suggests a particular burden on African vegans to negotiate the cultural importance of meat.

Meat-eating, then, carries associations in South Africa with misogyny
and white supremacy, but also separate associations with various African cultural traditions. Veganism is likewise a complex and multivalent
signifier. Given these complexities, Caitlin E. Stobie underscores that "a
flexible and situational understanding of praxis would help to immunize
vegan studies against . . . classism and racism."[72] *October* intervenes in this
cultural field via situated representations of coloured women engaged in
meat-eating, butchering, and meat refusal—all practices that can be lib-
eratory or oppressive.

Cape Cuisine, Meat, and Power in *October*

October follows Mercia Murray, a middle-aged South African woman liv-
ing in Scotland, as she revisits her hometown, Kliprand, in the Northern
Cape. A university lecturer in Glasgow, Mercia struggles with her sense of
superiority to her poorer, rural-dwelling sister-in-law, a butcher named
Sylvie. Cooking, especially preparing meat, catalyzes conflicts between
Mercia's cosmopolitan subjectivity and Sylvie's supposed provincialism.[73]
Using references to meat and Cape cuisine to situate cosmopolitan foods
and identities as contingent on colonization, enslavement, diaspora, and
neoliberal-era foodie culture, Wicomb extends ecofeminist thought to
reveal how clashes around meat-eating express not only white masculinism, but also multiple violences of globalization across many historical
stages. Even as *October* associates industrial meat production with patriarchalism and eugenicist thinking, interactions with meat also empower
Sylvie to reclaim agency from racially supremacist men and to evade the
capitalist efficiencies of industrial food. Underscoring that meat-eating
cannot be reduced to a single significance, *October* suggests the need for

context-specific food politics that avoid quests for purity, instead "staying with the trouble" of tainted foods.[74]

Mercia and Sylvie are haunted by memories of Mercia's deceased father Nicholas, who raped Sylvie in her childhood. Sections focalizing Nicholas intertwine racism, classism, and patriarchalism with attitudes about agriculture. Nicholas considers his own people "Scottish stock,"

> a good old colored family, evenly mixed, who having attained genetic stability could rely on good hair and healthy dark skin, not pitch-black like Africans, and certainly not like sly Slamse.... The Murrays had no further use for European blood; ... they ... kept their distance from others. Nicholas shook his head contemptuously at the people of Kliprand ... if one of their girls arrived from the white dorp [town] with a blue-eyed baby.[75]

Nicholas thinks race in terms of mixed "blood" and genetics, meaning biological essentialism. He considers his family superior to both Africans and other people classified as coloured, including "Slamse" (derogatory for Muslims) and the "Namaqualanders" of Kliprand, such as Sylvie (137).[76] Even as Nicholas takes pride in being coloured, he maintains the apartheid logic that condemns interracial procreation. Nicholas also disparages Namaqualanders as "too indigenous" to "till the land," implying that being an agriculturalist or pastoralist has inherent moral value (137). European settlers in many places justified the theft of hunting and foraging lands by invoking *terra nullius* (the doctrine that unenclosed land needs improvement); in southern Africa too, a "stereotype" is that Indigenous peoples "lack a concept of ... territoriality."[77] Nicholas also expresses eugenicist views and cajoles Sylvie into a sexual relationship by teaching her about sheep. While "fat-tailed Afrikaner sheep, prone to blowflies, needed antiseptic dips," Nicholas asserts:

> Just as we colored people have made progress—we no longer need the fat rumps of the Hottentots to see us through the lean months—better sheep are being bred, ones that don't succumb to pests and disease. [He] explained the crossing of Blackhead Persians with the Horned Dorset ... [to create] the new Dorper breed.... Sylvie should not like some backward, uneducated people think that this went against God's will.... The

Dorpers grew so fast, and their mutton was so good, that clearly the breeding had been sanctioned by God. (187–88)

Nicholas compares the Dorper—a sheep created in the 1940s via inter-se
techniques, in which closely related animals are crossbred—to coloured
people, linking animal breeding to a eugenicist vision of racial improvement as he hints that sex between himself and Sylvie would also be
"sanctioned by God."[78]
   Though Nicholas is a small-scale pastoralist, the character stands in
for commercialized industrial agriculture: Nicholas marries eugenicist
rhetoric with praise of agricultural modernization, exposing industrial
agriculture and racism as twin engines of violence. While breeding animals for certain qualities has long been a staple of animal husbandry,
Nicholas emphasizes the "way forward" and "scientific knowledge" (189).
He endorses new priorities for farmers in a consumer-capitalist economy
that multiplies animal death: Nicholas suggests wool is superfluous in
an era of "new, more convenient" synthetic fabrics, and Dorper sheep
are prized not for wool but for mutton and sheepskin (188).[79] Indeed,
an article from the Department of Animal Science at Oklahoma State
University suggests that the Dorper "reacts very favorably under intensive feeding conditions," a statement that raises red flags about animal
mistreatment.[80] Optimized for such conditions, the Dorper connotes an
industrial ideology in which homogenization, profit, and short-term
efficiency are valued over biodiversity, the ethical treatment of animals,
and stewardship of ecosystems. By expressing Nicholas's eugenicism and
his ensnarement of Sylvie through passages about sheep, Wicomb provokes readers to consider industrial meat production as aligned with
racism and sexual violence. Meat-eating likewise converges with patriarchalism in how Nicholas obligates his wife Nettie to cook and eat meat in
order to be a "good wife," despite her "distaste for meat"; Nettie responds
with "strategic dishing that would allow her to eat as little meat as possible" (114–115). Wicomb illustrates the ecofeminist idea that industrialized meat production and meat-eating express a logic of domination in
which speciesism intertwines with racism and misogyny.
   Yet meat-eating does not carry only negative connotations. Instead,
multiple meanings of both meat and Cape cuisine proliferate as Wicomb

contrasts Mercia and Sylvie through scenes of cooking, eating, and butchering. Cooking Cape food indexes long histories of globalization and expresses Mercia's contemporary diasporic and coloured identity. In her kitchen in Glasgow, Mercia

> would pound ginger and garlic with cumin and cardamom . . . for her signature dish of Moroccan lamb. . . . Mercia would turn up the music and dance. . . . She crooned along with David Kramer, ground her hips and dipped her shoulders hotnos style, waving her wooden spoon defiantly. . . . As the smell of fried cardamom rose, repeated its aroma and weaving through coriander and paprika revised its fragrance, she savored a bittersweet homesickness. (169–70)

With her "defiant" embrace of "hotnos style," Mercia reclaims a slur for Khoena-descended people. She takes pride in hybrid heritage through both Cape cuisine and the music of David Kramer, a singer, songwriter, and producer known for blending Afrikaans with English and celebrating Cape coloured communities.[81] "Moroccan lamb" and paprika, coriander, and cardamom are typical of Cape cuisine, and not unlike intersecting lines of melody, Mercia's spices "revise" their "fragrance" as they intermingle, connoting cultural creolization over time. Moreover, while Mercia recalls her own "homesickness" for the Cape, this scene appears as a flashback while she is visiting the Cape, as she fondly recalls cooking "back home in Glasgow" (169). Mercia's "home" is multiply located, combining coloured hybridity with a search for diasporic belonging.

While Mercia celebrates coloured heritage, Wicomb also situates cooking as a negotiation with imperial power dynamics. Mercia learns to cook, including her Moroccan lamb, "from Jane Grigson's recipes" (171). Grigson (1928–1990) was an English cookbook author and food columnist, credited with having "reminded" English cooks after World War II that "British cooking . . . had its own rich history."[82] Wicomb positions Grigson rather differently, as an "inventive English cook who borrowed, gloriously freed by the fact that there is no oppressive tradition of fine British cuisine which demands slavish adherence" (171). In this gloss, Grigson stands in for cultural appropriation by European colonizers, and for commodification, as her recipes translate folk knowledges into saleable print. Mercia retains agency by violating Grigson's recipe: she recalls the Afrikaans idiom *soos vinkel en koljander,* [*die een is soos die ander*] ("Like fennel and coriander, the one is like the other"), and decides that, while "the recipe does not call for fennel, . . . [she] cannot imagine coriander without a dash of its twin. They were lookalikes, meant to go together, inseparable" (170). Recombining the commodified recipe with regional folk knowledge, Mercia celebrates coloured identity—even as her power struggle with Grigson's recipe underscores that cooking practices and cultural identity exist within a consumer-capitalist world shaped by imperialism.

The power dynamics of culinary globalization also surface in a flashback to a dinner party that Mercia and her Scottish ex Craig hosted in Glasgow. Craig's idealizations of African authenticity clash with Mercia's sense of the often-violent creolization that produced Cape cuisine:

> [Craig] boasted about Mercia's Cape dishes, her use of spices, learned, he announced to guests, at her mother's knee. Mercia did not correct him. . . . Instead, Mercia dredged up stories of . . . the Cape as refreshment station . . . in the establishment of a spice route. Vinkel en koljander brought to Cape shores in exchange for scurvy-fighting fruit and veg. Once she spoke of slaves from Goa, Malaysia, East Africa, sizzling their spices in the shadow of Table Mountain, which was not nice, so that Craig explained that Mercia had had too much to drink. No one said that eating meat was not nice. (170–71)

This passage recounts the Cape's colonization, motivated by European appetites for spices and for vegetables that would cure sailors of scurvy. Mercia mentions the culinary influences of enslaved Asians and Africans, but Craig patronizingly silences her. To his white sensibility, discussing slavery is impolite. Silenced, too, is the killing of animals. The paragraph's final line (focalized through Mercia) links Craig's patriarchalism to "eating meat," and problematically even compares histories of colonization and enslavement to eating meat, as both are potentially "not nice," although "no one said" this. Craig's insistence that violence not appear at the dinner table does not extend to offering a vegan meal, because the very idea that meat-eating could be considered violent is suppressed. When read with a postcolonial vegan analytic, the scene reveals the obfuscation of multiple, incommensurable harms (racist, gendered, and speciesist) for the pleasure of guests consuming Mercia's cooking. Adding a postcolonial gloss, the logic of domination that ecofeminists associate with meat-eating and misogyny manifests as a product of colonization, racism, and the commodification of cuisine.

In Kliprand, cooking meat stokes the provincial–cosmopolitan conflict between Sylvie and Mercia, multiplying the potential meanings of meat-eating and its rejection. When Sylvie "triumphantly holds up a scraped sheep's head" for making brawn, "Mercia screams involuntarily" (167). She is startled by her own disgust: "What is happening to Mercia, the carnivore, here in Kliprand? Is this the measure of her distance from the place, from her home, her people? . . . Is Mercia growing fastidious about meat, about the killing of animals? . . . Is it connected with Sylvie, the butcher girl?" (168–69). Having joined a diasporic urban middle class, Mercia begins to associate meat-eating with poor rural people. Here, to reject meat-eating is to take a position of hierarchical power, while the opposite is true when Nettie tries to avoid compulsory meat-eating. For Stobie, *October* invites readers to think about veganism in relation to "situational animal ethics," where ethical resolutions need to be context-specific and flexible: although veganism can be a mode of feminist and environmental activism, "promoting veganism as 'the' feminist way of eating is problematic, because women's bodies and choices are already policed enough by patriarchal culture."[83] Revulsion about meat-eating can signify classism and metropolitan snobbishness when it is Mercia's reaction to Sylvie, yet can signify as an objection to patriarchal control in Nettie's case. The meanings of meat only multiply further when examining Sylvie's practice of sublimating meat into art.

Queer Time at the Butcher Shop

October destabilizes its own alignment of meat-eating with racist patriarchalism by associating meat primarily with Sylvie, who works in a butcher shop. Sylvie's guardians find her this job as a punishment, declaring Sylvie "pure evil" when they learn that Nicholas raped her (194). Thus linked to victim-blaming, the butcher shop also signifies to Sylvie the "dreariness of being trapped" in rural life (196). However, Sylvie finds ways to reclaim the butcher shop. First, she resists the rule that she wear a "black doekie," or small cloth covering the hair—a style expected for black women, as opposed to the "white polystyrene hat like the boer butchers wear" (101). Sylvie creates "ways of flouting the rules, finding pleasure in transgression" by folding in "a secret splash of color," "a flash of floral . . . at the brink of revealing itself" (101). She resists racial hierarchy quietly but creatively, transforming the doekie from a sign of control to a site of playful transgression. Transgression coalesces into an artistic practice as Sylvie begins dressing up and photographing herself:

> Here before her silver screen, Sylvie can be anyone. . . . She has borrowed Tiena's cream canvas jeans and tucked her cigarettes into the right pocket. Just so, on the hip, which she thrusts forward, so that the packet of Marlboros (she always transfers her ciggies into a Marlboro packet) shows. . . . Sylvie does not need a mirror for . . . pouting, . . . tilting her head like the girl with the glossy hair in the Clairol picture. (94)

Sylvie mimics consumer culture, telling herself that "this is the New South Africa" (93). Apartheid is over, and some see it as high time to embrace consumerism. But Sylvie puts off-brand cigarettes into the name-brand pack, has no mirror, and borrows her clothes. Much like Saluni in Zakes Mda's *The Whale Caller* (chapter 3), Sylvie play-acts consumer behavior that she cannot afford, underscoring how the promises of neoliberal capitalism diverge from the realities. Even as Sylvie reclaims agency through creative expression, Wicomb ironizes the narrative of conspicuous consumption as liberation, parodying the embrace of consumerism by some while underscoring its unavailability to others.

Preparing meat offers Sylvie an ambivalent agentic space in this consumer capitalist world: "It turned out to be not so terrible learning to make boerewors [Cape-style farmers' sausage], . . . better than unpicking hems, lengthening skirts, and squinting over invisible stitching. . . . Damp as babies, but she knows which she prefers" (99). Sylvie identifies butchery as an alternative to stereotypical women's work such as sewing and childcare. She reclaims the butcher shop as an art space, posing with the meat:

> Sylvie sets up the camera. . . . The right hand is slightly raised with loops and loops of sausage draped over it. She throws back her shoulder triumphantly. . . .

Only fear of someone bursting in prevents her from wrapping a length
of sausage around her neck. Like a rich silk scarf. . . . She could toss the
length of sausage over her shoulder . . . like [a] film star. . . . Instead, this
tame pose, but never mind. . . .

   Think of it as an advert in *Huisgenoot*. Healthy boerewors for the family, recommended by a healthy, smiling young butcher. (101–2)

Parodying how an ad in the popular magazine *Huisgenoot* (House companion) might invoke the middle-class family to sell meat, Sylvie's photography underscores that normative gendered and familial identities are
created via a consumptive logic for which meat-eating offers the perfect
metonym. Sylvie both feels and subverts the consumerist allure of creating an aspirational identity by buying things. By replacing "a rich silk
scarf" with a sausage, she ridicules the desire to consume luxury products
in order to assert upper-class femininity, even as she wants to be a "film
star." Meat expresses the racialized sex/gender norms and consumerist
class hierarchy that subordinate Sylvie; at the same time, meat animates
her creative practice that subverts those conventions. Meat represents
both disempowerment and its sublimation via parodic play.

   In distinction from ecofeminisms that reject meat-eating, Sylvie also
reclaims butchery as locus of feminist practice and anti-industrial temporality. She thwarts unwanted groping by her boss by threatening with
her axe, "we wouldn't want that bad old hand chopped off and parceled
up as soup bones, would we?" (195). Sausage-making becomes a redemptive process that locates Sylvie's astute suspicions of industrial food and
queers the temporality of food production:

Grind the meat in the big old mincer, add just the right amount of salt,
pepper, clove and coriander—although she cannot resist an extra dash of
coriander—then leave the mixture overnight. . . . No nasty cereals thrown
in as they do these days in town, nothing like that pink polony. . . . Time
[passed] . . . slowly, wrapped up in itself . . . mixed things through, drew
the flavors into each other. . . . It was time that brought something new
called boerewors. . . . That too is how a person gets through. You put up
with waiting. . . . Hers is the best boerewors in Namaqualand, all because
of the extra dash of coriander and the patience. (100)

Like Mercia in Glasgow, Sylvie alters a recipe by adding coriander. While Mercia challenges the authority of an English cook, Sylvie claims Cape cuisine as her own to use and adapt. Sylvie also values the "patience" of a small-scale rural operation, in contradistinction to "town," where industrial haste yields "pink polony." Sausage-making in "town" stands in for industrial meatpacking, which epitomizes the capitalist obsession with efficiency. (Such "efficiency" is of course false in an ecological sense, as industrial agriculture is carbon-intensive.) Sylvie's sausage-making resonates with ecofeminist thought: Adams finds meatpacking paradigmatic of capitalist production logics, noting that Henry Ford's assembly line took inspiration from the "disassembly line[s] of the Chicago slaughterhouses," where the bodies of animals are taken apart piece by piece.[84] Workers' identities are likewise subject to "fragmentation" by the inhuman industrial efficiency of the slaughterhouse or factory.[85] Sylvie's patient sausage-making queers time to interrupt the socially normative temporality of such capitalist efficiencies. If Sylvie's version of queer time seems backward-looking, valuing a smaller-scale mode of meat production associated with provincial life, this is both akin to the temporal irregularity that Freeman associates with queer disruptions to chrononormativity—such as anachronism, belatedness, and flashback—and a nod to eco/food movements that construct presents and envision futures based on small-scale, humane, and less carbon-intensive modes of production.[86]

While Sylvie critiques the haste of industrial meatpacking, she does not reject meat. Instead, Sylvie would concoct a new becoming out of dead flesh:

> Imagine, in the dark. . . . Stealing into Lodewyk's butchery. . . . An eerie, film-set light is cast over everything. . . . She, Sylvie, having stripped off all her clothes, would coil the sausage around her nakedness. . . . Neatly, like an Egyptian mummy, a queen wrapped in time. And if the sausage skin should break? Ag, the sausage meat would stay, plastered to her skin, grafted onto her. Sylvie, the Sausage Girl, brand-new as a baby, at one with her handwork. (102)

This posthuman image of meat "grafted" to Sylvie's skin rewrites the sexual politics of meat. Rather than solidarity between women and living animals, we have Sylvie's reinvention as "the Sausage Girl, brand-new," imagined through the intimacy of her flesh with dead flesh in which the animal is an "absent referent" (Adams's term for the discursive disappearance of the animal in statements such as "He treated me like a piece of meat").[87] In a disturbing necro-ecofeminism tainted by the death of animals, Sylvie fantasizes about mummification, a forever-time in death. Sylvie's patience may seem transmuted into a more moribund "waiting," a temporality that Barnard describes as typically South African but rejected in recent years of impatience for change.[88] Living with the transition's failures, the corruption of leaders such as Jacob Zuma, AIDS, the chasm between rich and poor, and very real environmental threats, South Africans may be tired of waiting for change. As I write in times of climate concern, pandemics, and global reckonings with anti-Black violence, the sense that waiting is moribund may be spreading. Sylvie's slow aesthetics of meat indulge troubling temporalities and desires even as they resist capitalist inefficiencies.

Still, Sylvie thinks beyond modes of futurity that might seem foreclosed to her (such as the reproductive futurity of the normative middle-class family) by refocusing on the posthuman necrofuturity of meat mummification, finding potentiality in queer temporalities and in tainted food. Her meat photography resonates with Emelia Quinn's concept of "vegan camp," an aesthetics that, "by laughing in the face of horror, forces an acknowledgement of the complicity of vegans in systems of global exploitation."[89] Vegan camp "detaches us [vegans] from the earnestness with which we might otherwise" approach the commodification of animal bodies, enabling vegans to not only "condemn exploitation" but also "foster . . . aesthetic enjoyment" and acknowledge that "vegan desires . . . are often implicated in complex ways in the practices of institutions and systems we abhor."[90] Sylvie is not vegan, but her photography practice similarly laughs in the face of her own subordination and of slaughter. Rather than lean away from racist body norms, consumerism, or the female body's association with meat (and with availability for consumption), Sylvie's photo-play reclaims these aesthetics.

Wicomb's representation of Sylvie does not contradict the position that industrial meat production is violent, nor that misogynistic, racist, and speciesist logics underwrite industrial agriculture. But October does complicate ecofeminist arguments on the relations among gender, race, and meat. Sylvie, the patient butcher, is a deviant figure for resisting industrial capitalism, racism, and sexism, and in this sense aligns with many vegan feminists. However, Sylvie also refuses white-centric dictates on the proper tools of feminist resistance: she queers the expectation that an ecofeminist text or praxis would earnestly reject meat-eating, instead creating an aesthetics rooted in parodic re-use of butchery's signs and products. In this reclamation of tainted food, *October* suggests that meat could be part of a creative and liberating practice, even as this emancipatory value is tinged by meat's more negative associations.

Everyone who participates in capitalism has "an inescapable complicity in exploitation," as Quinn notes of vegans.[91] Contesting the violences of globalized capitalism cannot entail total abstention from problematic products. Instead, resistance to intersecting oppressions may take tainted forms, such as parody, in which complicity with violence does not invalidate attempts to push back. Agency may begin by acknowledging that complicity, a responsible starting place for a vegan activist praxis, or indeed for any rethinking of one's relations with food. By locating Sylvie's agency with a tainted food, Wicomb insists that agency and oppression are not opposites, but entangled: resistance must work from within the violent global-capitalist system for which meat offers a metonym.

Conclusion: Reclaiming Tainted Foods

Eating supermarket fruit, preparing meat, and adapting Cape cuisine subvert racial capitalist logics in *Playing in the Light* and *October*. Marion and Brenda explore a newfound and disquieting intimacy as they eat peaches from Woolworths, even as the peaches locate Marion's alienation. Sylvie reclaims agency with her camera, her butcher's axe, and boerewors. Transgressive possibilities emerge by re-engaging the very foods that epitomize violences of neoliberal-era consumer culture and longer histories of colonization, racism, and misogyny. Wicomb's characters reclaim such tainted products to create temporalities, identity narratives, and interpersonal connections that exceed racist and cis-heteronormative capitalism.

Of course, these characters do not model "ethical eating." Instead, they may inspire new directions for food politics precisely because they do not sanitize or justify their own eating. Wicomb interrupts righteous claims— which food is "local," "organic," "humane," "fair trade"; what you should or should not eat—that all too frequently focus on white middle-class bodies and ideas, and that greenwash differences in food access. Read through queer and vegan analytics, her novels invite readers to stay with the trouble of a bad food system and acknowledge complicity as a starting point for resistance. In globalized food production, violence is not an exception isolable to specific products such as meat; it is the rule. This does not mean consumers shouldn't think conscientiously about their purchasing choices, if in a position to do so. It does mean, however, that the model of the ethical consumer-citizen has limits (as discussed in chapter 3). Looking for less righteous alternatives in food politics might mean re-examining tainted foods.

The politics of diet not only matter in the neoliberal present but also shape possible futures in an era of accelerating climate change. Building on this chapter's examination of meat-eating and veganism, the final chapter of *Precarious Eating* asks how cultural expectations about diet intersect with narratives of water injustice in Cape Town and Mumbai. I consider how novels by Henrietta Rose-Innes and Prayaag Akbar each revise public narratives of water emergency and disenchant problematic politicizations of diet as they envision climate futures.

PART III

Gastrohydropolitics and Climate Imaginaries

5

Purity and Porosity

Speculating Urban Water Justice and Future Diets

We've had the land wars, the gold wars, the diamond wars, the oil wars. . . . What do you think the next war is going to be about? I know you're going to say: food. Yes it will be about food, but there can't be no food without water.

—FRED KHUMALO, "Water No Get Enemy"

Food depends on water, as the narrator of Fred Khumalo's short story "Water No Get Enemy" observes. Drought and flooding can disrupt agriculture; rains can determine whether farmers repay loans or sink into debt; toxins in waterways are taken up in fish and crops. As climate change intensifies, conflicts over water are likely to reshape foodways. But conversely, how might ideas about eating shape access to water? Looking beyond the physical dependencies of food production on water, what are the less obvious ways in which cultural logics of consumption intersect water access?

In this concluding chapter, I consider how expectations about diet irrupt into narratives of water crisis in two cities: Cape Town and Mumbai. Many governmental, media, and "expert" narratives about their water management fall into one of two categories: a technocratic hubris in which problems can be resolved with existing engineering, or an assertion that (because of climate change) water-access issues are emergencies so sudden and unpredictable that governments should not be blamed. Neither of these simplifications reckons with the power relations that govern uneven access to water and drainage, as noted by many social scientists and other commentators who combine or complicate these positions. Seeking subtler narratives that recognize water infrastructures as ideological and political (not merely technical), this chapter will turn to two speculative consumption fictions: the 2011 *Nineveh* by South African writer Henrietta Rose-Innes and the 2017 *Leila* by Indian author and editor Prayaag Akbar.

In the ethnography *Hydraulic City,* Nikhil Anand remarks that "Mumbai is filled with stories of water"; however,

> many of these stories are now submerged in a new wave of crisis narratives. . . . As policy experts proclaim a future of water wars, scientists warn of imminent changes to our climate, and government officials, politicians, and researchers proclaim new emergencies around the state of cities; these emergency narratives often work to subdue and suppress the multivalence of water and its storytellers.[1]

As in Mumbai, also in Cape Town, the complexity of water stories may get lost in emergency narratives. Cape Town was catapulted into worldwide attention in early 2018 with media coverage of a drought-induced water crisis. The city government forewarned of "Day Zero," when municipal water levels would drop below 13.5% and the city would cut off private taps, requiring residents to queue for water. Headlines in the global North seized on this apocalyptic rhetoric, framing the "Dry City" as either a "wake-up call"—a warning for the rest of us to avert such a disaster—or a "harbinger of things to come."[2]

How can water troubles in Cape Town and Mumbai be narrated beyond these rhetorics of emergency? What futures might be imagined by thinking in more nuanced ways about water problems? In the speculative texts I examine, one narrative possibility emerges from a combined attention to hydro-infrastructures and diet. I define "hydro-infrastructures" expansively to include not only elements that directly manage water (such as pipes and pumps), but also walls, dwellings, roads, and other built features that impact how people experience water access and drainage. I understand hydro-infrastructures to be both powerful and precarious, influenced by Anand's definition of infrastructure as "a social-material assemblage that not only constitutes the form and performance of the liberal (and neoliberal) city but also frequently punctures its performances," as illustrated by how "Mumbai's hydraulic infrastructure is powerful, and yet is full of leaks and always falling apart."[3] I use the term "gastrohydropolitics" to name how struggles around hydro-infrastructures and water access can mirror, or can be structured by, the encoding of societal conflicts into notions of eating etiquette, proper food, and disgust. Examining novels that foreground both hydro-infrastructures and dietary norms, this chapter suggests a gastrohydropolitical viewpoint as a nonemergency narrative that can apprehend possible climate futures in terms of both present-day infrastructural injustices and hierarchies expressed through expectations about eating.

To elucidate this gastrohydropolitical viewpoint, I read *Nineveh* and *Leila* alongside ethnographic and urbanist scholarship on South African and Indian hydro-infrastructures. Resonating with Anand's description of powerful but leaky infrastructures, both Rose-Innes and Akbar attend to how walls, roads, and pipes separate people (by class, race, caste, religion, or place of origin), yet are porous to fluids, vapors, pollutants, and human social arrangements. These novels both center on hydro-infrastructural imaginaries, ruminating on walls, water access, and drainage. In so doing, they examine the dominant ideologies that infrastructural decisions reflect as well as the loopholes, surprises, failures, or transgressions that urban infrastructures allow. Both novels also obsess about what people eat as a way to explore conflicting social values. Building on scholarship on gastropolitics, I show how these fictions situate dietary norms as a cultural force that may shape climate futures. In *Nineveh,* different diets express conflicting modalities of engaging with nonhuman life and with other people, as do interactions with failing hydro-infrastructures. Gastropolitics and hydropolitics are copresent but divergent modes of thinking about adaptation to rising waters, to shifting economies, and to multiracial democracy. In *Leila,* gastropolitics and hydropolitics are articulated together: a gastrohydropolitical logic of "Purity" dictates how infrastructures differentiate access to clean air, urban space, and water in a future climate. With this attention to how dietary norms undergird inequality, Akbar positions lack of water access not as an aberration, but as a logical outgrowth of exclusionary narratives about who belongs to Indian cities.

Water Infrastructures, Water Crises: Cape Town and Mumbai

Media and local government have narrated both Cape Town and Mumbai as sites of water emergency. While residents do face dire limitations to water access, emergency narratives may obscure the long-term infrastructural insufficiencies that interact with weather to provoke water crisis and distribute impacts unevenly. Crisis narratives may also excuse egregious uses of government power and encourage antimigrant or anti-poor sentiments when precarious newcomers are framed as stealing scarce resources. Emergency narratives may also cast moments of shortfall or inundation as aberrations, obscuring that drought and flooding are seasonal recurrences whose shifts due to climate change require long-term planning. Narratives of water crisis, then, are telling: they can illuminate how cities are (or are not) preparing for climate adaptation and exemplify how municipal governments and the media produce ideas about who does and does not belong to a city.

Drought is hardly new in southern Africa. Segregationist-era archives reveal that, while some administrators were sympathetic to those rendered destitute by drought, others exploited drought-famine to extend state power. During a 1912 drought-famine, the chief magistrate of South Africa's Transkeian Territories asserted that "government has no intention of supplying grain to Natives, but looks to the people to help themselves by earning money. . . . There is a large field of labour open to them and it is for them to avail themselves of this means of supplying their needs. Thus, not only will there be fewer mouths to feed, but those who must necessarily remain will not continue in want."[4] Wage work as the only means of avoiding starvation had already sped colonization during the Xhosa "cattle killing" (chapter 2). The chief magistrate's suggestion that some leave home to work, leaving "fewer mouths to feed," looks flippantly on the splitting up of families that would become a hallmark of apartheid labor, suggesting how choices about managing drought and starvation enabled successive regimes of racial power. In a 1916 drought, the town council in Stellenbosch similarly proposed that children of "farmers impoverished by the present drought" and "degenerate Poor Whites" be sent to "relief sorting stations" for the purposes of "sifting out and testing [their] capabilities and character" so they might be employed in "farm work and house-wifery."[5] Dividing families, drought and famine "relief" enabled settler-colonial authorities to remold the lives of colonized and poor peoples to create cheap labor.

During apartheid, black and "coloured" Capetonians were displaced to townships in the arid Cape Flats, which receive four hundred millimeters per year of rain, compared to one thousand in nearby mountains. The Cape Flats are also prone to winter flooding because of low elevation, substandard infrastructure, and the density of impermeable surfaces in

Cape Town.[6] South Africa's 1996 constitution named every citizen's right to water access and sanitation, and various water legislation has been passed since. Yet infrastructure and public services remain inadequate in townships and informal settlements, amplifying seasonal drought and flooding. This is partly because market-oriented housing policy reproduced "apartheid-style ghettos," many in "far *worse* locations than apartheid era townships," often lacking sewage systems and stormwater drains.[7] In Khayelitsha, Cape Town's largest township, 10 percent of residents lack running water or toilets. Informal settlements generally have only communal taps.[8] In the 1990s, a serious drought was mismanaged by prioritizing white commercial agriculture rather than vulnerable citizens. Townships saw sudden cut-offs and repeated price hikes for both water and electricity, prompting a culture of distrust and protest (including against privatization) that remains important to contemporary struggles for resource equity.[9] As I write in late 2022, South Africa is again in the news, this time with regard to the intensifying rolling blackouts familiar to South Africans as "load-shedding."

Considering Cape Town's infamous 2017–2018 water crisis, then, requires recognizing that limited water access was nothing new for many Capetonians. New governmental and public narratives nonetheless emerged from the three-year drought that began in 2015. Surface water and groundwater are normally managed federally, but in 2017, the city of Cape Town assumed responsibility.[10] The city represented the drought as neither aberration nor business as usual, but "a slow onset event within an altered climatic regime, called the 'New Normal.'"[11] While the city characterized its approach as building "water resilience," it has been censured for using apocalyptic rhetoric as a motivator.[12] The 2017 "disaster plan" portending "Day Zero" sparked a "media frenzy" and encouraged panic.[13] "Public shaming and police" were used to "pressure" Capetonians to use less water, with the mayor reprimanding residents for "wasting water."[14] Daily water use was restricted to fifty liters per person. Water management devices (WMDs) were installed to measure household use and enable shut-offs. WMDs have been touted as pro-poor, allowing consumers to avoid tariffs that escalate at higher consumption levels. However, WMDs and tariffs are based on water consumption per household, with an assumed maximum of four inhabitants, which is far from the reality in many homes. Poorer infrastructure also makes leaks likely in townships, which can result in water being shut off even when residents are obeying restrictions.[15] Water-demand reduction has inevitable limits and raises ethical questions about placing responsibility on citizens already living in a "highly uneven waterscape."[16] The city's emphasis on demand reduction sharply contrasts the access and rights-oriented rhetoric of, say, the nonprofit group Viva con Agua, whose slogan "Water for All, All for Water" appears in a mural in Cape Town by Mozambican street artist AfroIvan (Figure 8).[17]

While poor Capetonians are likelier to face insufficient hydro-infrastructures, some wealthy Capetonians responded to the crisis by installing private boreholes, which affect the overall water table and can disturb aquifers. Thus, wealthy people who reduced their municipal consumption were not always using less water, raising further doubts as to the effectiveness of WMDs. The inequities deepened by such privatized

Figure 8. Mural by artist AfroIvan in partnership with Baz-Art Organisation, sponsored by Viva con Agua Foundation and featuring its slogan "Water for All, All for Water." Buitengracht Street, Cape Town. Photo by the author, October 2022.

solutions are illustrated in Simon Wood and Francois Verster's 2018 minidocumentary, *Scenes from a Dry City* (produced by Field of Vision). This twelve-minute film juxtaposes wealthy gardeners getting boreholes installed with township car-wash operators getting arrested. White golfers relax while black protestors denounce water privatization. Certainly not all wealthy residents approached the crisis like those depicted in *Scenes from a Dry City*; others outfitted their homes with do-it-yourself gray-water systems or joined neighborhood groups.[18] But if "the prospect of queueing at public taps was a panic-inducing threat to some Capetonians," still "to others it has been a lived reality for years."[19] By scaring some Capetonians with the prospect of inadequate water access, the city sidelined this reality. In the short term, consumers did curtail their water usage, rains came, and "Day Zero" never occurred. However, "scare tactics," combined with poor communication and new tariffs that seemed like an "unfair punishment" after Capetonians had reduced consumption, likely exacerbated long-term distrust.[20]

Rhetorics of emergency have likewise characterized water narratives in Mumbai, which shares with Cape Town a pattern of longstanding inequalities in water access and drainage. Anand details how public anxiety is piqued year after year as reservoir levels dip: "*Every year,* as the summer begins, . . . engineers and administrators . . . nervously announce the danger of failing monsoons and the likelihood of water cuts. Every year, the front page in several city newspapers features a small graphic indicating the water levels in each of the city's five dams. . . . Some also prominently display, in days, the amount of water Mumbai has left."[21] Mumbai's government and media produce emergency narratives quite like those of Cape Town in 2018, complete with day-by-day countdowns to catastrophe. According to Anand, this happens annually, then the monsoon comes, averting the crisis. Pressed in an interview, a former chief engineer admits that Mumbai actually has enough water: "Talk of water scarcity" is simply produced in order "to encourage Mumbai's public to save water"—the same tactic used in Cape Town.[22]

Without denying that Mumbai's water supply is dependent on the monsoon, whose patterns could be altered by climate change, Anand casts "scarcity talk" as "the key strategy through which the city's hydraulic state has been continuously extended," provoking public concern to stoke political power.[23] This reinforces ethnonationalist narratives of the city as threatened by migrants encroaching on a dwindling water supply, when in fact, Anand and others argue, water scarcity for particular residents is produced by problems in the *distribution* of an adequate supply. According to Stephen Graham, Renu Desai, and Colin McFarlane, Mumbai has increasingly entrenched "water revanchism: an attempt by the middle class to 'claim back' the city's hydrological commons from the poor through a discourse that casts themselves as tax-paying citizens" whose water is taken by "'encroaching' slum dwellers."[24] This politics has escalated into police raids destroying pipes and pumps in informal settlements. The 54 percent of Mumbai's population living in informal settlements often has to buy water for drinking and sanitation at many times the municipal rate, even as Mumbai is dotted with swimming pools in luxury housing enclaves, a situation describable as "hydrological apartheid."[25]

The narrative that migrants are causing water emergency not only dismisses their right to live in the city, but obscures actual causes of water problems. According to Lisa Björkman, India's restructuring since 1991 has provoked a "steady deterioration" of the water department's capacity.[26] Liberalization inspired Maharashtra to turn Mumbai into a "world-class" financial services center, prompting demolitions and new construction.[27] Meanwhile Mumbai has approached affordable housing by marketizing development rights: the city incentivizes developers and landowners to surrender land or "build amenities for social purposes" in exchange for "rights to develop above and beyond heights and densities allowed by the city's development plan."[28] This pattern remakes "the face of Mumbai without consulting the pipes," as it delinks development from water planning.[29] Many engineers acknowledge that the total water supply is adequate; the difficulty is how to follow unpredictable demand in this rapidly rebuilding city in order to deliver water where and when it is needed. (Mumbai has a "sump and pump" system wherein water is supplied to different zones on a rotating basis; more than eight hundred valves must be manually opened and closed daily.[30]) Liberalization also occasioned debates about privatizing water, and Björkman argues that, although privatization never occurred, years of controversy led to understaffing and disrupted the water department's record-keeping, undermining its efficacy.[31] This is not to suggest that water and sanitation in Mumbai were perfect before the 1990s; instead, problems originate in a "complex colonial and planning legacy of half-built improvements" and in the colonial decision to found this city in a flood-prone estuarine region.[32] Recent decades, however, have seen an ideological reconfiguration of water from a "public good to be . . . distributed collectively to benefit all urban residents" (Graham et al.) into an "*economic* good" for those who can afford it (Björkman).[33] Injustices in rural water access, meanwhile, disrupt agriculture and increase migration into cities, where migrants are often needed for their labor yet rejected as city residents. In Mumbai as in Cape Town, a discourse of overall water scarcity becomes a way to stratify, producing actual scarcity for some while spurring xenophobic or ethnonationalist discourses of unbelonging.

How does climate change fit into this picture? Some commentators have castigated the city of Cape Town for emphasizing a "New Normal" in an altered climate. Mike Muller, for example, claims that city officials used climate uncertainty as an alibi for their "poor management."[34] Muller frames drought as a technical problem that can be solved by conventional engineering: existing hydrological models should continue to be reliable "for the next few decades," he argues, and the city can increase water security by building more dams.[35] (At present, six dams supply 95 percent of Cape Town's water; numerous natural springs and rivers are channeled under the city straight to the ocean, wasting millions of litres of freshwater each day![36]) Without letting the city off the hook, I would suggest that Muller's view exemplifies the "Holocene mentality" critiqued by Nicholas Simpson, Clifford D. Shearing, and Benoit Dupont, which "places confidence in scientific modelling, technocratic solutions and statistical approaches."[37] A Holocene mentality would view water supply as dependent on "two things: rain and dams," believing "that it will rain again at some stage and that dams are needed because the drought is both normal and temporary."[38] While perhaps a welcome counter to apocalyptic rhetoric, such a viewpoint downplays climate change, ignores social and environmental harms of dam-building, and resists the idea of reducing water consumption at all, in favor of multiplying extant infrastructure.[39]

Other experts, however, critique the city even as they both acknowledge drought as recurring and emphasize uncertainties introduced by climate change. Lucy Rodina, for example, suggests that existing water management paradigms are unprepared "to deal with uncertainty."[40] Conventional approaches to water management rely on past data to predict future trends, but this data does not account for additional uncertainty introduced by climate change, which tripled the likelihood of the 2018 drought.[41] Prior to 2018, Cape Town planned for a drought severity typical of those projected to occur every fifty years, similar to the international standard. However, 2015–2018 constituted a 311-year drought.[42] The crisis, then, was caused both by climate-change-related drought amplification *and* by poor planning, which failed to account for how a 311-year disaster could become likely. This illustrates the need for "a paradigm shift (such as reframing how risk and probability are estimated)" in our era of climate change.[43] Such a shift should mean accounting for greater uncertainty without using uncertainty as an excuse to abdicate responsibility.

Water infrastructures and environmental futures are not only the domain of scientific and technical models that attempt to quantify uncertainty and risk but also the territory of speculative fiction. Indeed, the speculative work of novels, which can dwell in the unknown, becomes culturally urgent with the need to account for greater uncertainty. Fiction can offer alternative ways to project from present injustices to possible futures, raising questions about whether and how cities might change course, and what shifts in public thinking and consumption culture this might require. Speculative consumption fictions can keep marginalized populations, uneven infrastructures, and cultural divisions—often driven by expectations about diet—at the center of a conversation about evolving resource management in an age of climate change, as I'll now explore.

Speculating Climate Futures through Diet and Hydro-Infrastructures in *Nineveh*

Emergent Capetonian writer Henrietta Rose-Innes describes her recent "loose trilogy of environmentally themed novels," *Nineveh, Green Lion,* and *Stone Plant,* as all "set in a slightly future or alternative Cape Town."[44] Suggesting that "estrangement" is "one way to approach writing about the non-human," Rose-Innes describes how her recent writing

> edge[s] towards the speculative, without delving into outright fantasy. . . . The space I'm interested in exploring . . . is not exactly Narnia, and perhaps not even The Wood Between the Worlds, but perhaps the *wardrobe*: that space of possibility, where we have the first inkling that a break in perceived reality is imminent.[45]

I interpret Rose-Innes's "wardrobe" to mean the space of a liminal generic and temporal mode, situated between realism and speculative fiction, between the present and the future. This mode, which I'll describe as "slightly-speculative," inheres in *Nineveh*'s tendency to describe present-day diets and hydro-infrastructures in terms of the futures they might engender. Considering what this mode adds to consumption fiction's tool kit for representing climate change, I argue that the slightly-speculative hinges imaginations of climate futures on an ongoing examination of how past injustices have orchestrated contemporary hydro-infrastructures and consumption cultures.

Nineveh is the story of Katya Grubbs, a Cape Town small-business owner who specializes in "humane" removal of unwanted critters: "Putting the wild back in the wild. . . . Policing borders."[46] Katya is hired by real estate mogul Mr. Brand to address a beetle problem at his gated housing development, Nineveh. At first, Katya sees "no sign of life whatsoever" in the securitized estate, whose beetles are elusive (until flooding causes them to swarm) and whose human tenants have not yet moved in (116). Nineveh's "sterility" contrasts the "profuse and teeming wilderness" of a wetlands "beyond the white retaining wall" (116). Also beyond the wall lies an informal settlement, creating an uncomfortable analogy between human–nonhuman borders and borders of race and class. Yet the novel exceeds an allegorical logic in which nonhuman life would be only a "symbol of the social"; instead, "these two levels constantly overlap and shift one into the other."[47] Concerned with the multispecies assemblages that constitute Cape Town, *Nineveh* raises uncomfortable comparisons in order to consider the interplay between neoliberal apartheid and disruptions to nonhuman life.[48]

Several scholars have explored Rose-Innes's depictions of pests and urban environments.[49] Largely unremarked, however, is the lexicon of appetite, revulsion, and consumption that textures *Nineveh*'s engagements with racialized class inequality and interspecies relations. In its dual attentions to eating and flooding, I suggest, *Nineveh* offers a series of gastropolitical and hydropolitical ruminations on possible futures emergent in the present. By contrasting different diets (meat-eating and veganism) and differing usages of hydro-infrastructures (formal and informal), the novel explores a range of orientations to the neoliberal city, scrutinizing each as a potential way to adapt to rising waters, changing economic structures, and interactions across lines of social difference.

Bully Beef and Vegans of the Future

Nineveh situates dietary choices as expressions of raced, classed, and gendered identities that shape how individuals will (or will not) adapt to climate futures. Meat-eating is a locus of combined delight and disgust, paradigmatic of an industrial food system, as emerges in the novel's obsessive references to "bully beef" (minced corned beef canned in gelatin). Bully beef is initially associated with Reuben, Nineveh's security guard, when he delivers groceries to Katya:

> He unpacks: two cans of corned beef; a loaf of white bread, sliced; a tube of polony; a block of processed cheese; three bottles of bright red Sparletta; a tin of pilchards in peri-peri tomato sauce; a tin of condensed milk; a can of instant coffee; two rolls of toilet paper; a sack of sugar. She's amused but not disturbed by the proletarian cast of the food before her. It's clear that Reuben has taken it on himself to buy the food for her—she cannot imagine the glamorous Zintle stocking up on bully beef. (63)

Resembling a grocery list, this passage itemizes industrial products that range from basic necessities to unhealthy processed foods. Katya associates such groceries with a difference in taste and needs between Reuben and herself. In Reuben's hands, "the bags had seemed stuffed and heavy," as if these could be his groceries for the full week, but once "laid out" in Katya's lodgings, the food "seems rather meagre," insufficient for her (63). While the contrast between Reuben and the "white woman" Katya is implicitly racialized, the primary difference in Katya's conscious mind is class (92). Such "proletarian" food would not have been purchased by "the glamorous Zintle," a higher-up at Mr. Brand's company who represents the rise of South Africa's black middle class. (By the end of the novel, the corrupt Mr. Brand has sunk and Zintle has started her own PR firm [191].) The scene also implies a mismatch between Katya's personal habits—this isn't what she normally eats—and class associations with her job: "Perhaps this is what is considered suitable fuel for a pest-relocation expert, a Worm Lady" (63). These groceries index the interplay of race and class signifiers in the new South Africa: Zintle's middle-class identity differentiates her from working-class Reuben, yet Katya uses her whiteness to disidentify with "proletarian" foods despite the liminal status entailed by her occupation.

Katya finds the bully beef "toxic, fluorescent almost, but she can't resist," a combination of revulsion and relish suggesting the addictive qualities of industrial food, which she soon rejects: "That stuff will kill you" (86). Katya codes this rejection in terms of her perceived right to differently classed food: "Decent groceries: it must be possible to obtain them. She is not a particularly discerning eater, but there are a few things she craves: tea with milk; wholegrain bread, proper cheese, tomatoes and avocado. To say nothing of a bottle of wine or two" (91). This second grocery list connotes middle-classness. Buying fancier groceries indicates Katya's aspiration to distance herself from her working-class job and upbringing, pursuing the ease of wealthier white people.

Yet the bully beef hangs around, contributing to a gustatory lexicon that unsettles assumptions about race and class. Katya chops some into bait for the beetles, but instead attracts Len, her abusive and estranged father, who appears seemingly by accident. (It later becomes evident that Len was hired as exterminator prior to Katya and has been squatting since.) In the morning, Katya finds that Len has "got out the bully beef and he's digging in. With relish. It's not lost on her: this is the prey she was luring, with her silly cubes of meat" (155). Katya herself resumes eating "the processed meat. She doesn't even consider making him a different meal, one using the food she bought so hopefully for herself. She knows what Len likes. . . . She feels it sliding down her throat, staining her insides" (164). Katya has aspired to upward mobility and independence from her familial past, buying "proper" groceries "hopefully," but surrendering these aspirations at Len's return. Katya's reacceptance of the bully beef expresses emotional harm inasmuch as it is linked with reaccepting her father, but in a gastropolitical reading it signifies as Katya easing her ideology of class superiority. Ultimately, Katya will relinquish her goal to become a long-term employee and resident at Nineveh, ending the novel committed to having no fixed address. This arc opposes the reassertion of privilege in Katya's momentary desire for "proper" groceries, and aligns with her return to bully beef, a complex signifier

that represents working-class sensibilities yet also expresses the poisonous nature of an industrial food regime (as aligned with the patriarchal
violence of Len). Katya's trajectory is unsettling rather than satisfying, an
incomplete redress either to white privilege or to childhood trauma and
a nonanswer to problems with industrial food.

Images of Len "gorging himself on lurid meats" further associate meat-
eating with brutality (170). Yet Len's carnivorous cruelty makes him
somehow well adapted: "The world is a messy business and he is the man
for messy business: he's in there wrestling with it, bloodstained and dripping juices. *Got to get your hands dirty, my girl*" (173). With these images
of blood and flesh, Len is presented as the quintessential white male
meat-eater. He is a figure of the rugged masculinist survivalist, likely to
withstand environmental apocalypse because of his ruthlessness. Yet, even
as Len's characterization aligns meat-eating with patriarchal violence, Len
is also a figure for working-class practicality: he eats affordable canned
meat (as contrasted with Katya's middle-class nibbles) and forges friendly
business connections with low-income black characters, adapting to the
informal economic activity that proliferates in the shadows of global
neoliberal capitalism (as I'll discuss in a moment). Len not only con-
sumes but also resembles the bully beef: quasi-indestructible. Bully beef
stands for gendered violence and an unjust system of industrial foods,
yet also for a working-class capacity to withstand climate futures.

Even as *Nineveh* both abjures and revalues tainted meat (much like
Wicomb's *October,* discussed in chapter 4), the novel offers a counterpoint to Len in Katya's vegan nephew Toby. Katya thinks of Toby as "a
young tree. . . . He has a kind of springy resilience, like green wood. And
there is the vegetable greenness of the veins beneath his skin, his slightly
sappy body scent. *I'm a vegan now,* he told her recently. Perhaps that's
why he's growing so fast: photosynthesis" (20–21). Plant-eating slips into
plant-likeness. Rather than masculinist mastery over nature, Toby represents a softer masculinity and a porous relation with the nonhuman,
enacted by veganism. Such species liminality is emphasized in a scene
of salad-eating, in which teenage Toby and several other "kids look like
pretty insects to [Katya]: busy little garden helpers, mandibles moving.
Toby is lean and long, with those giant eyes and triangular chin, mantis-
like. He even has his hands held up and clasped, unconsciously praying for
something" (137). By eating salad, human becomes insect. This imagined

species conversion is not degrading, but edifying, making youth into "garden helpers" and associating them with prayer, work, and benefits to other species. A plant-based diet is framed as purification for a peaceful future of interspecies cooperation.

However, veganism as constructed in relation to Toby also connotes whiteness and middle-class pretensions. This is not to say that South African veganism is always coded as privileged, white, or a Western imposition. Indeed, in *The Postcolonial Animal,* Evan Maina Mwangi offers a vegan-inflected study of how many African literary and cultural texts reject excessive violence toward animals and situate respect for oppressed humans, nonhumans, and the environment as intertwined; moreover, veganism is a multiracial trend in South Africa.[50] Nonetheless, veganism is a bourgeois, white practice in Toby's case, inviting skepticism around its place within the rise of foodie culture in Cape Town. Moreover, while meat-eating has a strong association with white patriarchy, attributions of revolting meat consumption can also function to denigrate other groups. (I am thinking, for example, of the xenophobic images of Nigerian immigrants butchering meat in Neill Blomkamp's 2009 sci-fi film *District 9.*) Vegan advocacy can all too easily slip over into casting racist aspersions on meat-eaters who are not white, as discussed in chapter 4. There are reasons to question Rose-Innes's idealization of Toby as the sensitive vegan of the future, not least because *Nineveh* never reckons with Toby's racial and economic privilege. Rose-Innes does mock Toby's sensitivity on several occasions, as when Katya watches him sniffle over the corpse of a frog: "This humane stuff, it's a joke really. . . . Eradication is the future. And this poor boy, he's just not cut out for it" (145). "Eradication" is associated with Len's grittier model of future durability. Toby's veganism indexes a residual hope that, beyond living off the "lurid meats" and other preserved foods of a contemptible past, younger people might learn to tread lightly on the earth. But this is a troubling model of outsourcing environmental responsibility to posterity, in a privileged key.

Contrasting this light-footed but privileged veganism to hefty but violent meat-eating, Rose-Innes offers two opposing visions of climate futurity; each diet is examined in terms of its adaptive potential for the future and found to have pitfalls. While differently classed, both diets are primarily associated with white characters, situating diet as an arena of negotiation for white anxieties about how to relate to environment and to life in a multiracial city. This focus suggests the limitations of individual dietary choices as modes of imagining or adapting to environmental futures—if consumptive modes are held separate from broader questions of resource access and infrastructural inadequacy. Yet *Nineveh* does invoke those broader questions, considering relations with hydro-infrastructures as an arena for imagining past, ongoing, and future power dynamics.

Hydro-Infrastructures of the Formal and Informal City

Nineveh connects a formal Cape Town whose hydro-infrastructures reflect capitalist-colonialist logics to the informal Cape Town that supports it while operating at the margins of global capitalism and the nation-state. Characterizing colonial, apartheid, and neoliberal development as modes of water mismanagement, the novel's hydro-infrastructural imaginary suggests both the harms of present urban patterns and their unsuitability for a future of rising waters. *Nineveh* thus presages a collapse of the formal city in the face of climate change. More stalwart, however, are the modes of adaptation, informality, and communal living represented in the novel, and this suggests that preparing for climate futures requires creative rethinking of the infrastructures that colonialism, apartheid, and neoliberalism have created. Rose-Innes's representations of informality range from realist depictions of how informal settlements today experience water to speculations on the possible futures emerging as Capetonians repurpose infrastructures against the grain of neoliberal ideology.

Characteristic of the formal and neoliberal city, the walled Nineveh epitomizes enclave-style real estate, attempting but failing to police borders (whilst drawing its labor force from the informal city just beyond its gate). Real-estate development in postapartheid Cape Town has been characterized by "speculative building of holiday condos and other havens of 'careless' living," a form of "speculation" that "rests on shifting ground" in the face of climate change.[51] Such patterns make developers rich quickly, ignoring the need for affordable housing. They also lead to collapse, as Rose-Innes intimates by mentioning the 2008 financial crash: "The recession has not been good to anyone, and a lot of the luxury estates are failing, lying half-empty. . . . [Katya] imagines everything gone: Nineveh erased" (192). The Nineveh estate is metonymic of the real estate and financial practices that led to the 2007 housing market crash in the United States, spawning the global economic downturn to which a liberalized South Africa was vulnerable.[52] With such depictions of neoliberal-era infrastructure, *Nineveh* critiques land and water usages that impede preparedness for disasters and exacerbate injustice.

Rose-Innes situates neoliberal-era construction within longer patterns of predatory water management and urban development centered on "reclaiming" land. Katya flips through a book of past and present photographs of Cape Town, noting images of the "bleakly triumphal foreshore . . . pushing back the sea by force of will" (95). Part of Table Bay was filled in to create Cape Town's extensive foreshore, largely in the 1930s–1940s (although changes to the shoreline began in the 1800s).[53] Construction of the Duncan Dock "pushed back" the sea and "more than doubled" the metropolitan area, creating the Central Business District, today home to hotels, office buildings, the N1 highway, the central train station, and the Cape Town International Convention Centre.[54] Street names such as "Strand" ("Beach") and "Waterkant" ("Waterfront") recall that these streets, now deep in the Central Business District, were once beside the water (Figure 9).

Figure 9. High-rises where water once flowed. Facing southeast on pedestrian bridge where Waterkant ("Waterfront") Street crosses Buitengracht Street in central Cape Town. Photo by the author, October 2022.

In addition to moving the shoreline, foreshore planning dovetailed with the Slums Act of 1934 to encourage the deterioration of living conditions in areas such as District Six, later providing an excuse for its demolition.[55] (The destruction of this diverse working-class neighborhood would become an infamous example of apartheid removals.) Foreshore development, based on filling in more of the bay and removing residents of color, was in fact a centerpiece of the Le Corbusier–inspired notions of modernizing the city that would characterize apartheid development. The Foreshore Plan created in 1945–1946 used the 480 acres "reclaimed" by building the Duncan Dock to redesign how traffic would enter Cape Town, constructing new railway and maritime terminals, a "Grand Parade" envisioned as "a monumental approach from the harbour to the city—a 'Gateway to South Africa,'" and "a new Grand Boulevard sweeping down the mountainside from the east" (Figure 10).[56] Planners sought to replace the architectural "hotch-potch" of old Cape Town with a design suited to "modern urban life"—an ideology that built a city of removals and racial segregation.[57]

Nineveh alludes to such histories when Katya gazes down from Mr. Brand's corporate offices atop a skyscraper and sees the "foreshore: land stolen from the sea" (34). "Stolen" land connotes aggressive coastline development that converts water to unstable ground. At the same time, "stolen" land gestures to histories of displacing human inhabitants: Indigenous Khoena and black, "coloured," and Indian Capetonians forcibly moved during apartheid. Like the foreshore, Nineveh is imagined as a place built on land stolen from the water, or in the real-estate euphemism, land that was "reclaimed" (59). This term has a long history in Cape Town, used as early as 1894 in plans to construct a sea wall "for the purpose of *reclaiming* the foreshore of . . . Table Bay."[58] Using the same word to describe the unstable ground under Nineveh, Rose-Innes connects neoliberal development to colonial and apartheid histories by situating an appropriative logic of land-claiming as the root of both risky water management and iterative displacements.

But infrastructures intended to separate lives and dominate water are leaky. Both informal uses of infrastructure and nonhuman movements spill across the formal city's borders, as *Nineveh* encapsulates by representing the movement of water. Gurgling noises remind Katya that pipes connect her to nonhuman others: taking a bath, she hears "indistinct noises

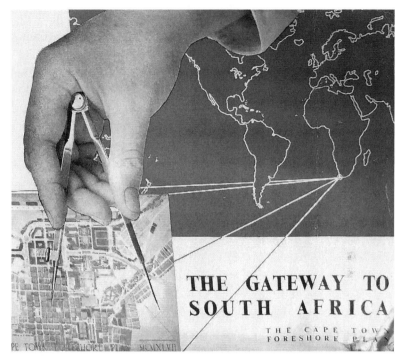

Figure 10. The white hand of a modernist planner pinches the city of Cape Town with a compass. Cover of "The Gateway to South Africa: Description of the Cape Town Foreshore Plan," brochure published by South African Railways, May 1947. Reproduced by permission of Western Cape Archives and Records Service.

coming through the pipes" and thinks of "the deeps beneath the city, alive with a million worms" (29); when she runs a tap, she "imagines the course the water is taking, down the pipes . . . and into the sewers; flowing ultimately, perhaps, into the depths of the swamp itself" (87). The "poorly drained property" of Nineveh attempts to keep water and swamp life out, but instead creates "a magnet for all kinds of damp-loving pests: water-snakes, slugs and especially mosquitoes. The rising water and its travelers always find a way back in" (59). The flow of water expresses interconnection among unlike coresidents. Flows of water also become metonymic of economic porosity when Katya notices that tiles and other materials from Nineveh are being smuggled out: "This place is not as impermeable as she had thought. There are channels, trade routes out and in" (109). The luxury development has become a scrapyard, enmeshed within circuits of salvage. If the Nineveh estate represents neoliberal capitalism, offering decadent and unsustainable lifestyles to the rich, then this salvage practice exemplifies the informal economies that repurpose neoliberal development's excess materials to sustain people living on the margins. Salvaging turns out to be an arena of cooperation between unlikely allies: Len, who has drilled a hole in Nineveh's floor to facilitate the removal of tiles and copper scrap, and collaborators from the informal settlement (more on them in a moment). Len's hole also perpetuates the need to hire an exterminator, as the beetles swarm through when the water is high, leaving Katya "flushed with a kind of admiration for Len's fiefdom: it's import/export. Beetles in, building material out. It's the kind of breaching of boundaries that someone like Mr. Brand could not be expected to . . . anticipate, or guard against" (160). Len becomes a praiseworthy figure of informal economic activity that adapts to rising waters and repurposes infrastructure against the designs of unscrupulous developers. His "import/export" business flouts the boundaries between the informal settlement and the luxury estate, as well as those between human and nonhuman life. A porous Nineveh thus illustrates how lives intermingle even when enclave-style infrastructures purport to separate them.

At the same time, porosity and flow mark the precarity of informal dwellings and the need for infrastructural justice. A climactic rainstorm floods both Nineveh (with its "terrible drainage") and the neighboring informal settlement, where "the water seems to lap right up against the outer shacks and infiltrate the muddy alleys between them. It must be hellish" (157, 167). As this passage indexes, the other side of Cape Town's well-publicized drought is flooding.[59] Water infrastructures in townships and informal settlements are inadequate in terms of not only where to get drinking water, but also drainage.

Attentive both to the antineoliberal potentiality and the precarity of the informal city, *Nineveh* reads contemporary Cape Town for signs of an ambivalent future in which infrastructural informality and inadequate water access will expand. So Khayelitsha township is seen through Katya's eyes:

> . . . a dusty ocean of tin roofs and walls, wind-battered, the color of sand and smoke. . . . The place is bigger every time she drives this way. The road

is barely holding, lapped by drifts of sand. . . . The shacks are being forced towards the sea by the pressure of the makeshift metropolis behind them. She thinks about the cluster of wood and tin homes near Nineveh. That's growing too, creeping outwards through the marshland. Reaching out to the next informal settlement and the next. . . . Perhaps this is the real city, and the patches of brick and plaster are the oddities, the stubborn holdouts too rigid to move or grow. (120–21)

In *Nineveh*'s slightly-speculative gaze, the present landscape bears signs of an emergent future. The oxymoron "dusty ocean" captures both dryness, or the scarcity of potable water in townships, and the proximity of the literal ocean. This description of the present connotes climate futures characterized by both drought and rising sea level, with encroaching but undrinkable waters intensifying contestations over land. If this passage initially seems to cast Khayelitsha as an invasive development overspilling its borders, by the end of the paragraph Katya hypothesizes that the troublesome presence is actually the formal city: both climate change and racial justice demand that the exclusive, bourgeois Cape Town "move or grow," debunking a capitalist teleology of endless accumulation. Yet this imagined dissolution of the formal city is not an ideal future of redistribution, so much as a likely future where expanding infrastructural and economic informality spread poverty rather than wealth. A longer climate future in which *all* human infrastructures break down is also presaged in the "Ozymandias"-like image of sand lapping away the road.

Yet, even as *Nineveh* forewarns that expanding informality will broaden exposure to drought and flooding, the novel invests hope in adaptive and communal modes of informality that could flourish as the neoliberal consensus collapses. Repurposing neoliberal infrastructures is a wily survival strategy associated with the character Nosisi, a resident of the informal settlement whom Katya encounters selling tiles liberated from Nineveh. After rains inundate both the luxury estate and the informal settlement, Katya exits the flooding Nineveh through a watery tunnel and emerges onto the beach to encounter Nosisi cleaning metal scrap. Nosisi reveals that Len provides her with scrap from inside Nineveh, which she resells, in exchange for food and cigarettes. Katya, who foolishly removed her shoes before wading underneath Nineveh, notices that Nosisi's feet are "sensibly encased in blue rubber gumboots like the ones they wear in a slaughterhouse. Katya's own feet are almost the same color" (187). Nos-isi's rubber boots index her ability to live in this difficult economy and waterscape, while Katya's cold blue feet signal naivete or ill-suitedness. Nosisi is presented as "sensibl[e]," opportunistic in her scavenging, and able to meet adversity with a sense of humor: she encourages Katya to go home, and then, "with a laugh, she's off again into the veils of rain" (187). Nosisi skillfully navigates her circumstances in the shadow of the global economy and in this watery, capricious microclimate, challenging as those circumstances may be.

I read Nosisi as a *bricoleur* figure, drawing on Sofia Samatar's sense of *bricolage* in Afrofuturism. Originally Claude Lévi-Strauss's term for a "jack-of-all trades" associated with "primitive" thought, the bricoleur is reclaimed in Nnedi Okorafor's novel *Who Fears Death* as a figure for "one who uses all that he has to do what he has to do."[60] Such Afrofuturist bricolage "prize[s] . . . the discarded," repurposing "the products of a domi-nant technoculture" to assert "black people's right to use whatever is at hand" in crafting new futures.[61] A similar logic informs Jesmyn Ward's fiction of the climate present, *Salvage the Bones,* in which a Black family in rural Mississippi survives poverty and Hurricane Katrina by salvaging. Rose-Innes is not a black author, nor would I describe her as an Afro-futurist. However, Rose-Innes is in conversation with writers such as Okorafor and Ward inasmuch as *Nineveh*'s most resourceful characters reclaim the discards of neoliberal capitalism to suit their own purposes, carving out space against an order that has done them no favors. Nosisi in particular ekes out a marginal living by repurposing objects from the neoliberal economy (of which the Nineveh estate is metonymic) within the informal economy. She is adept at surviving rising waters, whereas Mr. Brand's Nineveh project collapses, allegorizing the collapse of neo-liberalism in the face of climate change.

The salvage economy expands at the novel's end to encompass the entire Nineveh estate in ways that epitomize an emergent future of adap-tive living. Mr. Brand flees the country, "pursued by bankruptcy and law-suits" (191). Katya revisits Nineveh and finds that the estate finally has human occupants:

> There's a hole knocked in the bricks here, giving access. . . . Half of the gate
> is gone, perhaps taken for scrap metal. . . . Inside, someone seems to have

inhabited the guardhouse: there's colored cloth up in the windows. . . .
Some children are playing soccer in the central space, where grass grows
patchily. The apartments are also clearly lived in. . . . Here and there,
people have sunk half-bricks and pieces of wood into the muck, to step
on. (193–94)

Squatters have made it easier to enter and exit Nineveh and to cross
the central area, improvements oriented towards mobility and communal space, as opposed to Mr. Brand's walls and locks. Given the dual pressures of a shifting natural environment and the need for redistribution,
this version of Nineveh better suits most Capetonians. The new Nineveh
encapsulates both the breaking down of borders and the salvaging of
leftovers, exemplifying what Cajetan Iheka describes as the "infinite re-
sourcefulness crucial for ethical living . . . in a time of finite resources."[62]
This bricoleur orientation enables human futurity amidst infrastructural
inequality, climate change, and the oncoming demise of neoliberalism.
But while emphasizing its openness, Rose-Innes avoids romanticiz-
ing this new Nineveh as a utopia where everybody loves all their neighbors. For one, Nosisi has some understandable distaste for her nonhuman
neighbors, the beetles. In the beach scene, she advises Katya to "go inside,"
because, "when the rain stops, oh! . . . These goggas come again! It's terrible!'" (187). In the new Nineveh, Nosisi assures Katya that the goggas
(bugs) are "gone forever"; Katya "wants to say that nothing is certain.
Although that is maybe not true for Nosisi: she seems to stand squarely
on this ground, sure of her footing" (194). This description both reiter-
ates Nosisi's capability, in contrast to Katya's uncertainty, and leaves open
the question of whether the goggas are really gone. Symbolically, the real
"pests" have left: Mr. Brand and perhaps Katya herself, the white woman
Brand had enlisted in creating an exclusive Nineveh. Though Rose-Innes
at turns identifies either Nosisi or the goggas with reclaiming Nineveh's
shell from its intended wealthy human occupants, she avoids aligning
them: Nosisi can live around the beetles by learning their patterns, but
does not like them. This is interspecies coexistence with all of its frictions.
Intraspecies cohabitation also remains tense: Katya asks Nosisi whether
she has seen Nineveh's former security guard Pascal, an immigrant from
the Democratic Republic of the Congo; Nosisi "shakes her head, her face
unreadable. 'No, I don't know him.' And Katya wonders how welcome he

was here, the man from the DRC" (194). Gesturing toward xenophobia in contemporary South Africa, Rose-Innes refuses to romanticize relations in the informal settlement or reduce its residents to a monolith.

This closing vision of Nineveh, then, is one in which improvements to land or resource allocation are partial, improvised, and still contentious. Rather than Nosisi coexisting with a ruinous environment in some kind of idyllic harmony, her repurposing of infrastructures shows that she is prepared for climate futures because she *already* survives by making do on the margins of an imploding system, weathering shifting waterscapes by repurposing neoliberal society's discards into survival tools. There is potential for such a characterization to sugarcoat the unjust and often unlivable circumstances that neoliberal capitalism accords to the poor. However, I do not think that Rose-Innes's positive characterization of Nosisi countenances the circumstances of informal settlements. Rose-Innes simply refuses to present Nosisi as a victim, instead crafting a figure of resourceful endurance. Moving beyond a narrative of either progress or catastrophe, Rose-Innes's characterization of Nosisi and the salvage economy does what Anna Tsing calls "asking what else is going on"— paying attention to what exists neither inside nor outside the global economy, but on its edges, operating in relation to neoliberal capitalism yet suggesting possible other worlds.[63]

In *Nineveh,* diets and interactions with hydro-infrastructures each express ways that characters might adapt to climate presents and futures characterized by housing informality, frequent flooding, limited access to resources, and both multiethnic and multispecies coexistence. The repurposing of the Nineveh estate is invested with hope perhaps because it transforms a characteristic architecture of privatization into a communal space. The dietary choices of various white characters, meanwhile, fall short as modes of adapting to climate futures because they are too individualized. Even Len is appealing to the degree to which he forms relations with others in the informal economy, although unredeemable in the eating habits that symbolically express his abusiveness. Thus, *Nineveh* emphasizes the importance of rejecting logics of privatization and embracing greater communalism in how the novel holds individual diets in parallel to interactions with infrastructure. In *Leila,* however, experiences of hydro-infrastructures do not parallel diet so much as depend on it: normative attitudes about eating are leveraged to justify uneven infrastructures that differentiate access to water, clean air, and housing.

Purity versus Porosity: Gastrohydropolitics and *Leila*

The debut novel by Indian journalist and author Prayaag Akbar, *Leila* unfolds in a near-future city characterized by political repression, warming climate, and infrastructure inadequacy. For E. Dawson Varughese, *Leila* forms part of an emergent canon of millennial Indian fiction in English that uses speculative modes to explore urban precarity and fraught ideas of Indianness.[64] Having written the novel in Mumbai, Akbar describes its setting as combining elements of that city and Delhi, both of which create "an isolated, insular experience."[65] In Akbar's unnamed city, intensifying heat and water scarcity collide with a political regime of "Purity" that separates "communities" by caste, class, and religion, fixating on what may or may not enter whose neighborhood or body. This regime links notions of sexual purity and group identity to dietary proscriptions.

Food frequently signifies as a vehicle of pollution (and alimentary regulation as purity) in cultures in South Asia, according to thinkers such as Arjun Appadurai. In a 1981 ethnography of Tamil Brahmin households, Appadurai describes a "vaunted Hindu preoccupation with 'purity and pollution,'" expressed through a "vast plethora of rules about contact."[66] In this milieu, "food, along with blood and semen, is a particularly powerful medium of contact," linking eating, sex, the body, and group identity.[67] Vegetarianism offers a "culinary orthodoxy" in which avoiding certain foods can function to "signal caste or sect affiliation, lifecycle stages, gender distinctions, and aspirations toward higher status."[68] Social transactions with food are highly charged, sometimes erupting into "conflict or competition over specific cultural or economic resources" in what Appadurai calls "gastro-politics."[69]

Broadening the account of gastropolitics beyond Brahminical alimentary orthodoxies, Parama Roy notes that social and political relations in South Asia are forged via intermingling ideas about food and embodiment that stem from a range of caste identities and religious groups, including those of European colonizers.[70] While Appadurai's seminal usage of "gastro-politics" specifies conflicts that arise when different actors apply shared principles of food etiquette, I invoke "gastropolitics" to more broadly describe relations in which power, unequal access to resources, and even physical violence are undergirded by ideas about food. The recent global resurgence of ethnonationalism has in India manifested as gastropolitical, with "cow politics" offering a rallying point for the Hindu right. Electoral manifestos released by the Bharatiya Janata Party (BJP) in 1998, 2004, 2009, and 2014 all "pledge to preserve India's culture through central laws on cow protection."[71] Protecting cows may sound positive from a multispecies justice perspective; however, when cows are positioned as symbols of the Hindu majority under threat, cow protection can intrude on religious freedoms, disrupt the poor's right to food, and encourage violence, including numerous attacks on Dalits and Muslims by vigilantes accusing them of eating beef. In one such incident in 2002, five Dalit men were beaten and tortured; groups from the Hindu nationalist cultural association Vishwa Hindu Parishad (VHP) allegedly justified this attack by arguing "that a cow's life was more valuable than that of humans."[72] Such attacks have been implicitly sanctioned by judicial decisions supporting cow protection, which, according to Sambaiah Gundimeda and V. S. Ashwin, demonstrate a "judicial lack of neutrality" by favoring Hindu majoritarianism and denying "space for diversity."[73]

Hindu-right gastropolitics reached a chilling extreme in the 2002 anti-Muslim pogrom in Gujarat. According to Parvis Ghassem-Fachandi, many Gujarati Hindus rationalized this pogrom by mobilizing an affect of disgust and moral condemnation toward meat-eating, associated with Muslims. Ghassem-Fachandi's ethnography *Pogrom in Gujarat* tracks how a narrative of nonviolent vegetarianism was not only leveraged to sanitize the image of Gujaratis after the extreme violence of the pogrom, but indeed invoked as a rationale *for* violence, which would ostensibly purify Gujarat of harmful meat-eaters. Narendra Modi, chief minister of Gujarat at the time and subsequently prime minister of India, launched a "Vibrant Gujarat" PR campaign that countered bad press by framing *ahimsa* vegetarianism as evidence that Gujaratis are "nonviolent," invoking Mohandas Gandhi as the vegetarian figure of both Indian nationalism and regional Gujarati pride.[74] Rather than an isolated incident, the 2002 pogrom was arguably a pivotal moment in the political self-fashioning of Modi and the BJP, consolidating a Hindu nationalist discourse of vegetarian purity leveraged to label some Indians as outsiders. Such Hindu nationalism also manifests in other regional variations: Shiv Sena in Maharashtra, for example, has exemplified a Marathi-centered Hindu nativism that regards Muslims and migrants from elsewhere in India as outsiders encroaching on Mumbai.[75]

It is important here to differentiate Hindu nationalism (also called Hindutva) from Hinduism. According to Gundimeda and Ashwin, cow protection relies on "very particular readings of Hinduism, Indian history and Indian culture" to center the "sanctimony of the cow" as an (exclusively) Hindu value.[76] Cow politics exemplify Hindutva's selective gastropolitical interpretation of Hinduism, rather than generalities in Hindu culture. Similarly, Shakuntala Ray notes that, while "Hindutva politics paint Hinduism as largely heteronormative, as well as Hindu food culture as largely uniform in its understanding of purity," there in reality exist "rich tradition[s] of androgyny, homoeroticism and same-sex desire within Hindu mythology and philosophy, . . . as well as diverse positions and a range of reversals of purity within intricate Hindu food systems."[77] This cornucopia of desires and alimentary attitudes risks being flattened in what Ray describes as "an increasingly intolerant Hindutva-driven political climate," in which "a politics of enforced vegetarian-based purity, functioning as a mark of authenticity and ideal nationalist identity, intersects with liberalisation of the economy and globalisation."[78] Right-wing sexual politics and gastropolitics take shape and must be understood in relation with neoliberalism—and, I will suggest, with climate change and water scarcity.

To this end, I read *Leila* as a speculative account of how today's gastropolitics and hydropolitics might evolve toward future intensifications of resource stratification as climate change and privatization accelerate. While the novel implies a critique of Hindutva, Akbar does not suggest that harmful gastropolitics are an Indic particularity (an attitude that Roy has cautioned against).[79] Instead, *Leila* attributes exclusionary gastropolitics and a misogynistic discourse of sexual purity to multiple cultural groups, examining how local ethnopolitical formations entangle with neoliberal capitalism. Thinking in a moment of resurging right-wing nationalisms in many countries, I regard Akbar's textual India as an exemplary site from which to imagine how such structures, joined with a gastropolitics of proscription and purity, could shape water-scarce climate futures.

In the dystopian city of *Leila,* "Purity for all" refers to separation of religious groups, castes, and classes into walled sectors. The narrator Shalini recalls how the cosmopolitan and foliated city of her childhood disappeared into "hundreds of walls," each "fifty-nine feet high and two feet thick."[80] Within each sector, a community follows its own cultural rules. Even as "Purity" has become a regulated governmental regime, these "localities were self-enclosing" (43): walls are built and financed by the communities rather than the municipality. Intersecting vectors of public and private power, then, have enabled this situation, an extension of the logics of neoliberal-era governance. By the time Shalini grows up, "walls were everywhere. In ten years they'd appeared like a malignancy all over the city, as if the water pipes bubbled with this septic lymph" (79). Shalini describes the city as a diseased body, illuminating a connective logic between the infrastructural project of community separation, the delivery of resources such as water, and disgust attached to bodily fluids such as "lymph." Similarly, the "Purity" regime views the "community" as an extension of the human body. Purity is constructed through norms about what may enter or leave one's body. With constant references to bile, phlegm, flesh, food, breath, belches, sweat, and smells, Akbar represents societal anxiety about the body's potential "pollution" by external elements, and its potential to pollute. "Purity for all" is a fantasy of controlling such porosity in an urban environment "polluted" both by cosmopolitan cultural influences and by environmental contaminants.

While "Purity for all" entails marrying within one's community, Shalini (a middle-class Hindu) flouts these norms by marrying a Muslim man, Riz, and moving to the East End, one of few wealthy neighborhoods that has refused to build a sector wall, where they have a daughter named Leila. While the names Shalini and Riz mark respective Hindu and Muslim backgrounds, the name Leila, "depending on how it is pronounced, . . . could be considered Hindu, Muslim or even Christian in origin," signaling hybridity or inherent "impurity" in the eyes of the regime, and arguably signaling Shalini and Riz's resistance to such norms.[81] Yet Shalini possesses the same biases that undergird the regime. After her friend Dipanita suggests that Leila's nanny, Sapna, is too familiar in kissing the toddler's face, Shalini recoils at "the thought of [Sapna's] saliva on my daughter. I imagined faint, near-invisible lines of spit, slowly soaking into my daughter's skin, becoming part of her. That night I told Sapna she wasn't allowed to kiss my daughter anymore" (229). Though critical of the regime's rules against intercommunity marriage, Shalini has been socialized into its class and caste logics. The thought of saliva on skin locates anxieties about the permeability of bodies, and of communities that hire labor from "outside."

Imagining the community as a body that must be protected from such porosity, the regime relies upon gastropolitical norms, as Shalini reflects: "What we put into the body is so personal, intrinsic to family, belief. No politician dared argue against walls built around food. Purity came to have different meanings. Some people wanted no meat at all, some would eat only fish. In other areas Muslims were evicting anyone who drank alcohol or ate pork" (41). This description throws into relief the potential hegemony of diet whenever proscriptions become mandated to create social separations (something that Akbar suggests is already happening in Mumbai housing societies where "food choices decide your eligibility to stay on rent").[82] *Leila* attributes such exclusionary uses of dietary proscriptions to multiple religious communities, each with its own definition of "Purity." This hasn't stopped right-wing commentators from accusing Akbar's novel and the Netflix serial it inspired of being "Hinduphobic."[83] That charge—perhaps partly a reaction to Akbar's identity as a person with Muslim and Christian parents—recognizes Akbar's implied critique of the BJP but ignores the novel's even-handed suggestion that any set of gastronomic and sexual norms can become harmful when used to exclude.[84]

While the regime claims that each community can live by its own rules in peace, it differentiates access to water, clean air, and physical safety. "Slummers," or migrants and the urban poor, reside outside the sector walls with polluted air, piles of garbage, and precarious water access. Shalini shares a similar fate: cast out because of her intercommunity marriage, she is sent to "Purity Camp" to learn to respect the rules, with other women whose crimes range from queer relationships to protesting female circumcision. After camp, these women live in the crumbling "Towers" outside the city walls. Shalini is sent here because of her supposed crimes against "Purity"; however, she experiences living outside the walls as unwanted porosity. Particulates in the air make it hard to breathe and "pick at your eyes, . . . all day secretly seeping through your lids, by evening the rim around each eye inflamed" (11). Polluted air is described as one of many unwanted external elements entering the body. Those who live near burning landfills cannot stay "pure," instead experiencing their bodies as porous to pollutants. The problem with "Purity," then, is not just the punishing of harmless porosity (such as love across religious communities), but also that some members of society are exposed to harmful porosity, such as breathing polluted air. Porosity represents a cosmopolitan opposite to "Purity," but also exposure to environmental risk.

Porosity also indexes unwanted physical and sexual contact, to which "Tower women" and "Slummers" are most exposed. When Shalini requests a work transfer, she must go before a tribunal, where she is instructed to lie in "[a] high bed, like in a doctor's office" with the tribunal men around her (170). Shalini's thoughts flash on "a documentary, a movie maybe, Japanese women stretched naked on tables with sushi arranged across their shining satin bodies, so diners can slather over the topography of their vaginas, the ridges of their knees, the smooth scalloped breasts. I adjust my blouse" (170). Recalling the practice of *nyotaimori* (or eating sushi off female bodies), Shalini understands her experience with the tribunal as part of a gastropolitics that connects the pleasure of consuming food to the exploitation of women. When the leader, Mr Vijay, violently fondles Shalini, Akbar's descriptions center on penetrability to touch, vapors, fluids, and smells: "Mr Vijay is smelling me, taking soulful whiffs . . . beads of saliva on his lips. . . . He slides his finger underneath my bra"; "He has my nipple between the tips of his fingers and his eyes are large as a fish on ice. The pain is roasting and pink. . . . Blood might spurt from my ducts" (175–77). These descriptions connect food (breast milk replaced by blood, "a fish on ice") with sex, death, and penetration, exemplifying how a gastropolitical logic links diet to a range of concerns about what enters and exits the body. Shalini is later subjected to a body cavity search, similarly described as a process of unwanted entries and exits by breath, smells, bodily fluids, and fingers (251). These two scenes connect the "Purity" regime to a misogynistic patriarchalism that uses the claim that women are impure to violate their bodily autonomy— especially that of women at the bottom of the social hierarchy. Gendered and classed violations express a gastropolitics that constructs valuation and power around bodily porosity.

Leila not only illustrates power as gastropolitical but also insists that social hierarchies are produced infrastructurally. While "Tower women and Slummers" live among garbage, the sectors are connected by "fly-roads" high in the air: cars enter through elevated gates, keeping passengers "above all the mess" where it is "[e]asier to breathe" (174, 11). Mr Vijay boasts that the flyroads have made the city "beautiful": "Everything so clean. Our network of flyroads known all over the world. From Singapore, America, everywhere they're coming to see it" (174). This dystopian South Asian city is not an aberration, but a model for new built forms of neoliberal governance, with infrastructural insulation from one's own environmental impacts becoming the ultimate privilege. This privilege is temporary, however: pollutants from landfill fires start to affect even those inside the walls (223). These fires exemplify how environmental degradation will advance from impacting the marginalized, first, to impacting everyone.

Yet, in Akbar's dystopia, corporate-driven infrastructural innovation shields the privileged for a bit longer, as walls and flyroads are joined by "Skydomes": massive structures that privatize the air. The first Skydome encloses the city's exclusive political sector. From inside, a "[n]ear see-through . . . latticework of plastic venules across the sky" masks the "grey pall" of pollution and provides a bubble of climate-controlled air (219). Chants at a "Sealing" ceremony extol this triumph of privatization and advertise the product:

Why share the air? . . .
[No] outside impurities.
100% ClimaControl.
Breathe easy. . . .
Imported tech.
Tell your Council rep today! (219)

The rhetoric of "Purity" meets that of environmental "impurities," against which the wealthy enclose themselves. Skydome epitomizes how extreme liberalization ensures the resource-intensive comfort of some by exposing others to environmental risk. When a fire in the informal settlement Mahaan Nagar ("Great City" in Hindi) kills six children, a resident attributes the disaster to "those things that are coming up all over the city. . . . Sk . . . y. Daum. When you build a roof you keep something outside. . . . They put one of their massive air-conditioning units right next to Mahaan Nagar. Pumping out hot air, all day, all night. One hut caught fire, then another" (236). Skydome becomes a metonym for how privatization works: to create comfort "inside" of privilege, it "keep[s] something out-side," creating zones of sacrifice. Skydome also illustrates how environ-mental inequality can occur by infrastructural privatization overtaking the logics of governance: wealthy communities pay to enclose their air, rather than government allocating water or air as a public good. While the regime's ideologues claim to honor religious and cultural tradition and reject Westernization, "Purity" actually extends neoliberal logics first im-posed on India by Western financial institutions.

Representing Skydome as the epitome of infrastructural privatization undergirded by gastropolitical apartheid, Akbar shows that this dysto-pian future is not a radical departure from our present, but rather a logical outgrowth of neoliberal globalization operating in lockstep with reactionary politics. Indeed, even as *Leila* portrays a speculative future, its infrastructural details approach a realist rendition of the present. While Shalini narrates how the sector walls changed the city, for exam-ple, Akbar invites readers to question this. Shalini and Riz move to the East End because "the residents had long ago decided against putting up a sector wall, everyone could come and go" (80). Yet it is still an enclosed community with a "boundary wall," as Riz's brother Naz points out: "What's different about it? Why did the guards let us in just now? Imagine if we had come walking. . . . You think they'd let us in?" (80, 81). Naz's comment reframes the sector walls as existing on a continuum with present-day securitization, increasingly a part of Mumbai and other cities as affluent residents "secede from the public city through complexes involving gated communities, new raised highways, [and] private malls," drinking bottled water to "insulate themselves from the perceived health risks of piped municipal water."[85] In comparison, Akbar describes a home in an informal settlement as small but "spotless," with "columns of water pots" and a "flaking blue water drum" (230–31). Strikingly similar details are captured in Anand's ethnography of Mumbai, including descriptions of how the urban poor repurpose "three-hundred-liter blue drum[s]," formerly used to store petrochemicals, to save water.[86] Both luxurious and informal dwellings in Akbar's dystopian city resemble those of today.

Indeed, Akbar suggests a gradual (and realistic) transition from the present to his dystopia, as right-wing politics and infrastructural injus-tice intensify with the advance of climate change. Shalini recalls:

Every year the temperatures rose and the water problem worsened. . . . The
air was so dry you could hardly sweat. . . . Leila began to get dizzy spells. . . .
We had to . . . make sure she got lots of water. We all felt it, an intense
warmth like an infection, heat and anger rising inside you. . . . Sometimes
Sapna would get it, sometimes one of the other servants. You couldn't help
but explode. (86–87)

This passage links climate and affect: rising temperatures intensify rage,
which Shalini directs against her servants. This unfairness mirrors the
unfairness of water distribution: "No one followed the rules: the construction boom and the factories took the groundwater almost to zero,"
and Shalini's wealthy family takes extra water (understandably) to care
for their heat-stricken toddler, while "on TV they'd show clips of wail-
ing Slum women, banging brass pots. . . . Children . . . breathed in jerky,
rapid gulps and cried without tears" because of dehydration (88). Akbar
emphasizes how neoliberal development captures scarce resources at the
expense of the poor. Water scarcity and climate stress create the political
conditions for the rise of the "Purity" regime, as the politician Joshi gar-
ners populist support by falsely promising to return municipal water to
bastis (informal settlements) that have been cut off (111–12). Infrastructures of differentiated resource access manifest as features of the present
that may speed reactionary politics as climate change accelerates.

Conclusion: Consumption Fiction and Climate Futures

Leila explores how a gastropolitical preoccupation with moral, bodily,
and communal "pollution" impinges on a consideration of pollution in
the material sense (environmental contamination). A gastrohydropolitical
reading of *Leila* suggests that right-wing nationalisms may look to notions
of purity and disgust to justify uneven access to water and clean air, dis-
proportionate exposures to environmental pollution and sexual violence,
and socioeconomic stratification. This reading suggests also that such uneven resource access is buttressed by approaches to water infrastructure
that mask precarity by proposing technocratic "solutions." The potential
for gastropolitics to be leveraged in this way is not unique to India: indeed,
something similar is afoot in the post–9/11 masculinist, white U.S. nationalism whose association with meat-eating Laura Wright traces in *The*

Vegan Studies Project, for example. A gastrohydropolitical framework for apprehending consumption fiction reveals the environmental futures encouraged by today's seemingly contradictory conjuncture of right-wing nationalisms and neoliberalism in a moment increasingly stressed by drought, flooding, and other features of climate change.

Connecting today's cultural logics to disturbing climate futures emerges as an important facility of consumption fiction that is realized, I want to suggest, by a convergence of realism and speculation. *Nineveh* and *Leila* both couple future speculation with the realist work of depicting how hydro-infrastructures and gastropolitics already determine uneven resource access. Although *Nineveh*'s setting resembles contemporary Cape Town, Rose-Innes's cityscapes gesture toward possible futures, creating a slightly-speculative realism in how she depicts the flow, management, and absence of water, and in how her protagonist queries the future-appropriateness of various diets. Hydro-infrastructures and gastropolitics in the present thus emerge as determinants of climate futures. *Leila* is a more obviously "speculative" novel, set in a dystopian future city. Yet *Leila* hews closer to realism than this setting might suggest: Akbar's depictions of housing, transit, and water infrastructures echo ethnographic work on present-day Mumbai, while gastropolitics in *Leila* resemble Hindutva logics of alimentary purity. Both of these texts suggest, in the mutual contexts of urban social inequalities and climate change, a narrowing of the gap between realist fiction (which would mimetically represent everyday experiences in the writer's present) and speculative fiction (which would comment on the present by exploring future or alternate worlds). Narrowing this genre gap, I want to suggest, offers an alternative to narratives of apocalypse or emergency: a novelistic strategy that situates climate change, resource injustice, and gastropolitically justified violence neither as problems for a distant future nor as aberrations, but as characteristic features of an urgent present whose gastrohydropolitics will shape climate futures. With this narrowing of genre boundaries, a wider public is asked to recognize that—as marginalized peoples have known for many generations—dystopia is now.

There is potentially another narrowing of genre gaps present here: between consumption fiction and climate fiction. While in chapter 2 I emphasized the distinction between these categories, *Nineveh* and *Leila* arguably fit both rubrics. But if these novels from the global South can be characterized as climate fiction, it is not because of preoccupations with some future rupture caused by climate crisis; it is instead because they trace how a changing climate might intensify existing dynamics of uneven exposure to environmental risk, intimately connected with unequal access to food and water. Consumption fictions from the global South invite readers to remember the continuities of possible climate futures with histories of colonialism and capitalism, and the ongoing social inequalities that structure environmental precarity.

Acknowledgments

While the scholarly monograph often presupposes a single author, writing this book has instead been a process of conversations: both with the thinkers I've been lucky enough to meet, and with those I've encountered only through their writing.

At the University of Delaware, many wonderful colleagues offered feedback on parts of this project, advice about the publication process, and support with grant applications, including Siobhan Carroll, Emily Davis, Lowell Duckert, John Ernest, Laura Helton, Ed Larkin, Lindsay Naylor, Keerthi Potluri, Sarah Wasserman, and Julian Yates. Arline Wilson, my graduate research assistant and now colleague, aided with secondary literature review. Pam Brice, Ann Marie Green, Tanya Kang, Kaylee Olney, Cheryl Rodriguez, Laura Schmidt, and Jessica Venturi make it possible to get our work done. This book project was carried out with the support of the University of Delaware General University Research fund, which enabled both Arline's assistance and my research travel.

Stephanie Kerschbaum's commitment to mentoring junior faculty was crucial to my successful landing at UD, and I found years of support from a writing accountability group first facilitated by Stephanie. Jenny Lambe, Sharon Mitchler, Sarah Singer, and Elliot Tetreault kept this book alive through our weekly Zoom check-ins, particularly during the most isolating days of the Covid-19 pandemic. Feedback from my Penn Pals writing group—Najnin Islam, Dianne Mitchell, and Clare Mullaney—helped me tighten (and not hate) several chapters. Thanks in particular to Clare for organizing us!

Many other friends, interlocutors, and reviewers offered feedback on parts of this project over the years, including Aaron Bartels-Swindells, Vikrant Dadawala, Micah Del Rosario, Augusta Irele, Catherine Keyser, Ava Kim, Travis Lau, Jessica Martell, Riley McGuire, Nico Millman, Kristina Mitchell, Howie Tam, and Mary Zaborskis. Cristina Archer, Akua Banful, Dustin Crowley, Ted Howell, A. R. Siders, Maria Sulimma, and Dana Veron invited me to present from this work. This project has also benefited from conversations and collaborations with Scott Barton, Andrea Broomfield, Eve Buckley, Sarah Dimick, Mónica Domínguez Torres, Ursula Heise, Jess Holler, Denisa Krásná, Desiree Lewis, Sarah Lincoln, Lynn Mafofo, Gita Mistry, Rituparna Mitra, Rebecca Oh, Dana Phillips, Shakuntala Ray, Parama Roy, Eckard Smuts, Jennifer Wenzel, Délice Williams, and many others. Archivists Erika Le Roux (at the Western Cape Archives and Record Service) and Abhijit Bhattacharya (at the Centre for Studies in Social Sciences, Calcutta) facilitated crucial access to documents and images. Thank you to the Oxford Food Symposium and Mark McWilliams for including material from chapter 5 in the *Proceedings of the Oxford Symposium on Food and Cookery 2023*.

Precarious Eating originated from my dissertation at the University of Pennsylvania, where my thinking benefited from the energies of many mentors, formal and informal. Rita Barnard offered invaluable insights about South African literature and culture. Ania Loomba provided thoughtful and direct feedback and suggested several texts that enriched this project's archive. Jed Esty crafted the phrase "hunger versus taste" and supported me through many hurdles of academic life. In addition to my dissertation committee, numerous current and former Penn faculty and staff have offered support, encouragement, intellectual guidance, and friendship over the years, including Gwendolyn Beetham, David Eng, Al Filreis, Michael Gamer, Tsitsi Jaji, Suvir Kaul, Rahul Mukherjee, Paul Saint-Amour, Melissa Sanchez, Emily Steinlight, and Chi-ming Yang.

At the University of Minnesota Press, Doug Armato expressed enthusiasm about this project when I was still imagining its constituent parts, and strengthened the manuscript with his clear and strategic suggestions. Anonymous reviewers offered both generative feedback and belief in this book. Members of the board provided important correctives and directions for expansion, while the production team did a fabulous job preparing the book to go to press. Zenyse Miller kept everything organized and fielded my numerous questions. Thank you all!

I am grateful to my oldest friend, Emily Guthrie, whose expertise and conversation helped nuance my narrative around the challenges of interdisciplinary communication about GMOs. My neighbors cheered me up during the worst of the pandemic with outdoor chats and game nights, especially Rebecca Lacher and Orli Smith. Many other friends and chosen family have helped me through graduate school, life in the professoriate, and life in general. They include Eric Adamus, Mary Bowden, Dan Connolly, S. E. Eisterer, Thea Goodrich, Declan Gould, Ben Guthrie, Hanna Halperin-Goldstein, Peter Harvey, Russ Kinner, Erica Moltz, Libby Nachman, Laura Paul, Walter Plotkin, Martín Premoli, Gretchen and Doug Seibert, Jess Shollenberger, Alexa Smith, Sean Tandy, Andrew Tripodo, Joyce Tromba, Sophie Unterman, Chelsea Wahl, and Libby Watts.

Many people over the years encouraged me to pursue a PhD in English and an academic career. I am grateful to all of them, including Simone Dubrovic, Ivonne García, Sarah Heidt, Ted Mason, Janet McAdams, Kim McMullen, and especially my mom, Jo Ann Stanley. My dad, Kerry Stanley, inspired my attention to the nonhuman environment and my commitment to listening. My sibling, Corinne Stanley, challenges me to be a better version of myself. Thank you and love to Mom, Dad, and Corinne; to my indexer and father-in-law, Charles Knittle; to my mother-in-law, Jamie Preston; to my bonus parents, Bruce and Anne, and my cousin Jules; to my aunt and fellow postcolonialist Mary Spalding; to my dog and cats; and to the rest of my family, especially Brian Stanley and Helen Morgan, whom I love and miss. This book would not exist (and neither would dinner) without my favorite scholar, savviest reader, and partner, Davy Knittle.

My greatest gratitude goes to the many writers, activists, filmmakers, chefs, farmers, and fishers whose intellectual and material labor has inspired this book. I am energized every day by the possibilities for social justice and environmental futures that you imagine.

Notes

Introduction

1. India Express Web Desk, "Covid-19 India Timeline: Looking Back at Pandemic-Induced Lockdown and How the Country is Coping with the Crisis," *The Indian Express,* March 23, 2021, indianexpress.com; Sukhpal Singh, Barbara Harriss-White, and Lakhwinder Singh, "Agrarian Crisis and Agricultural Market Reforms in South Asia," *Millennial Asia* 12, no. 3 (2021): 267, doi.org/10.1177/09763996211063444.

2. Manveena Suri, Vedika Sud, Arpit Goel, and Rhea Mogul, "India's Prime Minister Modi to Repeal Controversial Farm Laws Following More than a Year of Protests," CNN, November 19, 2021, cnn.com.

3. Lakhwinder Singh and Baldev Singh Shergill, "Separating Wheat from the Chaff: Farm Acts, Farmers' Protest and Outcomes," *Millennial Asia* 12, no. 3 (2021): 394, 391, doi.org/10.1177/09763996211063600.

4. Singh and Shergill, 401.

5. Singh and Shergill, 391.

6. Singh, Harriss-White, and Singh, "Agrarian Crisis," 265; Suri, Sud, Goel, and Mogul, "India's Prime Minister Modi."

7. Singh and Shergill, "Separating Wheat," 405.

8. Singh and Shergill, 392.

9. Singh and Shergill, 393.

10. Singh and Shergill, 396.

11. Mahasweta Devi, "Strange Children," in *Of Women, Outcastes, Peasants, and Rebels: A Collection of Bengali Short Stories,* ed. and trans. Kalpana Bardhan (Berkeley and Oxford: University of California Press, 1990), 233. Subsequent references to "Strange Children" in this introduction are indicated parenthetically.

12. I follow the Bengali convention of referring to authors such as Mahasweta Devi and Tarashankar Bandyopadhyay by their given names.

13. By "agro-food systems," I mean arrangements for producing and disseminating food, from cultivation all the way to consumption.

14. See Lisa Lowe, *The Intimacies of Four Continents* (Durham, N.C.: Duke University Press, 2015).

15. See Mike Davis, *Late Victorian Holocausts* (New York: Verso, 2002), and chapter 1 of the present work.

16. Allison Carruth, *Global Appetites: American Power and the Literature of Food* (New York: Cambridge University Press, 2013), 4, 44–45.

17. Elizabeth DeLoughrey and George Handley, "Introduction: Toward an Aesthetics of the Earth," in *Postcolonial Ecologies: Literatures of the Environment,* ed. DeLoughrey and Handley (Oxford: Oxford University Press, 2011), 13.

18. DeLoughrey and Handley, 13.

19. Nixon explains the intertwining of environmental "slow violence" and economic destabilization by describing Stephanie Black's film documentation of structural adjustment programs in Jamaica: "planes disgorging federally subsidized American milk, onions, and potatoes at prices that destroy unsubsidized Jamaican farmers. . . . To compensate for the resultant agricultural collapse and the rising debt that follows from importing more subsidized American food, Jamaica must increase its dependence on tourists" (*Slow Violence and the Environmentalism of the Poor* [Cambridge. Mass.: Harvard University Press, 2011], 20). That this disruption manifests through foodstuffs, as vividly described by Nixon, is a tangential concern for him. I am interested in making such concerns with food central for the postcolonial environmental humanities, as well as making "environmental" the discussion of food in postcolonial studies more broadly—much as concerns with food sovereignty have long been central to work at the intersection of Indigenous studies and environmental humanities by scholars such as Winona LaDuke, Joni Adamson, Kyle Powys Whyte, and Elizabeth Hoover.

20. Sophie Sapp Moore and Aida Arosoaie, "A Syllabus for Plantation Worlds," *Edge Effects,* June 7, 2021, https://edgeeffects.net.

21. Graham Huggan and Helen Tiffin, *Postcolonial Ecocriticism: Literature, Animals, Environment,* 2nd ed. (New York: Routledge, 2015), 156n4.

22. See, e.g., Kyla Wazana Tompkins, *Racial Indigestion* (New York: New York University Press, 2012), 2, noting that the American explosion of "foodie" culture coincided with the emergence of "food studies," leading some to consider this academic field "scholarship-lite" or too bourgeois. Such dismissals ignore serious work on imperialism, slavery and indenture, race, migration, environmental justice, and labor undertaken by scholars in food studies, including those just mentioned and Sidney Mintz, Eric Holt-Giménez, and many others. Still, food studies has room to grow by engaging further with literature from the global South. This book advances that aspect of the field.

23. Tompkins, 2.

24. Philip McMichael, "A Food Regime Genealogy," *The Journal of Peasant Studies* 36, no. 1 (2009): 140, doi.org/10.1080/03066150902820354.

25. Valeria Sodano, "Food Policy and Climate Change: Uncovering the Missing Links," in *Climate Change and Sustainable Development: Ethical Perspectives on Land Use and Food Production,* ed. Thomas Potthast and Simon Meisch (Wageningen, Netherlands: Wageningen Academic, 2012), 254.

26. P. R. Shukla et al., "Summary for Policymakers," in *Climate Change and Land: An IPCC Special Report on Climate Change, Desertification, Land Degradation, Sustainable Land Management, Food Security, and Greenhouse Gas Fluxes in Terrestrial Ecosystems,* ed. Shukla et al. (Geneva, Switzerland: Intergovernmental Panel on Climate Change, 2019), 10.

27. Shukla et al., 9–10, 17–18, 20.

28. Amartya Sen, *Poverty and Famines: An Essay on Entitlement and Deprivation* (New York: Oxford University Press, 1992); Josué de Castro, *The Geopolitics of Hunger* (1946; repr. New York: Monthly Review, 1977). I am grateful to Eve Buckley for mentioning de Castro's work.

29. Vandana Shiva, *Biopiracy: The Plunder of Nature and Knowledge* (Boston: South End, 1997).

30. See, e.g., Vishwas Satgar and Jane Cherry, "Climate and Food Inequality: The South African Food Sovereignty Campaign Response," *Globalizations* 17, no. 2 (2020): 321, doi.org/10.1080/14747731.2019.1652467.

31. Shukla et al., "Summary for Policymakers," 7.

32. Noah Zerbe, "The Global Politics of Local Food: Community Resistance and Resilience in Durban, South Africa," *Association of Concerned Africa Scholars* 88 (2012): 36.

33. Preethi Krishnan and Mangala Subramaniam, "Understanding the Right to Food Campaign in India," *The Global South* 8, no. 2 (2014): 101–18.

34. Julie Guthman, *Agrarian Dreams: The Paradox of Organic Farming in California,* 2nd ed. (Berkeley: University of California Press, 2014), 222.

35. As Josée Johnston and Shyon Baumann note, "foodie" denotes "a person who devotes considerable time and energy to eating and learning about good food, however . . . defined" (*Foodies: Democracy and Distinction in the Gourmet Foodscape,* 2nd ed. [New York: Routledge, 2015], x).

36. Jennifer Wenzel, "Consumption for the Common Good? Commodity Biography Film in an Age of Postconsumerism," *Public Culture* 23, no. 3 (2011): 598, doi.org/10.1215/08992363-1336426.

37. Johnston and Baumann, *Foodies,* x.

38. Tellingly, Guthman's seminal account of California organic farming credits "[a]n Englishman, Sir Albert Howard" with being "one of the first to articulate an alternative to agriculture as usual, on the basis of his work in India" (*Agrarian Dreams,* 4). Missing is an acknowledgment of Indian actors or their long history of agroecology, collapsed here into "his work." Moments like this illustrate the

need for a postcolonial lens to complement important work by scholars such as Guthman.

39. Shameem Black, "Recipes for Cosmopolitanism: Cooking Across Borders in the South Asian Diaspora," *Frontiers* 31, no. 1 (2010): 4–5, doi.org/10.1353/fro .0.0071.

40. Anita Mannur, *Culinary Fictions: Food in South Asian Diasporic Culture* (Philadelphia: Temple University Press, 2010), 7.

41. Berry is associated with new agrarianism, Erdrich with the Native American Renaissance, and Berg with bioregionalism. See Wendell Berry, *The Art of the Commonplace: The Agrarian Essays of Wendell Berry*, ed. Norman Wirzba (Washington, D.C.: Counterpoint, 2002); Louise Erdrich, "Where I Ought to Be: A Writer's Sense of Place," *The New York Times*, July 28, 1985, nytimes.com; Peter Berg, *The Biosphere and the Bioregion: Essential Writings of Peter Berg*, ed. Cheryll Glotfelty and Eve Quesnet (New York: Routledge, 2014).

42. Cajetan Iheka, *African Ecomedia: Network Forms, Planetary Politics* (Durham, N.C.: Duke University Press, 2021), 19.

43. DeLoughrey and Handley, "Introduction," 4.

44. Susie O'Brien, "Articulating a World of Difference: Ecocriticism, Postcolonialism and Globalization," *Canadian Literature* 170/171 (Autumn/Winter 2001): 142.

45. Dipesh Chakrabarty, "The Climate of History: Four Theses," *Critical Inquiry* 35, no. 2 (2009): 213.

46. Satgar and Cherry, "Climate and Food Inequality," 319.

47. Satgar and Cherry, 319.

48. See, e.g., Heather Davis and Zoe Todd, "On the Importance of a Date, or Decolonizing the Anthropocene," *ACME* 14, no. 4 (2017): 761–80; Kathryn Yusoff, *A Billion Black Anthropocenes or None*, Manifold ed. (Minneapolis: University of Minnesota Press, 2019); Nicholas Mirzoeff, "It's Not the Anthropocene, It's The White Supremacy Scene; or, The Geological Color Line," in *After Extinction*, ed. Richard Grusin (Minneapolis: University of Minnesota Press, 2016), 123–49; Jason W. Moore, *Capitalism in the Web of Life: Ecology and the Accumulation of Capital* (New York: Verso, 2015).

49. McKittrick explores the "interplay between geographies of domination" and "a different sense of (black) place" in *Demonic Grounds: Black Women and the Cartographies of Struggle* (Minneapolis: University of Minnesota Press, 2006), x.

50. Byron Caminero-Santangelo, "In Place: Tourism, Cosmopolitan Bioregionalism, and Zakes Mda's *Heart of Redness*," in DeLoughrey and Handley, *Postcolonial Ecologies*, 291–307; Sverker Sörlin, "Scaling the Planetary Humanities: Environmental Globalization and the Arctic," in *The Routledge Companion to the Environmental Humanities*, ed. Ursula Heise et al. (Florence: Routledge, 2017), 438; Thomas Lekan, "Fractal Earth: Visualizing the Global Environment in the Anthropocene," *Environmental Humanities* 5 (2014): 171–201, doi.org/10 .1215/22011919-3615469.

51. Rebecca Walkowitz, *Born Translated: The Contemporary Novel in the Age of World Literature* (New York: Columbia University Press, 2015), chapter 3; Alexander Beecroft, *An Ecology of World Literature: From Antiquity to the Present Day* (New York: Verso, 2015), 283; Debjani Ganguly, *This Thing Called the World: The Contemporary Novel as Global Form* (Durham, N.C.: Duke University Press, 2016), 4, 21.

52. Ursula Heise, "Globality, Difference, and the International Turn in Ecocriticism," *PMLA* 128, no. 3 (2013): 637, doi.org/10.1632/pmla.2013.128.3.636. "Global novel" scholarship often seeks to correct problems with "world literature" as articulated by Franco Moretti, Pascale Casanova, and David Damrosch, which adapts world-systems theory to literary study in ways that are arguably Western-centric. See Shu-mei Shih, "Global Literature and the Technologies of Recognition," *PMLA* 119, no. 1 (2004): 16–30; Aamir Mufti, "Orientalism and the Institution of World Literatures," *Critical Inquiry* 36 (2010): 458–93.

53. Heise, 638.

54. Laura Wright, "The Township Gaze: A Postcolonial Ecofeminist Theory for Touring the New South Africa," in *Contemporary Perspectives on Ecofeminism,* ed. Mary Phillips and Nick Rumens (London: Routledge, 2015), 152. On South Asia's overidentification with "Indian food," see chapter 2 of the present volume.

55. On *dabbawallas,* see chapter 1 of Anita Mannur, *Intimate Eating: Racialized Spaces and Radical Futures* (Durham, N.C.: Duke University Press, 2022).

56. Joël Cabalion and Delphine Thivet, "Introduction: Who Speaks for the Village? Representing and Practicing the 'Rural' in India from the Colonial to the Post-Colonial," in "Representations of the 'Rural' in India from the Colonial to the Postcolonial," special issue, *South Asia Multidisciplinary Academic Journal* 21 (2019): 4, doi.org/10.4000/samaj.5384.

57. Andy Clarno, *Neoliberal Apartheid: Palestine/Israel and South Africa after 1994* (Chicago: University of Chicago Press, 2017), 11.

58. In this book, I capitalize "Black" when referring to North America and to the field of Black studies, out of respect to Black writers and activists who situate this as an empowering gesture, and to understandings of Black as a transnational political and intellectual identification in resistance to white supremacy. Similarly, I capitalize "Indigenous" when referring to the field of Indigenous studies and to Indigenous peoples in what is commonly called North America and/or in contexts of broadly transnational solidarities, where this tends to be the preferred practice. However, I do not capitalize "black," "white," "coloured," or "indigenous" when referring to South Africa, where capitalization of racial terms has a very different history associated with apartheid nomenclature. My choice about this follows Asanda Ngoasheng, who frames using "small letters for racial identifiers" as a "political statement to remind us that race is a social construct" ("Debunking the Apartheid Spatial Grid: Developing a Socially Just Architecture Curriculum at a University of Technology," *Journal of Asian and African*

Studies 56, no. 1 [2021]: 147n2, doi.org/10.1177/0021909620946856), and Amanda Lock Swarr, whose writing brought Ngoasheng's work to my attention (see *Envisioning African Intersex: Challenging Colonial and Racist Legacies in South African Medicine* [Durham, N.C.: Duke University Press, 2023], 17, 174n35).

While there are varying ideas in the United States about capitalizing "white," I never do, because I reject the violent usages of capitalization by white supremacist groups.

The term "coloured" is discussed at length in chapter 4. I maintain its South African spelling as a way of noting the word's history, "contestation," and ongoing administrative and community use in South Africa, following Zimitri Erasmus (*Race Otherwise: Forging a New Humanism for South Africa* [Johannesburg: Wits University Press, 2017], 147n2).

59. Clarno, *Neoliberal Apartheid,* 31–34.

60. Deborah Posel, "Races to Consume: Revisiting South Africa's History of Race, Consumption, and the Struggle for Freedom," *Ethnic and Racial Studies* 33, no. 2 (2010): 158, doi.org/10.1080/01419870903428505.

61. C. P. Chandrasekhar, "Notes on Neoliberalism and the Future of the Left," *Social Scientist* 39, no. 1/2 (2011): 24.

62. Ravinder Kaur, "'I Am India Shining': The Investor-Citizen and the Indelible Icon of Good Times," *The Journal of Asian Studies* 75, no. 3 (2016): 627.

63. Mukti Lakhi Mangharam, "Revealing Fictions: Neo-liberalism, Domestic Servants, and Thirty Umrigar's *The Space Between Us,*" *ariel: A Rreview of International English Literature* 49, no. 1 (2018): 83, doi.org/10.1353/ari.2018.0003.

64. See, e.g., Andrew van der Vlies, *Present Imperfect* (Oxford: Oxford University Press, 2017); Rita Barnard and Andrew van der Vlies, ed., *South African Writing in Transition* (New York: Bloomsbury Academic, 2019).

65. "Ocean Grabbing: Robbing People of Dignity and Livelihoods," in *The Journalist,* September 3, 2014, thejournalist.org.za, accessed November 21, 2022.

66. Christiana Louwa et al., "Carbon Trading and Geoengineering Not the Solution to the Climate Catastrophe: Statement of the World Forum of Fisher Peoples (WFFP)," November 14, 2022, worldfishers.org, accessed December 1, 2022.

67. Rozena Maart, *Rosa's District 6* (Ontario: Coach House / TSAR, 2004), 16–17.

68. Shaun Viljoen, introduction in Tina Smith et al., *District Six Huis Kombuis: Food & Memory Cookbook* (Rondebosch, South Africa: Quivertree, 2016), 9.

69. Smith et al., *District Six Huis Kombuis,* 32, 34, 59, 69, 187, 233, 265.

70. Smith et al., 195.

71. See Rejoice Mazvirevesa Chipuriro and Kezia Batisai, "House of Hunger: The Weaponisation and Politicisation of Food (Protests) in South Africa during COVID-19," in "South African Food Studies," ed. Ben Jamieson Stanley, Desiree Lewis, and Lynn Mafofo, special issue, *Matatu* 54, no. 1 (2023): 134-154, doi.org/10.1163/18757421-05401008.

72. David Arnold, "Pandemic India: Coronavirus and the Uses of History," in *The Pandemic: Perspectives on Asia* (New York: Columbia University Press, 2020), 18–19, 16.

1. From Famine to Farmer Suicides

1. Lee's suicide has been repeatedly covered in global media; see, e.g., Peter Tinti, "In 2003, A Farmer Killed Himself to Protest Globalization. Little Has Changed," *Vice,* September 12, 2019, vice.com.

2. Joël Cabalion and Delphine Thivet, "Who Speaks for the Village? Representing and Practicing the 'Rural' in India from the Colonial to the Post-Colonial," 14, in "Representations of the 'Rural' in India from the Colonial to the Postcolonial," ed. Cabalion and Thivet, special issue, *South Asia Multidisciplinary Academic Journal* 21 (2019), doi.org/10.4000/samaj.5384.

3. Cabalion and Thivet, 2.

4. See Rajender Kaur, "The Vexed Question of Peasant Passivity: Nationalist Discourse and the Debate on Peasant Resistance in Literary Representations of the Bengal Famine of 1943," *Journal of Postcolonial Writing* 50, no. 3 (2014): 279, doi.org/10.1080/17449855.2012.752153.

5. Rakhshanda Jalil, "Almost Entirely Ignored by Urban India, the Farmer Once Held Pride of Place in Literature and Poetry," *Scroll.in,* December 1, 2018, scroll.in. See also Swasti Pachauri, "Decolonising the 'Idea of the Farmer' through the Eyes of Munshi Premchand," *Down to Earth,* April 23, 2019, https://www.downtoearth.org.in.

6. Cabalion and Thivet, "Who Speaks for the Village?," 2; Food and Agriculture Organization of the United Nations, "India at a Glance," FAO, fao.org.

7. Cabalion and Thivet, "Who Speaks for the Village?," 4.

8. Paul R. Greenough, *Prosperity and Misery in Modern Bengal: The Famine of 1943–1944* (Oxford: Oxford University Press, 1982), 55.

9. Greenough, 61, 65, 69–70, 78, 81–83, 73.

10. Srimanjari, *Through War and Famine: Bengal 1939–45* (Hyderabad, India: Orient BlackSwan, 2009), 159, 94; Amartya Sen, *Poverty and Famines: An Essay on Entitlement and Deprivation* (New York: Oxford University Press, 1992), 65.

11. Srimanjari, *Through War and Famine,* 90, 164.

12. British rulers did prohibit the export of rice in 1942, but allowed so many exceptions that the order was ineffectual. The prohibition was actually to Bengal's disadvantage, because Bengal could not then import from other parts of India (Srimanjari, 152–53, 161–63; Sen, *Poverty and Famines,* 77).

13. Srimanjari, *Through War and Famine,* 100.

14. Greenough, *Prosperity and Misery,* 89, 94.

15. Srimanjari, *Through War and Famine,* 101, 119–20.

16. Srimanjari, 118.

17. Srimanjari, 119–20.

18. Sen, *Poverty and Famines,* 71–72.

19. Sen, 57.

20. Sen, 57.

21. Srimanjari, *Through War and Famine*, 169–70, 201.

22. Srimanjari, 210–11.

23. Srimanjari, 186.

24. Sen, *Poverty and Famines*, 52.

25. Srimanjari, *Through War and Famine*, 155; Greenough, *Prosperity and Misery*, 264–65.

26. Greenough, *Prosperity and Misery*, 265, 272.

27. Sen, *Poverty and Famines*, 1.

28. Sen, 45.

29. Sen, 45, 49.

30. Sen, 49.

31. Sen, 49 (emphasis original).

32. Greenough, for one, critiques a "nationalist" approach that blames "foreign rulers," recognizing how caste, class, gender, and rural status structured vulnerability (*Prosperity and Misery*, 272–73). Nonetheless, inequalities within Bengali society were themselves exacerbated by British rule. Whereas Greenough excuses actions by the British governments of India and Bengal as mistakes, most scholars acknowledge deliberate violence or at least criminal negligence. Srimanjari holds British wartime policy responsible, while noting that the air of unease prompted by the British administration encouraged hoarding and speculation among Bengali elites (*Through War and Famine*, 157). For Cormac Ó Gráda, hoarding by Indian elites has been overemphasized, distracting from the main problem: British "lack of political will to divert foodstuffs from the war effort" (*Eating People is Wrong, and Other Essays on Famine, Its Past, and Its Future* [Princeton, N.J.: Princeton University Press, 2015], 90).

33. Devereux finds Sen fixated on economics to the exclusion of politics ("Introduction: From 'Old Famines' to 'New Famines,'" in *The New Famines: Why Famines Persist in an Era of Globalization*, ed. Stephen Devereux [New York: Routledge, 2007], 9; see also Devereux, "Sen's Entitlement Approach: Critiques and Counter-Critiques," in *New Famines*, 66–89), but I see commonality between Sen's entitlement approach and Devereux's "'new famine' thinking": *Poverty and Famines* doesn't separate economics from politics, but rather suggests that stratified "exchange entitlements" are rooted in policy choices that are themselves failures of political accountability.

34. Devereux, "Introduction," 9, 21. On common pro-GM arguments, see Ian Scoones, "Can GM Crops Prevent Famine in Africa?," in Devereux, *New Famines*, 312–35.

35. Scoones, "Can GM Crops Prevent Famine in Africa?," 315.

36. Dan Banik, "Is Democracy the Answer? Famine Prevention in Two Indian States," in Devereux, *New Famines*, 300, 290.

37. Sourit Bhattacharya, *Postcolonial Modernity and the Indian Novel: On Catastrophic Realism* (Cham, Switzerland: Palgrave Macmillan, 2020), 71.

38. Kaur, "Vexed Question," 273–74.

39. Bhattacharya, *Postcolonial Modernity,* 54–55.

40. Bhattacharya, 47, 45, 59.

41. See B. Stanley, "Paddy, Mangoes, and Molasses Scum: Food Regimes and the Modernist Novel in *The Tale of Hansuli Turn*," in *Modernism and Food Studies*, ed. Jessica Martell, Adam Fajardo, and Philip Keel Geheber (Gainesville: University Press of Florida, 2019), 261–77.

42. Tarashankar Bandyopadhyay, *The Tale of Hansuli Turn,* trans. Ben Conisbee Baer (New York: Columbia University Press, 2011), 224–25, 345. Subsequent references will be to this translation text as *Hansuli Turn* and indicated parenthetically in this chapter; references specifically to the language in the original will be marked with the original title, *Hansuli Banker Upakathā.*

43. Ben Conisbee Baer, "Introduction" in Tarashankar, *Tale of Hansuli Turn,* xxii.

44. Angela Eyre, "Organized Peasant Resistance in Fiction: *The Sword and the Sickle* and *The Lives of Others,*" 14, in Cabalion and Thivet, "Representations of the 'Rural' in India," doi.org/10.4000/samaj.5498.

45. Eyre, 25.

46. I am influenced by Carruth's own efforts to instead consider agrarian and gastronomic discourse together (*Global Appetites: American Power and the Literature of Food* [Cambridge: Cambridge University Press, 2013], 8).

47. Baer, "Introduction," x.

48. Kyla Wazana Tompkins, *Racial Indigestion: Eating Bodies in the 19th Century* (New York: New York University Press, 2012), 4.

49. Parama Roy, *Alimentary Tracts: Appetites, Aversions, and the Postcolonial* (Durham, N.C.: Duke University Press, 2010), 62.

50. Roy, 46.

51. Baer, "Introduction," xix.

52. Baer, xvi.

53. See Stanley, "Paddy, Mangoes, and Molasses Scum."

54. Scoones, "Can GM Crops Prevent Famine in Africa?," 330, note 2.

55. Certain transgenic crops require less spraying, such as Bt (*Bacillus thuringiensis* gene) varieties that contain their own insecticides. However, others are engineered to resist herbicides, and therefore may encourage increased spraying for weeds, such as Monsanto's Roundup Ready varieties.

56. Devereux, "Introduction," 21.

57. Ian Scoones, "Mobilizing against GM Crops," *Journal of Agrarian Change* 8, nos. 2–3 (2008): 333.

58. Annika J. Kettenburg, Jan Haspach, David J. Abson, and Joern Fischer, "From Disagreements to Dialogue: Unpacking the Golden Rice Debate," *Sustainability Science* 13 (2018): 1470, doi.org/10.1007/s11625-018-0577-y.

59. Cabalion and Thivet, "Who Speaks for the Village?," 5.

60. Cabalion and Thivet, 5.

61. Scoones, "Can GM Crops Prevent Famine in Africa?," 313; Akhil Gupta, "Farming as a Speculative Activity: The Ecological Basis of Farmers' Suicides in India," in *The Routledge Companion to the Environmental Humanities,* ed. Ursula Heise et al. (London: Routledge, 2017), 190.

62. Anne-Lise François, "O Happy Living Things: Frankenfoods and the Bounds of Wordsworthian Natural Piety," *Diacritics* 33, no. 2 (2003): 63, jstor .org/stable/3805795.

63. Two weeks after this acquisition closed, a lawsuit claiming that Roundup causes cancer succeeded, holding Bayer responsible for $289.2 million in damages (later cut back to $78.5 million). This led a *Wall Street Journal* commentator to dub Bayer's acquisition of Monsanto "one of the worst corporate deals in recent memory" (Ruth Bender, "How Bayer-Monsanto Became One of the Worst Corporate Deals—in 12 Charts," *Wall Street Journal,* August 28, 2019, wsj.com).

64. Luca Lombardo, "Genetic Use Restriction Technologies: A Review," *Plant Biotechnology Journal* 12 (2014): 995, doi.org/10.1111/pbi.12242.

65. Lombardo, 996.

66. Lombardo, 1000.

67. See Eda Kranakis, "Patents and Power: European Patent-System Integration in the Context of Globalization," *Technology and Culture* 48, no. 4 (2007): 689–728, jstor.org/stable/40061325.

68. Lombardo, "Genetic Use Restriction Technologies," 996, 1000, 1002.

69. Scoones, "Mobilizing against GM Crops," 316–20.

70. Lombardo, "Genetic Use Restriction Technologies," 996.

71. It might seem that "the monitoring of patent right infringement by unauthorized use of seeds, if not impossible, is at least time-consuming and expensive," leading to the interests of biotech companies in GURTs (Lombardo, 1000). However, avenues of forcibly broadening intellectual property protection (even without GURTs) are demonstrated by Monsanto's behavior in relation to Roundup Ready soybeans cultivated in Argentina. Because Monsanto's patent on future progeny was valid in Europe but not in Argentina, Monsanto demanded testing of soybeans imported from Argentina to Europe, confirmed traces of its patented gene, and sued European importers for patent infringement. This led to attempts to pass costs on to Argentina and its farmers, forcing Argentina to bring its patent regulations in line with those of the European Patent Office (EPO). (EPO's decision to allow patents that involve multiple plant varieties and that cover future plant progeny are themselves controversial, given objections to the patenting of life-forms.) This constitutes a significant attack on Argentina's sovereignty, as well as a burden passed on to farmers. See Kranakis, "Patents and Power," 721–23. On TRIPS, see Amy Kapczynski, "Harmonization and Its Discontents: A Case Study of TRIPS Implementation in India's Pharmaceutical Sector," *California Law Review* 97, no. 6 (2009): 1571–649, jstor.org/stable/20677920.

72. Vandana Shiva, *Biopiracy: The Plunder of Nature and Knowledge* (Boston: South End, 1997), 5.

73. Shiva, 2.

74. Shiva, 66.

75. Scoones, "Mobilizing against GM Crops," 339.

76. Scoones, 340.

77. Barun S. Mitra, quoted in Per-Åke Holmquist and Suzanne Khardalian, *Bullshit* (New York: Cinema Guild, 2005), film, 51:32.

78. The 2020 Baker Creek Heirloom Seeds (LLC) catalog invites customers to "support the GMO-free food chain" and to join the Spring Planting Festival held at the Gettle family's farm in Mansfield, Mo., featuring Vandana Shiva, pictured grinning and holding a pumpkin (pp. 2, 4).

79. Vandana Shiva, *Making Peace with the Earth* (London: Pluto, 2013), 3.

80. Vandana Shiva, interviewed in Bill Moyers, "Vandana Shiva on the Problem with Genetically Modified Seeds," episode of *Moyers & Company* (Doctoroff Media Group), July 13, 2012, video, 3:43–7:19.

81. For more on this argument, see B. Stanley, "Global Gardens: Beyond the Human in Zoë Wicomb's Fiction," *Global South* 14, no. 2 (2020): 68–84, jstor.org/stable/10.2979/globalsouth.14.2.05.

82. Scoones, "Mobilizing Against GM Crops," 326; see also 337–38, 334.

83. Ravinder Kaur, "'I Am India Shining': The Investor-Citizen and the Indelible Icon of Good Times," *Journal of Asian Studies* 75, no. 3 (2016): 634–35, jstor.org/stable/44166281.

84. Kaur, 635.

85. While the "investor-citizen" idea is epitomized by the India Shining campaign, Kaur argues that this problematic figure has, like the Bharatiya Janata Party (BJP) and like neoliberalism, outlived the colossal failure of India Shining itself ("I Am India Shining," 624). India Shining provoked outrage and contributed to the BJP's defeat in 2004 elections, but the BJP and Narendra Modi have returned to power since and maintained similar rhetorics. As Cabalion and Thivet remark, it is as if 2004's "lessons regarding the rural–urban divide and myth of the Indian middle class had been obliterated in the BJP's memory" ("Who Speaks for the Village?," 8).

86. India Shining campaign ad quoted in Kaur, "I Am India Shining," 638–39.

87. Kaur, 638–40.

88. See Vandana Shiva and Kunwar Jalees, *Farmer Suicides in India* (New Delhi: Research Foundation for Science, Technology, and Ecology, 2005), 3.

89. Gupta, "Farming as a Speculative Activity," 185.

90. Gupta, 185–86; Daniel Münster, "Farmers' Suicides as Public Death: Politics, Agency and Statistics in a Suicide-Prone District (South India)," *Modern Asian Studies* 49, no. 5 (2015): 1592, jstor.org/stable/24495439.

91. Gupta, "Farming as a Speculative Activity," 188.

92. See Shiva and Jalees, *Farmer Suicides*.

93. Gupta claims that activists such as Shiva may have obscured these larger structures by focusing the narrative on GM seeds ("Farming as a Speculative Activity," 185, 188). I would instead suggest that we view Shiva's critique of GM seeds as part of her larger condemnation of neoliberal extractivism since the Green Revolution. I see Shiva's and Gupta's works as aligned in their attention to how neoliberalism, combined with environmental degradation, produces peasant precarity.

94. Gupta, "Farming as a Speculative Activity," 192.

95. Gupta, 190, 189.

96. B. B. Mohanty, "'We Are Like the Living Dead': Farmer Suicides in Maharashtra, Western India," *Journal of Peasant Studies* 32, no. 2 (2005): 267, doi.org/10.1080/03066150500094485.

97. Nilotpal Kumar, *Unraveling Farmer Suicides in India: Egoism and Masculinity in Peasant Life* (New Delhi: Oxford University Press, 2017), 139.

98. Kumar, 164.

99. Kumar, 141–42, 145.

100. Kumar, 143.

101. Kumar, 147, 151.

102. Carruth, *Global Appetites,* 8.

103. Gupta, "Farming as a Speculative Activity," 192.

104. Kumar, *Unraveling Farmer Suicides,* 4.

105. Kumar details a "fake farm suicide" in which neighbors counterfeited debt transactions to make twin suicides by a wife and husband seem debt-motivated (rather than motivated by marital troubles) so the children might get compensation money (*Unraveling Farmer Suicides,* 197–98). But can marital problems be separated from an atmosphere of economic precarity, debt, and other farmers' deaths? Are these children not entitled to financial assistance from the state? The framework of "fake farm suicides" could, I worry, discredit arguments that neoliberalism really does harm marginal agriculturalists, and play into state attempts to limit financial assistance.

106. While there is a real village called Peepli in Rajasthan and a Pipli between Haryana and Uttar Pradesh, the film locates Peepli in "Mukhya Pradesh"—likely an ironic name for Madhya Pradesh in central India. (*Peepli Live* was filmed in Madhya Pradesh, using a number of Adivasi debut actors from that state; see "Aamir's *Peepli Live* Going to Sundance Film Fest," Sify Movies, December 7, 2009, sify.com.) *Mukhya* means "head" or chief in Hindi, whereas *Madhya* means "central" or "middle." In 2016, several years after the release of *Peepli Live,* urban development minister Venkaiah Naidu commented that top-level corruption in India has been resolved and that "Madhya Pradesh has become *mukhya* [chief] Pradesh with surplus water, electricity and good roads" ("Madhya Pradesh Has Now Become Mukhya Pradesh: Venkaiah," *Times of India,* October 24, 2016, timesofindia.indiatimes.com)—the type of portrait that the film debunks.

107. M. K. Raghavendra, "*Peepli Live* and the Gesture of Concern," *Economic and Political Weekly* 45, no. 39 (2010): 14, jstor.org/stable/25742112.

108. Anusha Rizvi, writer and director, *Peepli Live,* codirected by Mahmood Farooqui and produced by Aamir Khan and Kiran Rao (Mumbai: Aamir Khan Productions and UTV Motion Pictures, 2010), Netflix film, 12:37.

109. Rizvi, 1:21:42, 1:22:38. Quotations are from the film's English subtitles. Rakesh is speaking Hindi, while Nandita is speaking a combination of Hindi and English. Nandita's primary use of English marks her urban middle-class status in this film primarily in Hindi.

110. Rizvi, 1:23:45.

111. Rizvi, 1:23:29.

112. Rizvi, 1:40:05.

113. Rizvi, 1:41:46.

114. Boris Trbic, "Less Dancing, More Darkness: Peepli Live," *Metro Magazine* 166 (2010): 64–68.

115. Raghavendra, "*Peepli Live* and the Gesture of Concern," 14.

116. "Vidarbha Farmers Demand *Peepli* Ban," *Times of India,* August 15, 2010, n.p., timesofindia.indiatimes.com.

2. Nutmeg and Disordered Eating

1. Amitav Ghosh, *The Nutmeg's Curse: Parables for a Planet in Crisis* (Chicago: University of Chicago Press, 2021), 11.

2. Ghosh, 10.

3. Ghosh, 8.

4. See Sidney Mintz, *Sweetness and Power: The Place of Sugar in Modern History* (New York: Penguin, 1985); Erika Rappaport, *A Thirst for Empire: How Tea Shaped the Modern World* (Princeton, N.J.: Princeton University Press, 2017); Mark Kurlansky, *Salt: A World History* (New York: Walker, 2002).

5. Ghosh, *Nutmeg's Curse,* 92.

6. Julia Adeney Thomas et al., "JAS Round Table on Amitav Ghosh, *The Great Derangement: Climate Change and the Unthinkable,*" *Journal of Asian Studies* 75, no. 4 (2016): 936, doi.org/10.1017/S0021911816001121.

7. Amitav Ghosh, *The Great Derangement: Climate Change and the Unthinkable* (Chicago: University of Chicago Press, 2016), 15.

8. Ghosh, 16.

9. Ghosh, 17.

10. Ghosh, 61.

11. Introducing a 2018 special issue of *Studies in the Novel* on climate change fiction, Stef Craps and Rick Crownshaw cast Ghosh's "wholesale condemnation of modern literature for the absence of climate change within its pages" as representative of an ecocritical "pessimism" that their issue will contest ("Introduction: The Rising Tide of Climate Change Fiction," in "The Rising Tide of Climate Change Fiction," ed. Craps and Crownshaw, special issue, *Studies in the Novel* 50,

no. 1 [2018]: 1, doi.org/10.1353/sdn.2018.0000). Elsewhere literary critics invoke
Ghosh to discuss how a novel *can* meet the representational challenges of climate change, as in Shouhei Tanaka's reading of Karen Tei Yamashita ("The Great
Arrangement: Planetary Petrofiction and Novel Futures," *Modern Fiction Studies* 66, no. 1 [2020]: 190–215, doi.org/10.1353/mfs.2020.0008). Ghosh's comments
have also been raised—often with ambivalence or as a point to disprove—by one
or more panelists during seminars on climate change and fiction at the American Comparative Literature Association, in which I have participated, for several years running (2019–2021). However, the interdisciplinary roundtable on
The Great Derangement in *Journal of Asian Studies* cited in note 6 above mostly
praises the work. While a full catalog of responses to *The Great Derangement*
would be book-length, these examples suggests that many literary scholars find
Ghosh too pessimistic about fiction's potential to represent climate change, even
as his argument has been generative for interdisciplinary conversations.

12. Ghosh, *Great Derangement*, 9.

13. Ghosh, 79.

14. Ghosh, 80.

15. Literary historians such as Nancy Armstrong have long "lamented the
privatization of human experience" by European novels that reduce the political
to the psychological, as Stephanie LeMenager notes ("Climate Change and the
Struggle for Genre," in *Anthropocene Reading: Literary History in Geologic Times,*
ed. Tobias Menely and Jesse Oak Taylor [University Park, Pa.: Penn State University Press, 2017], 223). Postwar American fiction, as cultivated in MFA programs,
likewise provokes charges of being "self-involved" given its autoreferential interest in the psyche (see Mark McGurl, *The Program Era: Postwar Fiction and the
Rise of Creative Writing* [Cambridge, Mass.: Harvard University Press, 2009], 31,
32). Such elite realism and (post)modernism, valued by global Northern institutions such as the *London Review of Books,* the *New York Review of Books,* and
The Literary Journal, is what Ghosh defines as "serious fiction." This includes
fiction not only by authors from the North, but also by postcolonial cosmopoli-
tans such as Ghosh himself (raised in India, Bangladesh, and Sri Lanka; trained
at Oxford; living in New York) because British and American institutions governing the tastes of the "dominant culture" have an outsized influence on global
South writers (See Ghosh, *Great Derangement,* 7, 80, and "Biography," 2011,
accessed July 29, 2018, amitavghosh.com; see also Thomas et al., "JAS Round
Table," 929).

16. While "Anthropocene" and "climate change" are not equivalent, they are
arguably associated in the popular imagination, and are key terms in overlapping critical conversations about fiction.

17. Adam Trexler, *Anthropocene Fictions: The Novel in a Time of Climate
Change* (Charlottesville: University of Virginia Press, 2015), 12.

18. Trexler, 13.

19. LeMenager, "Climate Change," 223.

20. Ghosh dismisses "cli-fi" by describing it as a subset of science fiction that locates climate change solely in the future (Ghosh, *Great Derangement,* 24). This runs counter to the logic of much sci-fi, where a different world functions as an allegory for our own. (I am indebted to a conversation with Ursula Heise at the 2017 ASLE conference for this gloss.) Moreover, the literary-critical storm around cli-fi has addressed not only genre fictions such as sci-fi, crime, and romance, but also realism. For example, Adeline Johns-Putra (drawing on Sylvia Mayer) delineates two strands of climate change fiction: a "futurist" type indebted to science fiction, and a "realist strand" (*Climate Change and the Contemporary Novel* [Cambridge: Cambridge University Press, 2019], 37–38). LeMenager notes that "fictions that have been called cli-fi are remarkably diverse," ranging across "realism, sci-fi, and even memoir" ("Climate Change," 222–23). Kate Marshall identifies an emergent trend of realist "novels of the Anthropocene" that self-consciously locate themselves within geological or epochal time ("What Are the Novels of the Anthropocene? American Fiction in Geological Time," *American Literary History* 27, no. 3 [2015]: 529). Ranging beyond fiction to photography and soundscapes, a 2020 special issue of *Resilience: A Journal of the Environmental Humanities* theorizes an aesthetics of "climate realism" (Lynn Badia, Marija Cetinić, and Jeff Diamanti, eds., "Climate Realism," special issue, *Resilience* 7, no. 2–3 [2020]).

21. Ghosh, *Great Derangement,* 11.

22. See, e.g., Johns-Putra, *Climate Change*; Trexler, *Anthropocene Fictions*; Craps and Crownshaw, "Introduction."

23. The category "cli-fi" was coined by Dan Bloom, an American journalist whose "Cli-Fi Report Global" website (2021; accessed August 5, 2022, cli-fi.net/) offers a tool for educators and readers assembling lists of "cli-fi," but also exemplifies the unstated assumption that American texts would be at the center of the category. Bloom suggests that, for an "extensive bibliography," users consult Susanne Leikam and Julia Leyda's "Cli-Fi in American Studies," which explicitly centers on the United States because, "as one of the most prolific generators, disseminators, and adaptors of literary and cultural texts, North America participates at the forefront in the recent spate of cli-fi. . . . As one of the key fossil-fuel consumers with global political influence, North America, particularly the United States, features prominently in cli-fi narratives" ("Cli-Fi in American Studies: A Research Bibliography," *American Studies Journal* 62 [2017], doi.org/10.18422/62-08). While I agree on the importance of critiquing the U.S. role in carbon capitalism and geopolitics, I disagree with the assertion that countries beyond North America are less "prolific" in producing literary and cultural texts and can therefore be deemphasized.

24. Amitav Ghosh, *The Hungry Tide* (New York: First Mariner, 2006), 179. Subsequent references to this text are indicated parenthetically.

25. Ghosh, *Great Derangement,* 9. Climate change "became a matter of personal urgency" when research for *The Hungry Tide* acquainted Ghosh with sea

level rise in the Sundarbans (Ghosh quoted in Sabine Russ, "Amitav Ghosh and Curt Stager," interview over email, *Bomb* 139 [2017]: 44).

26. For an expanded version of this argument in the context of pedagogy, see Ben Jamieson Stanley and Emily Davis, "Climate Fiction and the Global South," in *Teaching the Literature of Climate Change,* ed. Debby Rosenthal (New York: Modern Language Association, 2024).

27. LeMenager, "Climate Change," 225.

28. Anita Mannur, *Intimate Eating: Racialized Spaces and Radical Futures* (Durham, N.C.: Duke University Press, 2022), 108.

29. Madhur Jaffrey, *A Taste of India* (New York: Atheneum, 1986), 10, 11.

30. Jaffrey, 13–14.

31. Mannur, *Intimate Eating,* 30, 65.

32. Shameem Black, "Recipes for Cosmopolitanism: Cooking Across Borders in the South Asian Diaspora," *Frontiers* 31, no. 1 (2010): 6. See also Parama Roy, *Alimentary Tracts: Appetites, Aversions, and the Postcolonial* (Durham, N.C.: Duke University Press, 2010), 28; Delores B. Phillips, "The Globe at the Table: How Madhur Jaffrey's *World Vegetarian* Reconfigures the World," in *Eating Asian America: A Food Studies Reader,* ed. Robert Ji-Song Ku et al. (New York: New York University Press, 2013), 371–92.

33. Rappaport, *Thirst for Empire,* 87.

34. Jayeeta Sharma, *Empire's Garden: Assam and the Making of India* (Durham, N.C.: Duke University Press, 2011), 17, 8.

35. Sharma, 3.

36. Ghosh, *Nutmeg's Curse,* 54.

37. Kyle Whyte, "Indigenous Food Systems, Environmental Justice, and Settler-Industrial States," in *Global Food, Global Justice: Essays on Eating under Globalization,* ed. M. Rawlinson and C. Ward (Newcastle upon Tyne: Cambridge Scholars), 3–4.

38. Sharma, *Empire's Garden,* 6; Roy, *Alimentary Tracts,* 6.

39. Although descended from Adivasi groups such as the Munda, Oraon, and Santhal, tea tribes are not Scheduled Tribes (STs) because they are not autochthonous to Assam. ST status would provide welfare, land rights, and educational opportunities, but could intensify conflict with other STs. Sectarian conflict has been significant in Assam in recent years, with insurgent groups critiquing the postcolonial state's extension of colonial exploitation but often asserting nativist claims to territory, rather than proposing to broaden social equality (see Indrajit Sharma, "Identity Politics and Search for Liberation: Tea Tribes of Assam," *Economic and Political Weekly* 53, no. 9 [2018], epw.in/journal; Sharma, *Empire's Garden,* 16).

40. Sharma, *Empire's Garden,* 9.

41. Gautam Bhadra, *From an Imperial Product to a National Drink: The Culture of Tea Consumption in Modern India* (Kolkata: Centre for Studies in Social Sciences, Calcutta, and Tea Board India, 2005), 12, 2.

42. Paul R. Greenough, *Prosperity and Misery in Modern Bengal: The Famine of 1943–1944* (New York: Oxford University Press, 1982), 76.

43. Bhadra, *From an Imperial Product,* 2, 17, 19.

44. Bhadra, 27.

45. Mannur, *Intimate Eating,* 136.

46. Salman Rushdie, *Midnight's Children* (New York: Random House, 2006), 529.

47. Pankaj Mishra, "Midnight's Grandchildren," *Prospect,* April 1997, https://www.prospectmagazine.co.uk/. Mishra is speaking specifically about Indian writing in English. He notes that literature in other languages has wider circulation within India but is ignored in the West.

48. Hurubie Meko and Lauren D'Avolio, "Rushdie Stabbed Roughly 10 Times in Premeditated Attack, Prosecutors Say," *New York Times,* August 13, 2022, accessed August 14, 2022, nytimes.com.

49. Roy, *Alimentary Tracts,* 157. On disordered eating, see Graham Huggan and Helen Tiffin, *Postcolonial Ecocriticism: Literature, Animals, Environment,* 2nd ed. (New York: Routledge, 2015), 156–58, esp. note 4.

50. Divya Victor, "C is for Comorin and not Chutney," lines 1–7, in *Kith* (Albany, N.Y.: Fence; Toronto: BookThug, 2017), 193 (emphasis original); reprinted by permission of Divya Victor, with gratitude.

51. Anita Mannur, *Culinary Fictions: Food in South Asian Diasporic Culture* (Philadelphia: Temple University Press, 2010), 108.

52. Mannur, 8. See also chapter 2, "Consuming India," in Graham Huggan, *The Postcolonial Exotic* (New York: Routledge, 2001).

53. Mannur, *Intimate Eating,* 61.

54. Richard Grove, *Green Imperialism* (Cambridge: Cambridge University Press, 1995).

55. Michael L. Lewis, *Inventing Global Ecology: Tracking the Biodiversity Ideal in India, 1947–1997* (Athens: Ohio University Press, 2004), 139–40.

56. Lewis, 139.

57. I follow Ghosh's usage "Morichjhãpi," except when quoting sources that use "Marichjhapi" or "Morichjhanpi." These three transliterations all refer to the same place.

58. The deaths at Morichjhãpi were reported in the Indian press but there was never a governmental inquiry. Mallick condemns an accompanying "silence" in the academic community yet notes that "[s]cholars are constrained not to criticize regimes that provide them with research access" ("Refugee Resettlement in Forest Reserves: West Bengal Policy Reversal and the Marichjhapi Massacre," *Journal of Asian Studies* 58, no. 1 [1999]: 112). Amnesty International and Human Rights Watch purportedly ignored messages from Mallick, while academic journals could not find peers willing to review Mallick's piece, such that Mallick's account was not published until 1999 (120). When fictionalized in *The Hungry Tide,* however, the massacre became a topic of discussion in the international literary academy and classroom.

59. Annu Jalais, "Dwelling on Morichjhanpi: When Tigers Become 'Citizens,' Refugees 'Tiger-Food,'" *Economic and Political Weekly* 40, no. 17 (2005): 1759; Mallick, "Refugee Resettlement," 107–8.

60. Jalais, "Dwelling on Morichjhanpi," 1761; see also Mallick, "Refugee Resettlement," 114.

61. Jalais, "Dwelling on Morichjhanpi," 1761.

62. Lewis, *Inventing Global Ecology*, 200.

63. Mallick, "Refugee Resettlement," 118.

64. Ghosh describes traveling in the Sundarbans with Jalais as an important part of his research ("Author's Note," *The Hungry Tide*, 331–32).

65. Ramachandra Guha and Joan Martinez-Alier, *Varieties of Environmentalism: Essays North and South* (London: Earthscan, 1997), 116.

66. Pheng Cheah, *What is a World? On Postcolonial Literature as World Literature* (Durham, N.C.: Duke University Press, 2016), 254.

67. See, e.g., Rajender Kaur, "'Home Is Where the Oracella [*sic*] Are': Toward a New Paradigm of Transcultural Ecocritical Engagement in Amitav Ghosh's *The Hungry Tide*," *ISLE* 14, no. 1 (2007): 127–28; Ursula Heise, *Imagining Extinction: The Cultural Meanings of Endangered Species* (Chicago: University of Chicago Press, 2016); Upamanyu Pablo Mukherjee, *Postcolonial Environments: Nature, Culture and the Contemporary Indian Novel in English* (New York: Palgrave Macmillan, 2010).

68. Ghosh, *Great Derangement*, 78.

69. Judith A. Carney and Richard Nicholas Rosomoff, *In the Shadow of Slavery: Africa's Botanical Legacy in the Atlantic World* (Berkeley: University of California Press, 2009), 34–36, 42.

70. Carney and Rosomoff, 43–44.

71. Steve Striffler and Mark Moberg, "Introduction," in *Banana Wars: Power, Production, and History in the Americas,* ed. Striffler and Moberg (Durham, N.C.: Duke University Press, 2003), 6, 14; Robert Gottlieb and Anupama Joshi, *Food Justice* (Cambridge, Mass.: MIT Press, 2010), 104–5, 26.

72. On *The Big Banana,* see chapter 2 in Cajetan Iheka, *African Ecomedia: Network Forms, Planetary Politics* (Durham, N.C.: Duke University Press, 2021).

73. As Cheah puts it, *The Hungry Tide* "self-reflexively alludes to its vocation as world literature" (*What is a World,* 250). The novel self-consciously enters a global literary canon both by making global economic and ecological systems manifest and by referencing intertexts as disparate as the poetry of Rainer Maria Rilke, the Bengali folk tradition of *jatra*, Joseph Conrad's *The Heart of Darkness,* and more. *The Hungry Tide*'s system of meanings, then, transpires in conversation with literature from many geographies.

74. Dan Koeppel, *Banana: The Fate of the Fruit That Changed the World* (New York: Hudson Street, 2008), 31; Striffler and Moberg, "Introduction," 9.

75. Susan Willis, "Learning from the Banana," *American Quarterly* 39, no. 4 (1987): 591.

76. Mannur, *Culinary Fictions,* 5.

77. Susan Sontag, *Illness as Metaphor* (New York: Farrar, Straus, and Giroux, 1977), 58–59.

78. Susan Bordo, "Not Just 'a White Girl's Thing': The Changing Face of Food and Body Image Problems," in *Food and Culture: A Reader,* ed. Carole Counihan and Penny Van Esterik, 3rd ed. (New York: Routledge, 2013), 265–75.

79. V. G. Julie Rajan, "Fragmented Self: Violence and Body Image among South Asian American Women," in *Body Evidence: Intimate Violence against South Asian Women in America,* ed. Shamita Das Dasgupta (New Brunswick, N.J.: Rutgers University Press, 2007), 95.

80. Rajan, 100.

81. Rajan, 102–3.

82. Sunita Puri, "Happiness in Quotation Marks," in *Stories of Illness and Healing: Women Write Their Bodies,* ed. Sayantani DasGupta and Marsha Hurst (Kent, Ohio: Kent State University Press, 2007), 265.

83. Bordo, "Not Just 'a White Girl's Thing,'" 268.

84. On fish's lack of appeal for conservation projects, see Heise, *Imagining Extinction,* 23.

85. Rob Nixon, *Slow Violence and the Environmentalism of the Poor* (Cambridge, Mass.: Harvard University Press, 2011), 151.

86. Ghosh, *Nutmeg's Curse,* 154–55.

87. Ghosh, 156.

88. Ghosh, 157.

89. Ghosh, 157–58 (emphasis mine).

3. Hunger versus Taste

1. "The Hermanus Whale Crier," hermanus.co.za, accessed December 8, 2016.

2. Zakes Mda, *The Whale Caller* (New York: Farrar, Straus and Giroux, 2005), 14. Subsequent references to this novel are indicated parenthetically.

3. "Coloured," a term for multiracial persons, has been variously debated, reclaimed, and rejected since the end of apartheid; see chapter 4.

4. Serge Raemaekers et al., "Review of the Causes of the Rise of the Illegal South African Abalone Fishery and Consequent Closure of the Rights-Based Fishery," *Ocean and Coastal Management,* 2011, 433–34, doi.org/10.1016/j.ocecoa man.2011.02.001.

5. Legacy of Slavery Art Exhibition, Cape Town Museum, capetownmu seum.org.za, accessed November 21, 2022; Tina Smith et al., *District Six Huis Kombuis: Food and Memory Cookbook* (Rondebosch, South Africa: Quivertree, 2016), 22.

6. Maria Hauck and Neville A. Sweij, "A Case Study of Abalone Poaching in South Africa and its Impact on Fisheries Management," *ICES Journal of*

Marine Science 56 (1999): 1028, doi.org/10.1006/jmsc.1999.0534; Raemaekers et al., "Review of the Causes," 438.

7. Raemaekers et al., "Review of the Causes," 433–38.

8. Lesley Green, *Rock | Water | Life: Ecology and Humanities for a Decolonial South Africa* (Durham, N.C.: Duke University Press, 2020), 190.

9. Edwin Muchapondwa, Kerrie Brick, and Martine Visser, *Abalone Conservation in the Presence of Drug Use and Corruption: Implications for Its Management in South Africa,* Environment for Development Discussion Paper Series, November 2012, 2, jstor.org/stable/resrep14970.

10. Green, *Rock | Water | Life,* 191.

11. Green, 194, 195–97.

12. Leftist commentators sometimes describe South Africa's transition as a move from racial apartheid to class apartheid: the mass democratic platform of the anti-apartheid struggle devolved into a neoliberal agenda as the African National Congress (ANC) transformed from a resistance movement to the reigning political party, leaving most black South Africans in poverty. See Patrick Bond, *Elite Transition: From Apartheid to Neoliberalism in South Africa,* revised and expanded ed. (London: Pluto, 2014).

13. Andrew Bennie and Athish Satgoor, "Deepening the Just Transition through Food Sovereignty and the Solidarity Economy," in *The Climate Crisis: South African and Global Democratic and Eco-Socialist Alternatives,* ed. Vishwas Satgar et al. (Johannesburg: Wits University Press, 2018), 297.

14. Ramachandra Guha and Joan Martinez-Alier, *Varieties of Environmentalism: Essays North and South* (London: Earthscan, 1997), xxi.

15. Ramachandra Guha, *Environmentalism: A Global History* (New York: Longman, 2000), 99–100.

16. Bram Büscher, *Transforming the Frontier* (Durham, N.C.: Duke University Press, 2013), 57.

17. Pheng Cheah, *What Is a World? On Postcolonial Literature as World Literature* (Durham, N.C.: Duke University Press, 2016), 255.

18. Büscher, *Transforming the Frontier,* 55.

19. Büscher, 59, 54. See also Steven Robins and Kees van der Waal, "'Model Tribes' and Iconic Conservationists? Tracking the Makuleke Restitution Case in Kruger National Park," in *Land, Memory, Reconstruction, and Justice: Perspectives on Land Claims in South Africa,* ed. Cherryl Walker et al. (Athens: Ohio University Press, 2010), 163–180; B. Stanley and Walter Dana Phillips, "South African Ecocriticism: Landscapes, Animals, and Environmental Justice," in *The Oxford Handbook of Ecocriticism Online,* ed. Greg Garrard (Oxford: Oxford University Press, 2017), doi.org/10.1093/oxfordhb/9780199935338.013.154.

20. Laura M. Pereira et al., "Chefs as Change-Makers from the Kitchen: Indigenous Knowledge and Traditional Food as Sustainability Innovations," *Global Sustainability* 2, no. 16 (2019): 4, doi.org/10.1017/S2059479819000139; see also Chris Hattingh and John P. Spencer, "Homosexual Not Homogeneous: A

Motivation-Based Typology of Gay Leisure Travelers Holidaying in Cape Town, South Africa," *Journal of Homosexuality* 67, no. 6 (2020): 781, doi.org/10.1080/00 918369.2018.1555393.

21. Wine tourism in the Western Cape grew 16 percent from 2016 to 2017. When selecting wineries, 85 percent of tourists considered practices such as organic farming, carbon neutrality, and "social equality" ("2nd Annual South African Food and Wine Tourism Report in Partnership with Wesgro," *Explore Sideways: The Art of Wine and Travel,* March 12, 2018).

22. Christian M. Rogerson, "Developing Beer Tourism in South Africa: International Perspectives," in *African Journal of Hospitality, Tourism and Leisure* 4, no. 1 (2015): 3, ajhtl.com.

23. UNESCO Creative Cities Network, "Overstrand Hermanus," accessed November 22, 2021, en.unesco.org; "Hermanus Overstrand South Africa's First UNESCO City of Gastronomy," *Nosy Rosy* (blog), accessed November 22, 2021, nosyrosy.co.za/hermanus-overstrand-south-africas-first-unesco-city-of-gastro nomy/.

24. Agatha Herman, *Practising Empowerment in Post-Apartheid South Africa: Wine, Ethics and Development* (London: Routledge, 2018), 4.

25. Herman, 35.

26. Bennie and Satgoor, "Deepening the Just Transition," 297.

27. Mpumzi Zuzile, "Land Reform: Nearly 900 Underutilised Farms to be Made Available," *Sunday Times,* October 1, 2020, timeslive.co.za.

28. Jane Battersby, Maya Marshak, and Ncedo Mngqibisa, "Mapping the Invisible: The Informal Food Economy of Cape Town, South Africa," *Urban Food Security Series,* no. 24 (South African Migration Program, 2016), 1.

29. This reflects a pattern on the African continent and elsewhere in the global South in which "land grabs" by multinationals displace smallholders; see Nnimmo Bassey, "The Climate Crisis and the Struggle for African Food Sovereignty," in Satgar, *Climate Crisis,* 190.

30. Battersby, Marshak, and Mngqibisa, "Mapping the Invisible," 2; Pereira et al, "Chefs as Change-Markers," 4.

31. Battersby et al, 6–9.

32. Bennie and Satgoor, "Deepening the Just Transition," 297.

33. "Conserving the African Penguins; A Recipe for Success," *Cape Town Green Map,* updated October 7, 2022, accessed 18 October 18, 2023, capetown greenmap.co.za.

34. Pereira et al., "Chefs as Change-Makers," 4.

35. Pereira et al., 4.

36. Nompumelelo Mqwebu quoted in Melissa Twigg, "How Johannesburg Became the Foodie Capital of South Africa," *The Independent,* Feb 26, 2018, accessed November 22, 2022, independent.co.uk.

37. Nompumelelo Mqwebu, *Through the Eyes of an African Chef* (West Beach, South Africa: Quickfox, 2017), 19.

38. Kobus van der Merwe, *Strandveldfood: A West Coast Odyssey,* photography by Jac de Villiers (Paternoster, South Africa: Wolfgat, 2022), 14.

39. Van der Merwe, 16.

40. Van der Merwe, 14.

41. Renata Coetzee, foreword to van der Merwe, *Strandveldfood,* 13.

42. Van der Merwe, *Strandveldfood,* 19.

43. Van der Merwe, 19.

44. Gayle Ravenscroft, "Plight of Paternoster," *The Cape Times,* January 29, 1981, 12. Courtesy of the District Six Collection, University of the Western Cape Library.

45. The Journalist (website), "Ocean Grabbing: Robbing People of Dignity and Livelihoods," *The Journalist,* September 3, 2014, accessed November 21, 2022, thejournalist.org.za.

46. Jenny Willis, "Finding Herself at Home: Rochelle Karolus and the Wolfgat Restaurant," *Good Food Jobs* (blog), June 25, 2019, accessed November 27, 2022, goodfoodjobs.com/blog.

47. Pereira et al., "Chefs as Change-Makers," 4.

48. Van der Merwe, *Strandveldfood,* 19, 49.

49. Coetzee, foreword to *Strandveldfood,* 13.

50. Wolfgat, accessed November 21, 2021, wolfgat.co.za/bookonline.

51. La Via Campesina, "The International Peasant's Voice," *La Via Campesina,* July 7, 2017, brochure, 2, viacampesina.org/en (when originally accessed, this page was simply plain text, but the same definition is now found in the brochure there).

52. Raj Patel, "Food Sovereignty: Power, Gender, and the Right to Food," *PLoS Medicine* 9, no. 6 (2012): 1; Eric Holt-Giménez, "From Food Crisis to Food Sovereignty," in *Taking Food Public: Redefining Foodways in a Changing World,* ed. Psyche Williams-Forson and Carole Counihan (New York: Routledge, 2012), 595.

53. Food Sovereignty Campaign Coordination Committee, "Declaration of South African Food Sovereignty Campaign," *Climate & Capitalism,* 5 March 2015, climateandcapitalism.com.

54. The Journalist, "Ocean Grabbing."

55. Eric Holt-Giménez, "Introduction: Strategies to Transform Our Food Systems," in *Food Movements Unite!,* ed. Eric Holt-Giménez (Oakland, Calif.: Food First, 2011), 2.

56. Food Sovereignty Campaign Coordination Committee, "Declaration."

57. Food Sovereignty Campaign Coordination Committee, "Declaration;" Vishwas Satgar and Jane Cherry, "Climate and Food Inequality: The South African Food Sovereignty Campaign Response," *Globalizations* 17, no. 2 (2020): 326–29.

58. South African Food Sovereignty Campaign (website), "COVID-19 Solidarity," accessed January 21, 2021, safsc.org.za/.

59. Satgar and Cherry, "Climate and Food Inequality," 326–27.

60. Food Sovereignty Campaign Coordination Committee, "Declaration."

61. Tabara Ndiaye and Mariamé Ouattara, "Rural Women Create Thriving Food Systems in West Africa," trans. Deanna Drake Seeba, in Holt-Giménez, *Food Movements Unite!,* 53.

62. Ndiaye and Ouattara, 55–56.

63. Ndiaye and Ouattara, 55, 59–60.

64. Ndiaye and Ouattara, 66–67.

65. See Elaine Salo, "Food Is an African Feminist Issue," *Matatu* 54, no. 1 (2023): 17–23.

66. Born in 1948, Mda grew up under apartheid in Soweto and the rural Eastern Cape before moving to Lesotho to join his father in exile; he characterizes his own family as the "aristocrats of the revolution" (Rachel Donadio, "Post-Apartheid Fiction," *The New York Times Magazine,* December 3, 2006, nytimes .com). Mda studied internationally, writes in English, and travels between the United States and South Africa as professor emeritus of English at Ohio University, lecturer at Johns Hopkins, and "extraordinary professor" of English at the University of the Western Cape. He is also one of few black South African writers published in the global North (by Farrar, Straus and Giroux) and acclaimed internationally, with novels translated into twenty-one languages and numerous awards. See Zakes Mda and Elly Williams, "An Interview with Zakes Mda," *The Missouri Review* 28, no. 2 (2005): 63–65, doi.org/10.1353/mis.2006.0034; Zakes Mda faculty page, Johns Hopkins University, accessed August 14, 2023, advanced .jhu.edu/directory/zakes-mda/; Zanemvula Kizito Mda, *South African History Online,* accessed January 29, 2020, sahistory.org.za.

67. An exception is Katherine Hallemeier's work, which underscores the lack of attention to food in Mda criticism ("An Art of Hunger: Gender and the Politics of Food Distribution in Zakes Mda's South Africa," *The Journal of Commonwealth Literature* 53, no. 3 [2018]: 379–93, doi.org/10.1177/0021989416658783).

68. See, for example, Laura Wright, *Wilderness into Civilized Shapes* (Athens: University of Georgia Press, 2010); Meg Samuelson, "Historical Time, Gender, and the 'New' South Africa in Zakes Mda's *The Heart of Redness,*" *Sephis* 2, no. 2 (2006): 15–18; Astrid Feldbrügge, "The Human and the Non-Human World in Zakes Mda's *The Heart of Redness* and *the Whale Caller*" in *Local Natures, Global Responsibilities: Ecocritical Perspectives on the New English Literatures,* ed. Lauren Volkmann et al. (Amsterdam: Rodopi, 2010), 151–66; Byron Caminero-Santangelo, "In Place: Tourism, Cosmopolitan Bioregionalism, and Zakes Mda's *The Heart of Redness,*" in *Postcolonial Ecologies,* ed. Elizabeth DeLoughrey and George Handley (Oxford: Oxford University Press, 2011), 291–307; Jonathan Steinwand, "What the Whales Would Tell Us," in DeLoughrey and Handley, *Postcolonial Ecologies,* 182–99.

69. Allison Carruth, "Wily Ecologies: Comic Futures for American Environmentalism," in *American Literary History* 30, no. 1 (2018): 111, muse.jhu.edu/ article/685535.

70. Mda draws on Jeff Peires's 1989 historical account, *The Dead Will Arise* (Jennifer Wenzel, *Bulletproof: Afterlives of Anticolonial Prophecy in South Africa and Beyond* [Chicago: University of Chicago Press, 2010], 19).

71. Zakes Mda, *The Heart of Redness* (New York: Picador, 2000), 71. Subsequent references to this novel are indicated parenthetically.

72. For the seminal Americanist critique of "wilderness" ideology, see William Cronon, "The Trouble with Wilderness; or, Getting Back to the Wrong Nature," in *Uncommon Ground: Rethinking the Human Place in Nature,* ed. William Cronon (New York: Norton, 1995), 69–90. For a transnational view, see Guha, *Environmentalism.*

73. Rita Barnard, *Apartheid and Beyond: South African Writers and the Politics of Place* (Oxford: Oxford University Press, 2015), 166.

74. Meg Samuelson sees Mda's and Camagu's perspectives as aligned, which leads her to find Mda's novel antifeminist. She alleges that Mda uses "the female form to house his 'heart of redness,'" epitomizing the novel's "reliance on a set of gendered tropes spawned in both colonial and nationalist discourse" ("Historical Time," 17). While I share Samuelson's feminist commitments, this reading elides the savvy integration of subsistence food gathering and the tourism economy by female characters and, emphasizing Qukezwa's representation as "reproductive body," ignores Qukezwa's voice. At the least, the gender politics of *The Heart of Redness* are more complex.

75. European colonial authorities in South Africa and elsewhere ruled by "customary law," naming a member of each "tribe" as "chief." These chiefs possessed judicial, legislative, executive, *and* administrative power. As Mahmood Mamdani emphasizes, "one should not be misled by the nomenclature [chief] into thinking of this as a holdover from the precolonial era." Instead, customary law was based on colonialists ossifying one of many African political traditions, "the one with the least historical depth, that of nineteenth-century conquest states" (Mahmood Mamdani, *Citizen and Subject: Contemporary Africa and the Legacy of Late Colonialism* [Princeton, N.J.: Princeton University Press, 1996], 22–23).

76. Mqwebu, *Through the Eyes,* 35, 19.

77. Zakes Mda faculty page.

78. For Wendy Woodward, Sharisha's eventual death exemplifies how compassion arises only when animals are individualized ("The Killing (Off) of Animals in Some Southern African Fiction, or 'Why Does Every Animal Story Have to Be Sad?,'" *Journal of Literary Studies* 23, no. 3 [2007]: 301, 295–97, doi.org/10.1080/02564710701568139). For Harry Sewlall, *The Whale Caller* "celebrates the possibility of existing in harmony with nature" ("Border Crossings: Mapping the Human and the Non-Human in Zakes Mda's *The Whale Caller,*" *Scrutiny2* 12, no. 1 [2007]: 129–30, doi.org/10.1080/18125440701398612), whereas Graham Huggan and Helen Tiffin tackle the "profoundly difficult subject" of bestiality (*Postcolonial Ecocriticism: Literature, Animals, Environment,* 2nd ed. [New York: Routledge,

2015], 211). These three readings contextualize Mda's representation of human–whale relations differently, but they share a limitation: the authors engage only parts of the novel about whales, ignoring how Mda intertwines animal themes with social justice and consumerism.

79. Clare Barker argues that postcolonial writers represent disability as "radiant affliction": a sign of colonial violence and pain but simultaneously a trope that "sets in motion more positive stories of knowledge, care, and cultural strength." For Barker, postcolonial narratives of disability offer conceptual resources for recognizing notions of "normality" as culturally contingent and reimagining futurity ("'Radiant Affliction': Disability Narratives in Postcolonial Literature," in *The Cambridge Companion to Literature and Disability,* ed. Clare Barker and Stuart Murray [Cambridge: Cambridge University Press, 2018], 105). In Mda's novel, disabilities are troubling metaphors for the damages caused by neoliberal-era inequality, but also can be read as literal manifestations of that regime complexly intersecting with race and class. In this way, *The Whale Caller* proves problematic yet open to a recuperative reading of disability as *both* metaphor for other oppressions *and* material entanglement, the type of approach advocated by Sami Schalk (see chapter 1 in *Bodyminds Reimagined: (Dis)ability, Race, and Gender in Black Women's Speculative Fiction* [Durham, N.C.: Duke University Press, 2018]).

80. Deborah Posel, "Races to Consume: Revisiting South Africa's History of Race, Consumption and the Struggle for Freedom," *Ethnic and Racial Studies* 33, no. 2 (2010): 161, doi.org/10.1080/01419870903428505.

81. Marina Moskowitz, *Standard of Living: The Measure of the Middle Class in Modern America* (Baltimore, Md.: Johns Hopkins University Press, 2004), 3, 4.

82. Raj Patel, *Stuffed and Starved: The Hidden Battle for the World Food System* (Brooklyn, N.Y.: Melville House, 2012), 252–53.

83. Nehanda Radio, "Malema Ate Sushi off Naked Women with Me—Kenny Kunene," September 13, 2016, nehandaradio.com.

84. Township tours, which bring busloads of visitors into low-income areas, have been critiqued for invading people's homes and rendering poverty a spectacle. "Cultural villages" simulate or reenact African traditions, often with little cultural accuracy, as satirized in *The Heart of Redness.* See Laura Wright, "The Township Gaze: A Postcolonial Ecofeminist Theory for Touring the New South Africa," in *Contemporary Perspectives on Ecofeminism,* edited by Mary Phillips and Nick Rumens (New York: Routledge, 2015), 150–67; Morgan Ndlovu, "Cultural Villages and Their Idea of South Africa: A Decolonial Critique," *International Journal of Critical Diversity* 1, no. 2 (2018): 33–41, jstor.org/stable/10.13169/intecritdivestud.1.2.0033.

85. Julie Guthman, "Fast Food / Organic Food: Reflexive Tastes and the Making of 'Yuppie Chow,'" in *Food and Culture: A Reader,* ed. Carole Counihan and Penny Van Esterik, 3rd ed. (New York: Routledge, 2013), 506.

86. Julie Guthman, *Agrarian Dreams: The Paradox of Organic Farming in California,* 2nd ed. (Berkeley: University of California Press, 2014), 20.

87. See Susie O'Brien, "'No Debt Outstanding': The Postcolonial Politics of Local Food," in *Environmental Criticism for the Twenty-First Century,* ed. Stephanie LeMenager, Teresa Shewry, and Ken Hiltner (New York: Routledge, 2011), 231–46.

88. Jennifer Wenzel, *The Disposition of Nature: Environmental Crisis and World Literature* (New York: Fordham University Press, 2020), 73.

89. Wenzel, 76–77.

90. Posel, "Races to Consume," 173.

4. Queer/Vegan Reading

1. Graham Boynton, "South Africa: Raise a Glass to Cape Cuisine," *Telegraph,* January 30, 2016, accessed April 16, 2018, telegraph.co.uk.

2. Boynton.

3. "Cape Malay" refers to Muslim Capetonian culture with these multiple ancestries.

4. On how Eurocentric accounts elide enslaved people's influence on Cape cuisine, see Marlene van Niekerk, "The Eating Afrikaner: Notes for a Concise Typology," in *Reshaping Remembrance: Critical Essays on Afrikaans Places of Memory,* ed. Albert Grundlingh and Siegfried Huigen (Amsterdam: Rozenberg, 2011), 6–7.

5. A 2010 conference on Wicomb at Stellenbosch University positioned the Cape as a "site of global intersections . . . that sutured into a new global economy Atlantic and Indian Ocean worlds," leading to special issues in *Current Writing* and *Safundi*; see Meg Samuelson, "Reading Zoë Wicomb's Cosmopolitan, Domestic and Recursive Settings," *Current Writing* 23, no. 2 (2011): 89, doi.org/10.1080/1013929X.2011.602903. See also Kai Easton and Derek Attridge, eds., *Zoë Wicomb and the Translocal: Writing Scotland and South Africa* (New York: Routledge, 2017).

6. See Antoinette Pretorius, "'Does the Girl Think of Nothing but Food?' Food as a Marker of Unhomeliness, Inauthenticity and Violence in Zoë Wicomb's *October*," *Food, Culture & Society* 18, no. 4 (2015): 645–57, doi.org/10.1080/15528 014.2015.1088194; Caitlin E. Stobie, "'My Culture in a Tupperware': Situational Ethics in Zoë Wicomb's *October*," in *Through a Vegan Studies Lens: Textual Ethics and Lived Activism,* ed. Laura Wright (Reno: University of Nevada Press, 2019), 131–45; Derek Attridge, "'No Escape from Home': History, Affect and Art in Zoë Wicomb's Translocal Coincidences," in Easton and Attridge, *Zoë Wicomb and the Translocal,* 49–63.

7. Andrew van der Vlies, "Zoë Wicomb's Queer Cosmopolitanisms," *Safundi* 12, no. 3–4 (2011): 437, doi.org/10.1080/17533171.2011.586838.

8. Brenna Munro, *South Africa and the Dream of Love to Come: Queer Sexuality and the Struggle for Freedom* (Minneapolis: University of Minnesota Press, 2012), viii.

9. Neville Hoad, *African Intimacies: Race, Homosexuality, and Globalization* (Minneapolis: University of Minnesota Press, 2007), xviii, xxi.

10. Rahul Rao, "Global Homocapitalism," *Radical Philosophy* 194 (2015): 47, radicalphilosophy.com.

11. Hoad, *African Intimacies,* 73–74.

12. Natalie Oswin, "Producing Homonormativity in Neoliberal South Africa: Recognition, Redistribution, and the Equality Project," *Signs* 32, no. 3 (2007): 649, doi.org/10.1086/510337.

13. Roderick A. Ferguson, *One Dimensional Queer* (Cambridge: Polity, 2019), 3, 11.

14. Grant Andrews, "The Emergence of Black Queer Characters in Three Post-Apartheid Novels," *Tydskrif vir Letterkunde* 56, no. 2 (2019): 2, doi.org/10 .17159/2309-9070/tvl.v.56i2.5843.

15. Munro, *South Africa,* ix, xxv.

16. Andrew van der Vlies, "Queer Returns in Postapartheid Short Fiction: S.J. Naudé's *The Alphabet of Birds,*" in *South African Writing in Transition,* ed. Rita Barnard and Andrew van der Vlies (New York: Bloomsbury Academic, 2019), 210 (emphasis original).

17. Elizabeth Freeman, *Time Binds: Queer Temporalities, Queer Histories* (Durham, N.C.: Duke University Press, 2010), 3.

18. Freeman, 46.

19. Pheng Cheah, *What is a World? On Postcolonial Literature as World Literature* (Durham, N.C.: Duke University Press, 2016), 1.

20. Deborah Posel, "Races to Consume: Revisiting South Africa's History of Race, Consumption and the Struggle for Freedom," *Ethnic and Racial Studies* 33, no. 2 (2010): 159–60, doi.org/10.1080/01419870903428505.

21. Rita Barnard, "Introduction," in *South African Writing in Transition,* 4.

22. Barnard, 4.

23. Andrew van der Vlies, *Present Imperfect: Contemporary South African Writing* (Oxford: Oxford University Press, 2017), 18, 20.

24. Tendai Chiguware, "Assessing the Technological Relevance of South African Supermarkets in the Face of Changing Consumer Behaviour," in *Supermarket Retailing in Africa,* ed. Felix Adamu Nandonde and John L. Stanton (New York: Routledge, 2022), 92.

25. Stephen Peyton, William Moseley, and Jane Battersby, "Implications of Supermarket Expansion on Urban Food Security in Cape Town, South Africa," *African Geographical Review* 34, no. 1 (2015): 36–54, doi.org/10.1080/19376812.20 14.1003307.

26. Woolworths Holdings Limited, "Our History," 2017, accessed November 14, 2017, woolworths.co.za.

27. See, e.g., Dan Roodt, "Woolworths Boycotted Over Racist Hiring," *Space van Adriana: Afrikaner Boer Genocide Archive South Africa* (blog), September 3, 2012, accessed 30 August 2022, nolstuijt.wordpress.com.

28. Statement from Woolworths quoted in Fadia Salie, "Woolworths Douses Racial Fires," *News 24,* September 4, 2012, accessed August 30, 2022, news24.com.

29. Social media posts quoted in Verashni Pillay, "Woolworths: Y u no like whites?" on *Mail & Guardian,* September 5, 2012, accessed August 30, 2022, mg.co.za.

30. I retain the South African spelling of "coloured" to mark the term's specific meanings in South Africa. Zimitri Erasmus writes: "The spelling in South Africa should not be changed to that used in the USA because the meanings of these terms are context-specific. . . . In South Africa Coloured does not always mean black. . . . There is a history, from the 1920s to the present, of US projections of its black/white binary . . . onto the far more complex South African context." While race in the United States also exceeds a Black–white binary, "coloured" in South Africa is certainly not equivalent to "colored" in the United States—both because their meanings were never the same and because coloured in South Africa remains a category with more administrative and cultural currency today, even as it is also "contested." On my choice to capitalize "Black" in global Northern contexts but not capitalize "black" or "coloured" in reference to South Africa, see note 58 to the Introduction. Zimitri Erasmus, *Race Otherwise: Forging a New Humanism for South Africa* (Johannesburg: Wits University Press, 2017), 21.

31. Erasmus, 24.

32. Zoë Wicomb, "Shame and Identity: The Case of the Coloured in South Africa," in *Writing South Africa: Literature, Apartheid, and Democracy, 1970– 1995,* ed. Derek Attridge and Rosemary Jolly (Cambridge: Cambridge University Press, 1998), 93.

33. Zimitri Erasmus, "Reimagining Coloured Identities in Post-Apartheid South Africa," in *Coloured by History, Shaped by Place: New Perspectives on Coloured Identities in Cape Town,* ed. Zimitri Erasmus (Cape Town: Kwela, 2001), 20.

34. Erasmus, "Reimagining Coloured Identities," 16, 14.

35. Erasmus, *Race Otherwise,* 21, 89–90.

36. Zoë Wicomb, *Playing in the Light* (New York: New Press, 2006). At multiple points in the novel, Marion literally "is not hungry" (49) and "isn't hungry" (62); on a date, she has "no hunger for more information" about another person, metaphorizing lack of hunger as indicative of Marion's withdrawn personality (76). Subsequent references to *Playing in the Light* are indicated parenthetically.

37. Freeman, *Time Binds,* 39, 42.

38. I am riffing on the classic phrase that "race is the modality in which class is lived" in Stuart Hall, Chas Critcher, Tony Jefferson, John Clarke, and Brian Roberts, *Policing the Crisis: Mugging, the State, and Law and Order* (London: Macmillan, 1978), 394.

39. Van der Vlies, "Zoë Wicomb's Queer Cosmopolitanisms," 437.

40. Munro, *South Africa,* ix.

41. Van der Vlies, "Zoë Wicomb's Queer Cosmopolitanisms," 427.

42. Posel, "Races to Consume," 160.

43. Laura Wright, *The Vegan Studies Project: Food, Animals, and Gender in the Age of Terror* (Athens: University of Georgia Press, 2015), 109.

44. Laura Wright, "Doing Vegan Studies: An Introduction," in *Through a Vegan Studies Lens,* ix.

45. Wright, "Doing Vegan Studies," xvii.

46. Amie Breeze Harper, "Race as a 'Feeble Matter' in Veganism: Interrogating Whiteness, Geopolitical Privilege, and Consumption Philosophy of 'Cruelty-Free' Products," in "Women of Color in Critical Animal Studies," special issue, *Journal for Critical Animal Studies* 8, no. 3 (2010): 14, criticalanimalstudies.org (emphasis original).

47. Luis Cordeiro-Rodrigues, "The Racialization of Animal Advocacy in South Africa," *Ethnicities* 21, no. 4 (2021): 7, doi.org/10.1177/1468796820946762.

48. Wright, "Doing Vegan Studies," xvii.

49. Wright, xvii.

50. Anita Powell, "South Africa: Meet the Afri-Vegans: South Africa Slowly Embracing Veganism," *AllAfrica Global Media,* January 22, 2020, accessed January 4, 2021, allafrica.com; Cordeiro-Rodrigues, "Racialization of Animal Advocacy," 10.

51. Powell.

52. See the South African Vegan Society website at vegansociety.org.za/, accessed August 23, 2021.

53. Quoted in Marianne Thamm, "Fanon Meets Biko Meets J.M. Coetzee as UCT Academic Row over Food Highlights Racial Fault Lines," *The Daily Maverick,* July 13, 2016, accessed August 23, 2021, dailymaverick.co.za.

54. Thamm.

55. Quoted in Michael Glover, "Animals off the Menu: A Racist Proposal?," in *Animals, Race, and Multiculturalism,* ed. Luís Cordeiro-Rodrigues and Les Mitchell (Cham, Switzerland: Palgrave Macmillan, 2017), 177.

56. Glover, 177. As worldwide, most food in South Africa is produced via factory farming, itself a Western imposition that tends to increase meat consumption and related diseases. Economic benefits of factory farming accrue primarily to companies based in the global North (Cordeiro-Rodrigues, "Racialization of Animal Advocacy," 12).

57. Cordeiro-Rodrigues, "Racialization of Animal Advocacy," 15.

58. Cordeiro-Rodrigues, 5–6.

59. Maneesha Deckha, "Is Multiculturalism *Good* for Animals?," in Cordeiro-Rodrigues and Mitchell, *Animals, Race and Multiculturalism,* 79–80.

60. Deckha, 65–66.

61. Deckha, 66.

62. Stobie, "My Culture in a Tupperware," 134.

63. Evan Maina Mwangi, *The Postcolonial Animal: African Literature and Posthuman Ethics* (Ann Arbor: University of Michigan Press, 2019), 4.

64. Mwangi, 4.

65. Cordeiro-Rodrigues, "Racialization of Animal Advocacy," 11.

66. Zoë Wicomb, "Culture Beyond Color?" *Transition* 60 (1993): 31, jstor.org/stable/2934916.

67. Van Niekerk, "Eating Afrikaner," 9.

68. Van Niekerk, 9.

69. Stobie, "My Culture in a Tupperware," 133.

70. Author's observations, Cape Town, October 2022.

71. Anesu Mbizvo quoted in Powell, "South Africa."

72. Stobie, "My Culture in a Tupperware," 134.

73. On provincial–cosmopolitan postcolonial perspectives, see Meg Samuelson, "Unsettling Homes and the Provincial-Cosmopolitan Point of View in Zoë Wicomb's *October*," in Easton and Attridge, *Zoë Wicomb and the Translocal* 178–95.

74. "Staying with the trouble" is Donna Haraway's phrase to describe a praxis of "eschewing futurism," instead "learning to be truly present . . . as mortal critters entwined in myriad unfinished configurations of places, times, matters, meanings," refocusing our energies on how to live and die in multispecies "response-ability on a damaged earth" (*Staying with the Trouble: Making Kin in the Chthulucene* [Durham, N.C.: Duke University Press, 2016], 4, 1, 2). I invoke Haraway's language to suggest a food politics that would acknowledge and work within the complicities of eating with various forms of violence and damage, as a precondition to healing.

75. Zoë Wicomb, *October* (New York: New Press, 2014), 138. Subsequent references to *October* are indicated parenthetically.

76. On multiple identities of Namaqualanders as "Nama (Khoi), coloureds, *basters* (people of mixed ancestry—European, Khoi-San, Tswana), blacks and '*bruin Afrikaners*,'" see Steven Robins, "Fenced In By Ideas of Modernity: Land Struggles and Civic Activism in Namaqualand, 1980–93," in *From Comrades to Citizens: The South African Civics Movement and the Transition to Democracy*, ed. Glenn Adler and Jonny Steinberg (New York: St. Martin's, 2000), 131.

77. Sidsel Saugestad, *The Inconvenient Indigenous: Remote Area Development in Botswana, Donor Assistance, and the First People of the Kalahari* (Somerset, N.J.: Nordic Africa Institute, 2001), 89.

78. See "Dorper," *AGTR: Animal Genetics Training Resource,* February 18, 2010, accessed October 3, 2017, agtr.ilri.cgiar.org/dorper.

79. Oklahoma State University, "Breeds of Livestock—Dorper Sheep," OSU, June 4, 1999, accessed October 3, 2017, breeds.okstate.edu/sheep/dorper-sheep.html.

80. Oklahoma State University.

81. Mathilda Slabbert, "Animals and Nature: Mapping Storylines and Metaphors in David Kramer's Narratives," *Literator* 32, no. 1 (2011): 101.

82. Rachel Cooke, "Jane Grigson: Her Life and Legacy," *The Guardian,* March 2015, accessed August 30, 2021, theguardian.com.

83. Stobie, "My Culture in a Tupperware," 131, 140.

84. Carol J. Adams, *The Sexual Politics of Meat* (New York: Continuum, 1990), 52.

85. Adams, 52.

86. Freeman, *Time Binds,* xxii.

87. Adams, *Sexual Politics,* 40.

88. Barnard, "Introduction," 2, 4.

89. Emelia Quinn, "Notes on Vegan Camp," *PMLA* 135, no. 5 (2020): 927, doi .org/10.1632/pmla.2020.135.5.914.

90. Quinn, 921, 928.

91. Quinn, 922.

5. Purity and Porosity

1. Nikhil Anand, *Hydraulic City: Water and the Infrastructures of Citizenship in Mumbai* (Durham, N.C.: Duke University Press, 2017), vii–viii.

2. "Cape Town's Water Crisis Should Be a Wake-up Call," *Financial Times,* January 28, 2018, ft.com; "Cape Town Drought Is a Global Harbinger, Says NASA Scientist," *PBS NewsHour Weekend,* March 31, 2018, pbs.org/newshour.

3. Anand, *Hydraulic City,* 6.

4. Chief Magistrate of the Traskeian Territories, Umtata, to Resident Magistrate, Cofimvaba, December 31, 1912, source 1/COF, vol. 9/1/1, reference 7/6629/1912, Western Cape Archives and Records Service (WCARS), Cape Town. Reprinted by permission of WCARS.

5. Meeting minutes, town council of Stellenbosch, February 25, 1916, source 3/CT, vol. 4/1/3/68, reference 40/3, WCARS. Reprinted by permission of WCARS.

6. Johan P. Enqvist and Gina Ziervogel, "Water Governance and Justice in Cape Town: An Overview," *Wiley Interdisciplinary Reviews: Water* 6 (May 26, 2019): 3, doi.org/10.1002/wat2.1354; Lesley Green, *Rock | Water | Life: Ecology and Humanities for a Decolonial South Africa* (Durham, N.C.: Duke University Press, 2020), 48.

7. Patrick Bond, *Elite Transition: From Apartheid to Neoliberalism in South Africa,* rev. and expanded ed. (London: Pluto, 2014), 115–16.

8. Enqvist and Ziervogel, "Water Governance," 9, 5.

9. Pressured by the International Monetary Fund, South Africa privatized various services after the end of apartheid. French multinational Suez took over water management in Cape Town and Johannesburg, leading to fee spikes, supply cut-offs, a cholera outbreak, and protests. Protests against privatization were also a feature of Cape Town's 2017–2018 water crisis. See "Turning the Tide of Water Privatization—The Rise of the New Municipal Movement," Rapid

Transition Alliance, January 28, 2019, rapidtransition.org; Claudia Gastrow, review of *Scenes from a Dry City* (film, Simon Wood and François Verster, 2018), Africa is a Country, June 9, 2019, africasacountry.com; Bond, *Elite Transition*, 169.

10. This decision was probably motivated by competition between the African National Congress (ANC), in control of the national parliament, and the Democratic Alliance (DA) party governing the Western Cape Province and city of Cape Town (Enqvist and Ziervogel, "Water Governance," 8).

11. Nicholas Philip Simpson, Clifford D. Shearing, and Benoit Dupont, "When Anthropocene Shocks Contest Conventional Mentalities: A Case Study from Cape Town," *Climate and Development* 12, no. 2 (2020): 165, doi.org/10.1080/17565529.2019.1609402.

12. Simpson, Shearing, and Dupont, 165.

13. The City never (yet) reached "Day Zero," the popular name for the hypothetical second phase of the Critical Water Shortages Disaster Plan. Phase 1 began when the plan was published in October 2017; Phase 2, if dam levels dropped to 13.5 percent, would have meant turning off taps in homes (Enqvist and Ziervogel, "Water Governance," 8).

14. Lucy Rodina, "Water Resilience Lessons from Cape Town's Water Crisis," *Wiley Interdisciplinary Reviews: Water* 6 (August 4, 2019): 2–3, doi.org/10.1002/wat2.1376.

15. Enqvist and Ziervogel, "Water Governance," 9–10.

16. Rodina, "Water Resilience Lessons," 4.

17. Viva con Agua Foundation commissioned this work through Baz-Art Organisation, as part of a three-mural project intended to raise awareness about water and sanitation ("Viva con Agua Foundation," Baz-Art Organisation, baz-art.co.za, accessed July 31, 2023).

18. Eve Fairbanks, "Dry, the Beloved Country," *Huffington Post,* April 19, 2018, highline.huffingtonpost.com.

19. Enqvist and Ziervogel, "Water Governance," 12.

20. Enqvist and Ziervogel, 9–10.

21. Anand, *Hydraulic City,* 39 (emphasis original).

22. Anand, 40.

23. Anand, 40.

24. Stephen Graham, Renu Desai, and Colin McFarlane, "Water Wars in Mumbai," in *Infrastructural Lives: Urban Infrastructure in Context,* ed. S. Graham and C. McFarlane (New York: Routledge, 2015), 82.

25. Graham, Desai, and McFarlane, 66, 76.

26. Lisa Björkman, *Pipe Politics, Contested Waters: Embedded Infrastructures of Millennial Mumbai* (Durham, N.C.: Duke University Press, 2015), 1.

27. Björkman, 1; Graham, Desai, and McFarlane, "Water Wars," 63.

28. Björkman, *Pipe Politics,* 10.

29. Björkman, 11.

30. Björkman, 31.

31. Björkman, 61, 28–29, 32, 37.

32. Graham, Desai, and McFarlane, "Water Wars," 66; Amitav Ghosh, *The Great Derangement,* 38–9.

33. Graham, Desai, and McFarlane, 82; Björkman, *Pipe Politics,* 7.

34. Mike Muller, "Lessons from Cape Town's Drought," *Nature* 559, no. 7713 (2018): 175, doi.org/10.1038/d41586-018-05649-1.

35. Muller, 176.

36. Nicholas Philip Simpson, Clifford D. Shearing, and Benoit Dupont, "Gated Adaptation during the Cape Town Drought: Mentalities, Transitions and Pathways to Partial Nodes of Water Security," *Society & Natural Resources* 33, no. 8 (2020): 3, doi.org/10.1080/08941920.2020.1712756; Green, *Rock | Water | Life,* 45, 53.

37. Simpson, Shearing, and Dupont, "When Anthropocene Shocks," 164.

38. Simpson, Shearing, and Dupont, 166.

39. Mike Muller views Cape Town's crisis as symptomatic of distrust in "experts," i.e. engineers. While making a valid point that there is likely to be distrust in "a technical cadre" that is "still predominantly white and from the *ancien regime,*" Muller dismisses the social movements and "environmentalists"—such as groups hesitant about large-scale dam projects—on the other side of that divide ("Developmental States, the Role of Experts and Cape Town's Water Crisis," *New Agenda: South African Journal of Social and Economic Policy* 69, no. 69 [2018]: 17, journals.co.za/journal/nagenda/doi/abs/10.10520/EJC-e68657a6e).

40. Rodina, "Water Resilience Lessons," 3.

41. Enqvist and Ziervogel, "Water Governance," 2.

42. Enqvist and Ziervogel, 7.

43. Rodina, "Water Resilience Lessons," 3.

44. Henrietta Rose-Innes quoted in Gail Fincham, "Henrietta Rose-Innes in Conversation with Gail Fincham," *Tydskrif Vir Letterkunde* 56, no. 2 (2019): 89, journals.assaf.org.za. Popular within South Africa, Rose-Innes has not attained the global prestige of Amitav Ghosh, Zoë Wicomb, or Zakes Mda; however, she has gained international recognition since winning the 2008 Caine Prize for African Writing. Rose-Innes has now been translated into French and Spanish, the U.S. rights to *Nineveh* were acquired by Unnamed Press in 2016, and *Animalia Paradoxa* was published by Boiler House Press (based in East Anglia, UK, where Rose-Innes completed her MFA). See Aghogho Akpome, "Imagining Africa's Futures in Two Caine Prize-Winning Stories: Henrietta Rose-Innes's 'Poison' and NoViolet Bulawayo's 'Hitting Budapest,'" *Journal of Commonwealth Literature* 55, no. 1 (2020): 96–110, doi.org/10.1177/0021989418777840; Lily Meyer, "Henrietta Rose-Innes on Pests & Allegories: The South African Literary Star Talks about Her US Debut" (interview with Henrietta Rose-Innes), Electric Lit, November, 28, 2016, electricliterature.com.

45. Rose-Innes quoted in Fincham, "Henrietta Rose-Innes," 92 (emphasis original).

46. Henrietta Rose-Innes, *Nineveh* (Los Angeles: Unnamed, 2016), 99, 20. Subsequent references to *Nineveh* are indicated parenthetically.

47. Filippo Menozzi, "Invasive Species and the Territorial Machine: Shifting Interfaces between Ecology and the Postcolonial," *ariel: A Review of International English Literature* 44, no. 4 (2013): 194, doi.org/10.1353/ari.2013.0038.

48. "Neoliberal apartheid" is Andy Clarno's term for the restructured racial capitalism produced by "decolonization" and liberalization in South Africa and Palestine/Israel since 1994—characterized by surface-level claims to racial equality subtended by growing economic inequality and securitization, with "a rearticulation of the relationship between race and class" where some members of racially oppressed groups join an economic elite while the majority experience poverty and precarious employment (*Neoliberal Apartheid: Palestine/Israel and South Africa after 1994* [Chicago: University of Chicago Press, 2017], 11).

49. See Loren Kruger, "Cape Town and the Sustainable City in the Writing of Henrietta Rose-Innes," *Journal of Urban Cultural Studies* 2, no. 1–2 (2015): 15–33, doi.org/10.1386/jucs.2.1-2.15_1; Graham Riach, "Henrietta Rose-Innes and the Politics of Space," *Journal of Commonwealth Literature* 55, no. 1 (2020): 22–37, doi.org/10.1177/0021989418780937; Jennifer Wenzel, *The Disposition of Nature: Environmental Crisis and World Literature* (New York: Fordham University Press, 2020); Daniel Williams, "Life among the Vermin: *Nineveh* and Ecological Relocation," *Studies in the Novel* 50, no. 3 (2018): 419–40, doi.org/10.1353/sdn.2018.0028; Akpome, "Imagining Africa's Futures"; Menozzi, "Invasive Species."

50. Evan Maina Mwangi, *The Postcolonial Animal: African Literature and Posthuman Ethics* (Ann Arbor: University of Michigan Press, 2019).

51. Kruger, "Cape Town and the Sustainable City," 19.

52. The 2008 financial crisis prompted South Africa's steepest recession in seventeen years, with foreign investments and demand for exports crashing. Among African countries, South Africa was one of the worst affected because exports form a larger share of South Africa's economy; impacts rippled outward, however, to other countries in the Southern African Development Community (SADC). See Theresa Moyo, "Global Economic Crisis and South Africa's Manufacturing Industry: The Case of the Automotive, Textile and Clothing, and Mining Industries," in *The Global Financial and Economic Crisis in the South: Impact and Responses,* ed. José Luis León-Manríquez and Theresa Moyo (Dakar: CODESRIA, 2017), 119–53; Jennifer Cohen, "How the Global Economic Crisis Reaches Marginalised Workers: The Case of Street Traders in Johannesburg, South Africa," in "The Economic Crisis," special issue of *Gender and Development* 18, no. 2 (2010): 277–89, jstor.com/stable/25758904.

53. "The Changing Shoreline," sign at Waterkant and Bree Streets, Cape Town, sponsored by City of Cape Town, Cape Archives Depot, Nationaal Archief The Hague, and National Library of South Africa. Observed by the author on October 9, 2022.

54. "The Gateway to South Africa: Description of the Cape Town Foreshore Plan," *South African Railways*, May 1947, source 3/CT, vol. 4/2/1/1/685, reference 20/6/34K, WCARS, 7. Reprinted by permission of WCARS.

55. District Six Museum, Cape Town.

56. "Gateway to South Africa," WCARS, 21–23. Reprinted by permission of WCARS.

57. "Gateway to South Africa," 12, 14. Reprinted by permission of WCARS.

58. "Summary of Reclamation of the Foreshore, Table Bay," source PWD, vol. 2/7/14, reference 77, WCARS, my emphasis. Reprinted by permission of WCARS.

59. See Enqvist and Ziervogel, "Water Governance."

60. Sofia Samatar and Nnedi Okorafor quoted in Samatar, "Toward a Planetary History of Afrofuturism," *Research in African Literatures* 48, no. 4 (2017): 177, muse.jhu.edu/article/690428.

61. Samatar, 178.

62. Cajetan Iheka, *African Ecomedia: Network Forms, Planetary Politics* (Durham, N.C.: Duke University Press, 2021), 3.

63. Anna Lowenhaupt Tsing, *The Mushroom at the End of the World: On the Possibility of Life in Capitalist Ruins* (Princeton, N.J.: Princeton University Press, 2015), 61.

64. E. Dawson Varughese, "Post-Millennial Indian Dystopian Fiction: A Developing Canon of Precarity, (Im)purity and Ideas of India(nness)," *South Asia* 44, no. 6 (2021): 1042, doi.org/10.1080/00856401.2021.1972258.

65. Akbar quoted in Lopamudra Ghatak, "Urban Ghettos in Delhi and Mumbai Are Creating Isolated, Insular Experiences," review of *Leila* by Prayaag Akbar, *Economic Times,* April 29, 2017, accessed June 29, 2022, economictimes.indiatimes.com.

66. Arjun Appadurai, "Gastro-Politics in Hindu South Asia," *American Ethnologist* 8, no. 3 (1981): 507, doi.org/10.1525/ae.1981.8.3.02a00050.

67. Appadurai, 507.

68. Appadurai, 497, 498.

69. Appadurai, 495.

70. Parama Roy, *Alimentary Tracts: Appetites, Aversions, and the Postcolonial* (Durham, N.C.: Duke University Press, 2010), 7–8.

71. Sambaiah Gundimeda and V. S. Ashwin, "Cow Protection in India: From Secularising to Legitimating Debates," *South Asia Research* 38, no. 2 (2018): 157, doi.org/10.1177/0262728018768961.

72. Gundimeda and Ashwin, 157.

73. Gundimeda and Ashwin, 157.

74. Parvis Ghassem-Fachandi, *Pogrom in Gujarat: Hindu Nationalism and Anti-Muslim Violence in India* (Princeton, N.J.: Princeton University Press, 2012), 153, 155.

75. Graham, Desai, and McFarlane, "Water Wars," 67–68, 73.

76. Gundimeda and Ashwin, "Cow Protection," 157.

77. Shakuntala Ray, "Forbidden Tastes: Queering the Palate in Anglophone Indian Fiction," *Feminist Review* 114, no. 1 (2016): 29, doi.org/10.1057/s41305-016 -0013-z.

78. Ray, 19.

79. Roy, *Alimentary Tracts,* 20.

80. Prayaag Akbar, *Leila* (London: Faber & Faber, 2018), 38. Subsequent references to *Leila* are indicated parenthetically.

81. Varughese, "Post-Millennial Indian Dystopian Fiction," 1049.

82. Akbar quoted in Ghatak, "Urban Ghettos."

83. See Ashish Shukla, "Leila: Who Would Question Prayaag Akbar or Netflix?," OpIndia, June 21, 2019, opindia.com/.

84. Dolores Herrero, "Populism and Precarity in Contemporary Indian Dystopian Fiction: Nayantara Sahgal's *When the Moon Shines by Day* and Prayaag Akbar's *Leila,*" *ATLANTIS* 42, no. 2 (2020): 223, doi.org/10.28914/Atlan tis-2020-42.2.11.

85. Graham, Desai, and McFarlane, "Water Wars," 76.

86. Anand, *Hydraulic City,* 110.

Index

BEN JAMIESON STANLEY (they/them) is assistant professor of English at the University of Delaware.